DANTE, CINEMA, AND TELEVISION

Edited by Amilcare A. Iannucci

The *Divine Comedy* of Dante Alighieri (1265–1321) is one of the seminal works of Western literature. The poem has had an enormous impact on modern culture, nourishing a plethora of twentieth-century authors from Joyce and Borges to Kenzaburo Ōe. Although Dante's influence in the literary sphere is well documented, little has been written on his role in the evolution of the visual media unique to our times, namely cinema and television. *Dante, Cinema, and Television* corrects this oversight.

The essays in this volume, written by scholars from a broad range of disciplines, examine the impact of the *Divine Comedy* on film and television, focusing on specific directors, writers, producers, and actors, from cinema's silent era to the present. The essays also consider individual productions and the different modes of appropriation used in cinema and television. *Dante, Cinema, and Television* demonstrates the many ways, both subtle and bold, in which Dante's *Divine Comedy* has been given new life by cinema and television, and underscores Dante's vast legacy to modern culture.

(Toronto Italian Studies)

AMILCARE A. IANNUCCI is a professor with the Centre for Comparative Literature at the University of Toronto.

DANTE, CINEMA, AND TELEVISION

Edited by
Amilcare A. Iannucci

UNIVERSITY OF TORONTO PRESS
Toronto Buffalo London

© University of Toronto Press Incorporated 2004
Toronto Buffalo London
Printed in Canada

ISBN 0-8020-8601-2 (cloth)
ISBN 0-8020-8827-9 (paper)

Printed on acid-free paper

Toronto Italian Studies

National Library of Canada Cataloguing in Publication

Dante, cinema, and television / edited by Amilcare A. Iannucci.

(Toronto Italian studies)
Includes bibliographical references and index.
ISBN 0-8020-8601-2 (bound).   ISBN 0-8020-8827-9 (pbk.)

1. Dante Alighieri, 1265–1321 – Influence.   2. Motion pictures –
History and criticism.   I. Iannucci, Amilcare A.   II. Series.

PQ4433.D35 2004   791.43'6   C2003-905301-6

This book has been published under the aegis of the Charles Speroni Chair
of the Department of Italian, University of California Los Angeles, and the
University of Toronto Humanities Centre.

University of Toronto Press acknowledges the financial assistance to its
publishing program of the Canada Council for the Arts and the Ontario
Arts Council.

University of Toronto Press acknowledges the financial support for its
publishing activities of the Government of Canada through the Book
Publishing Industry Development Program (BPIDP).

Contents

Acknowledgments

The idea for this volume goes back a long way, to the spring of 1997, when I was the Charles Speroni Chair Visiting Professor in Italian at UCLA. In addition to teaching a graduate course on Dante, my duties included organizing a small conference on the general topic of my course. Since UCLA is a stone's throw away from Hollywood, I decided to put together a conference on Dante's influence on cinema and television, a subject which only very recently has begun to attract sustained scholarly attention. The conference generated considerable interest and sparked much lively discussion among the participants. Indeed, it was so successful that I decided to repeat the exercise on a grander scale in Toronto a few years later. The first major event of the new University of Toronto Humanities Centre (of which I am the founding director) was, in fact, a conference/film festival on Dante and cinema. The film festival was mounted by Cinemathèque Ontario over a ten-day period in March-April 2001. Cinemathèque screened some fifteen Dante-based and -inspired films, from such silent film classics as Milano Films' 1911 *Dante's Inferno* and Guido Brignone's 1926 *Maciste all'Inferno* to much more recent Dante-influenced films by directors as diverse as Fellini, Lynch, and Brakhage.

With two exceptions, all the essays collected in this volume were first presented at one of the two conferences described above. They have, of course, been completely revised (and in some cases greatly expanded) for publication. Although completeness (an impossible task) was not an objective of the volume, together these essays do cover the major areas of Dantean influence on cinema and television. I would like to thank the contributors for agreeing to have their work published in this volume. It was both a pleasure and an education for me to work with them.

An enterprise of this nature would be impossible to complete without the help of many people and organizations along the way. First, I would like to express my gratitude to all of the libraries and film archives which kindly allowed us to reproduce illustrations and stills from their collections. In Los Angeles, I would like to thank Marga Cottino-Jones, who in 1997 was Chair of the Department of Italian at UCLA. No stranger to medieval and cinema studies, she was naturally drawn to this project and made sure that the conference at UCLA was a huge success. Her support and encouragement was much appreciated, as was that of Luigi Ballerini and Massimo Ciavolella, two other members of the Italian Department who took a keen interest in the project. A special thanks goes to Carmela Speroni, who was instrumental in establishing the Chair at UCLA in memory of her husband, whose textbook, *Basic Italian* (prepared in collaboration with Carlo Golino), has introduced thousands of students to the Italian language since it was first published in 1958. The conference was organized under its aegis. She took an active role in the proceedings of the conference and has remained an enthusiastic supporter of the project in its subsequent phases.

In Toronto, too, there are many people to thank, first among them, John Tulk, my assistant at the Humanities Centre. He worked tirelessly first in the organization of the conference and film festival and then in the preparation of the manuscript of the book. Others who have in one way or another contributed to the project are Paul Perron, Principal, University College; Carlo Coen, Director, Italian Cultural Institute; Susan Oxtoby, Director of Programming, and Andrea Picard, Programme Coordinator, Cinemathèque Ontario; and Bart Testa, Cinema Studies, University of Toronto. Last, but certainly not least, I would like to thank Ron Schoeffel of University of Toronto Press. As one of the editors of the Press's Italian Series, I have had occasion over the years to work closely with Ron and it has always been a pleasure. Ron inaugurated the Italian Series several years ago and has nourished it since. Italian studies in North America owes much to him.

The two conferences on which this volume is based were supported by grants from the following organizations: the Charles Speroni Chair in Italian Studies, UCLA; the University of Toronto Humanities Centre; the Italian Cultural Institute, Toronto; and the Social Sciences and Humanities Research Council of Canada.This book is published under the aegis of the Charles Speroni Chair of the Department of Italian, UCLA, and the University of Toronto Humanities Centre. I gratefully acknowledge the generosity of all of the above.

Introduction

Dante's cultural predominance in the modern world is enormous. In institutes of higher learning, Dante studies abound, while numerous Dante commentaries and periodicals flood the scholarly market (Iannucci, 'The Presence of Italian Literature ... Abroad' 22ff). Moreover, translations of Dante's works continue to occupy the skills of eminent scholars and translators, maintaining, in the process, the pleasure of the reading public and the profitability of printing houses the world over. However, it is in the sphere of literary activity that Dante's impact on the modern world has been felt most acutely (cf. Havely 1ff). Dante has thus deeply affected the major British and American modernists, such as Joyce, Pound, Eliot, Auden, and Beckett, and has reverberated in a plethora of twentieth-century writers throughout the globe from west (Dante's engagement, for example, by Borges is well attested) to east (e.g., Kenzaburo Ōe and H. Yamada).

However, it is not only in a literary context that Dante's influence continues to be felt. Rather, Dante has also had a profound impact on the visual arts and on music, as a cursory glance at artists such as Gustave Doré (*Commedia*) and Dante Gabriel Rossetti (*Dante's Dream*) and composers such as Tchaikovsky (the symphonic fantasy *Francesca da Rimini*) and Rachmaninoff (*Francesca da Rimini*, for voice and piano) would amply testify. Just as importantly, his influence has spread decisively into the non-literary or para-literary world of the visual media unique to the twentieth century, namely cinema and television. In fact, Dante's poem has emerged as a vehicle ideally suited for both these media. For the *Commedia* represents a medieval knowledge system brought to perfection, a veritable encyclopedia the nature of whose cosmology is driven by visual images. This visual aspect has provided an ongoing source of inspiration not only to nineteenth-century visual artists such as Doré but also to the pioneers of early cinema who, before the advent of narrativity, were content to unfold images/tableaux of well-known material and, just as importantly, to their successors in both film and television who could count on these images for their instant appeal and recognition.

In short, appropriation of Dante has nourished both cinema and television from their inception down to the present day. At times such appropriation of the Florentine poet and his work has been holistic, spanning a director's (Fellini, Pasolini, Greenaway, Allen, Lynch) or an actor's/interpreter's (Gassman, Albertazzi, and Sermonti) whole career. At other times it has been less engaging, limited to an individual piece or performance (such as Harry Lachman's 1935 *Dante's Inferno* or the numerous 'performances' of Dante on television and radio in Italy in the 1980s), or restricted to a mere reference made for dramatic or comedic intent (one thinks here not only of Jim Carrey and his one Dantean inspired moment in *Liar Liar*, but also of Roberto Benigni's Academy Award acceptance speech, which included a thank-you to Dante). Dante, therefore, has left his mark on cinema and television, and both visual media have continually seized upon the potential of his text to shape their respective artistic representation. More importantly, they have recognized the visual potential of Dante's text and have reworked it in a host of ways from total appropriation (Milano Films' 1911 *Inferno*, Greenaway's *A TV Dante*, *The Devil's Advocate*) through incorporation of Dantean ideas, structure, and imagery (*Blue Velvet*, *The Sopranos*) to mere sight gags and fleeting allusions (*Totò al giro d'Italia*, the television sitcom *Frasier*) so as to acknowledge its dynamic fluidity and recognize it as perfectly suitable to, and adaptable for, the modern media of cinema and television.

The influence of Dante on cinema and television is the subject of this volume. Eleven of the essays are concerned with cinema and two with television. Leading off the former is a bird's-eye overview of Dante's influence on Hollywood, where Dante's sway has been, and continues to be, of major significance. There is, of course, good reason for this fact, given the primary characteristic of Dante's text. This is its malleability, its pliability, its producerly quality, which allows it to be reused and reworked forever anew in many different media and in myriad different ways. This is as true of silent cinema as it is of sound. In the silent era, Dante's text is incorporated cinematically from the very beginning, in one of the earliest cinema classics, Vitagraph's 1908 *Francesca da*

Rimini. This short film represents wholesale appropriation of Dante, as do Otto's 1924 *Dante's Inferno* and Griffith's 1928 *Drums of Love*. Moreover, Dante successfully made the transition to sound and has inspired a host of Hollywood directors. Some of these have been engaged holistically, such as Taylor Hackford and Woody Allen, although the latter, as in all matters, represents a mode of appropriation which is filtered primarily through cinema and secondarily through many other sources. Others have incorporated Dante and his material less forcefully, but leave no doubt that Dante is their principal source. The opening tercet from the *Inferno* which is highlighted before the beginning of the comedic action of Tom Shadyac's *Patch Adams* (1998) and the thematic structure of David Lynch's *Blue Velvet* (1986) make this abundantly clear. Dante's influence therefore has been a pervasive force in the cinema of Hollywood, and, indeed, of cinema and television around the globe. The remaining essays of this volume trace Dante's global influence on both in greater detail.

One of the impediments to researchers of the influence of Dante on cinema and television is the dearth of material from the history, especially early history, of these media. Many reasons account for this scarcity, but one of the most pervasive is the attitude, present in the formative genesis of these media, that they were inferior and not likely to last. Two of the essays in this volume are therefore welcome contributions to this problematic area. Vittoria Colonnese Benni, labouring in the penumbral world of early Italian silent cinema, employs an abundance of sources (preserved film clips, magazine articles, reviews) to piece together the solution to a tantalizing *lacuna*, namely, the Helios-Psiche film trilogy of Dante's *Commedia*. In spite of the decisive loss of this trilogy's *Purgatorio* and portions of its *Paradiso*, Colonnese Benni manages to recreate much of the monumental scale that these three films entailed and succeeds at restoring much of the films' overall content and structure. In so doing, she demonstrates that the film trilogy, in terms of its length, structure, and critical and audience reception, must have been a major accomplishment. Moreover, even though it is judged poorly in comparison to its near contemporary, the *Inferno* by Milano Films, Colonnese Benni convincingly argues that 'these three films, therefore, and most especially *Purgatory* and *Paradise*, constitute a watershed in the history of early Italian cinema.' Rino Caputo, much closer, chronologically, to his sources, sheds much light on the recent history of Italian television and radio. He uses an historically meticulous approach, akin to that of Colonnese Benni's, in order to survey the recreation of the *Comedy* on Italian radio and television in the last ten years. Arguing that Dante is a national icon, associated with Italy's political struggle, and that he is now as ever 'a naturally audio-visual author,' Caputo begins with the academic 'lectura Dantis' which Giorgio Petrocchi introduced for RAI in the mid-1980s. The result of this was a tendency to 'declaim' the *Comedy*, a tendency which was apparent in all subsequent broadcast events on television and radio, or in public performances, such as the dramatic readings by Sermonti and by Gassman. Caputo links the latter two by virtue of a common goal, namely, to 'declaim' the *Comedy*. But whereas the purpose of Sermonti's 'execution' is 'to allow the text to resonate freely, uninhibited by immediate critical reflection,' 'the "reading" of Gassman ... has its origin in his desire, perceived as an artistic and cultural challenge, to link together the theatre and the *Comedy*.' The result of all such approaches, Caputo argues, is the resurgence of a 'Dantemania' which is likely to influence in an ongoing manner these media well into the third millennium.

The remaining essays approach Dante's influence on cinema and television from a decidedly different methodological perspective or explore the manifold ways in which Dante's seductive sway has exercised itself. Thus John Welle applies a philological/historical approach to the emergence of Italian film and Italian film culture during its period of silent gestation and uses a nexus of relations associated with film to explore cinema's unfolding. Using Milano Films' *Inferno* as an example, Welle argues that the film 'is perhaps best understood as a bridge between the early cinema of attractions and a cinema in transition toward classical film narration.' He thus situates the film within the gradual move from transitory cinema venues to fixed ones and a similarly gradual transition toward longer narrative films. Examining such staples of early silent cinema as historical/literary epics, documentaries, and comedies, Welle locates the *Inferno* within the first category of literary epic and shows that the film was the most influential and important of all of the early Dantean inspired movies. Welle sees the film as seminal and, in conclusion, points 'to the film's participation in a broader set of dynamics involving the interaction of film and literature, whose interrelationship has helped to establish the parameters of Italian film culture.'

A far different approach is employed by Marguerite Waller and Gabrielle Lesperance. Waller surveys the language of post-war Italian film from a deconstructionist and feminist perspective. Arguing that the poetics of Dante's *Commedia* and the language of post-war Italian film share much in common, Waller engages five post-war films as intertextual intersects with Dante's poem. Analysing select scenes from each movie and juxtaposing them with texts from the *Commedia*, Waller contends that the common poetics running through all of them is that of 'a story about decentring patriarchal masculinities.' Thus, Rossellini's *Roma, città aperta* is a call to rethink identity and to revisit its various forms embedded in society; Fellini's *La dolce vita* is about the 'ruin' of representation, and 'ruining representation, becomes linked explicitly to questions of gender and sexuality, and understood to necessitate a radical decentring of patriarchal masculinities.' This enterprise of decentring is then pursued by Wertmüller's *Mimi metallurgico, ferito nell'onore*, which 'relentlessly exposes the seductions of identificatory masculinity,' and Cavani's *Portiere di notte*, which is an invitation to understand 'the performativity of identities.' Finally, Nichetti's *Volere volare* uses the poetics of *Paradiso* to suggest 'that the meaning of male sexuality is just as constructed and metaphorical as other significations.' Gabrielle Lesperance pursues a similar approach in offering some initial observations on Pasolini's final 'text,' *Salò*. Taking exception to recent criticism which sees the movie as constructed on Dante's principle of 'theological verticalism' and its 'perfect system of punishment,' Lesperance argues that the film instead presents a Hell that is morally relative, based on blind justice, and that it is this moral relativism which 'serves only to underscore the perfection and ideological symmetry in the *Divine Comedy*.' But even though there is an uneven bureaucracy in *Salò*, Lesperance argues that the film has an overwhelming symmetry shaped, in part, by its numerological, apocalyptically charged, use of four. This symmetry, in turn, calls into question the important issue of identity, and Lesperance, paying especially close attention to the scenes which involve the film's narrators, shows that through their confused identities 'the film suggests that what passes for identity is very slippery, indeed, and here degenerates into what could be better deemed prefabricated standardizations than true identity.' Through its use, therefore, of such blurred images and others, such as the cross-dressed libertines, Pasolini, Lesperance argues, 'is making us question the nature of power, gender, and position through his constant interplay of the same.'

Several essays explore the different ways in which Dante's influence has exerted itself on film and television. Sometimes, it has been holistic, occupying a director's whole career, while at other times it has been limited to selected works. Patrick Rumble examines the influence of

Dante on the lifelong work of Pier Paolo Pasolini, not only as a film-maker, but also as a writer. Pasolini's writerly debts to Dante are clear from his earliest poetic anthologies (his award-winning volume of po-etry from the 1950s, *The Ashes of Gramsci*, was composed almost entirely in Dantesque terza rima). Likewise, Dante is clearly an animating moral and stylistic force in the background of Pasolini's films of the 1960s and 1970s. This influence of Dante continues and is clearly discernible in Pasolini's last film, *Salò*. Here Rumble examines how Pasolini struc-tures his twentieth-century Inferno (allegorically representing both Ital-ian fascism and contemporary consumerist society) according to coordinates offered in the *Divine Comedy* – in particular, the various 'circles' that segment and order Dante's Hell. Rumble thus exposes the huge influence of Dante on Pasolini throughout his life, both in terms of theme and structure.

What Rumble does for Pasolini, Guido Fink does for Fellini. He first explores some of the common ground between Fellini and Dante. This includes the recurrent metaphor of pilgrimage, the use of real charac-ters in fictional works, the highly self-reflexive nature of the two artists' respective works, and the common interest in, and criticism of, Catholic religion 'as practised and understood in their times.' Most important for Fink is 'their obvious tendency to structure their work in circles.' But whereas Dante the pilgrim (who reverses the downward circular journey through Inferno to undertake the upward circular journeys through Purgatory and Paradise) is ever moving forward, Fellini's characters follow a circular route which brings them back to their starting points. Within each circle, however, the *modus operandi* of both filmmaker and poet is the same, for both 'seem interested in breaking up the usual narrative and/or visual pattern with sudden changes, apparitions, abrupt disappearances.' Fink concludes by asking whether Fellini's circles may be construed as 'infernal' and justifies his answer of 'not always, not entirely' by analysing Fellini's hesitancy to display moral repulsion at anything that could be conceived as human nature.

Victoria Kirkham explores the influence of Dante from the perspec-tive of urban imagery in a single work, Antonioni's *Red Desert*. Arguing that distinctive urban settings are a hallmark of modern Italian direc-tors such as Rossellini, Fellini, and Pasolini, Kirkham shows that Antonioni's evocation of Ravenna in *Red Desert* is unique. Furthermore, his vision of the city as 'a chilly, ugly, and dehumanized port synony-mous with the desert of the film's title' is derived from Dante. Dante, whose remains are interred in Ravenna, and the medieval past are invoked repeatedly throughout the film: the street where Giuliana, the female protagonist of the film, has her shop is Via Alighieri; above her bed there is a wooden panel of *St George and the Dragon*, one of the mainstays of medieval legend; an antique wooden chair, on which the sleepless Giuliana reclines and from which she narrates for her son the fairy tale about an island, is known as a Dante chair. But it is Dante's portrayal of Ravenna, together with his evocation of its *'pineta,'* to which the poet compared his Earthly Paradise (*Purgatorio* 28), that most inspires Antonioni's modern urban vision. For him, Dante's Edenic Ravenna is a thing of the past and has been replaced by a modern industrial Hell. Antonioni therefore uses Dante and his description of Ravenna as a reminder of past glory, and with that Dantean past Antonioni establishes a complete break to create an urban wasteland, a 'foggy, colour-drained, and polluted environment' which echoes the emotional barrenness of Giuliana.

Often Dante's influence on cinema is not direct, as it is with Antonioni, but indirectly mediated through the use of another film. A case in point is the independent African-American filmmaker Spencer Williams. As Dennis Looney argues, Dante's influence on African-American history and culture has been largely neglected by Dante scholars. To redress this imbalance, Looney uses Williams and his invocation of Dante, albeit mediated through the 1911 *Inferno*, in his film *Go Down, Death!* 'in an unprecedented way.' The theme of the movie is good versus evil. After the protagonist, Jim, kills his kindly landlady, Carrie, he wanders into a desert-like terrain and expires. Now occurring in rapid sequence are a mark-up shot of the Gates of Hell accompanied by a sign with the text 'Abandon all hope, ye who enter here,' and then several scenes from the *Inferno*. Although these scenes occupy less than a minute of film footage and although their quality is poor, they do not detract from the 'intelligent reading of Dante behind Williams's allusive adaptation of the cinematic *Inferno*.' For these scenes chronicle Jim's many sins and show us his ultimate destination, the ninth circle, which is reserved for his traitorous murder. Moreover, these scenes are grounded in Dante the pilgrim, who stands out as the only white presence in the film. Looney sees this presence as a bold act of incorporation whereby 'Williams uses Dante-the-character to integrate his "All-Negro Production" ... engaging in a charged act of creative imitation that we might call "artistic integration."' At the same time, it is Dante's moral cosmology that 'ultimately transcends issues of race' and that is used to reinforce the film's message, namely, that traffickers in evil, black or white, suffer the same dire consequences.

A problem that must be faced by all who attempt to 'translate' Dante into the modern visual media is the creative manner in which they render Dante's text intelligible to a present-day audience. As Andrew Taylor argues, this was a central and all-consuming problem for visual artist Tom Phillips, who, with Peter Greenaway, was one of the creators of *A TV Dante*. Years earlier, Phillips had confronted this problem head-on and, in a painting entitled *Beginning to Think about Dante*, had filtered out nearly all references to Dante's historical moment and had stressed 'instead the resonances which Dante's poem finds in modern experience.' But, as Taylor shows, the range of resonances which find expression in Phillips' painting become as arcane and as difficult for a modern audience to digest as the original text of Dante. Taylor contends that the same can be said for *A TV Dante*, which leaves a general audience at sea with its wealth of cryptic images and fails to satisfy a more academic and fastidious audience with its use of supposed 'experts.' Taylor then posits the interesting theory that the only audience that mattered to Phillips and Greenaway was themselves. He uses Nancy Vickers's analysis of *A TV Dante* ('Dante in the Video Decade' 263ff) to show that 'its primary object is to develop television as a "new vernacular."' Thus we can refer to *A TV Dante* as a 'volgarizzamento,' and, as such, it 'functions both as an accurate translation of an old masterpiece and as a technical exercise that showcased the potential of a new language – Television.' *A TV Dante*, Taylor argues, takes on the challenge of 'translation.' It is often successful, capturing the *Commedia*'s polysemy and raising the status of video as an art form, but it is not consistent, often deteriorating into gross simplification.

John Tulk explores the influence of Dante on Canadian cinema in its concern with filmic translation of vision. He analyses two Canadian films, one from the silent era and one from the sound era, linking them both to Dante's underlying vision. For him *Back to God's Country* is a primitive experimental film in which Nell Shipman shapes a vision of the epic battle of good versus evil along structural lines established by Dante in the first two *cantiche*. Similarly, R. Bruce Elder in *Illuminated Texts*, a modern-day experimental film, elaborates a culminating vision of ultimate infernal horror in a manner totally analogous to the way in which Dante elaborates his culminating vision of ultimate bliss at the end of the *Paradiso*. Tulk thus establishes the issue of vision as being a unique point of contact between Canadian filmmakers and the Florentine poet.

For Bart Testa it is the abyssal chasm of time that separates Dante from his modern audience. He therefore explores the works of three filmmakers who take up the issue of time as the central difficulty of 'translation.' Thus, Stan Brakhage in his short film *The Dante Quartet* imagines the *Commedia* paradoxically 'as an artist's interiority that can be known again, but for the first time, as kin to Dante's.' He creates 'a plausible analogon of the poem' which produces an 'all-at-once' temporal effect, recalling Dante as a temporal totality and allowing the *Commedia* to rise 'again' and yet for the 'first time.' Another 'diametrically different cinematic time' is at the centre of Antonioni's *Red Desert*, which is, Testa argues, a filmic *Purgatorio*. Thus, the protagonist, Giuliana, is a purgatorial soul in motion who moves in an 'in-between' time, between a bygone past and an unrealized future. But Antonioni, unlike Dante, folds both Hell and Heaven into his Purgatory and presents time as 'naked and accented,' a form of painful suspension. In so doing, Antonioni weaves into his film allusions that, in the end, become abysmal: Paradise has been lost; 'history has turned the world into deprival'; and Giuliana is caught up in time that does not stop and is suspended as 'individuation' in the Purgatory of our modernity. A relentless but radically decelerated time also occupies Canadian artist R. Bruce Elder and his *The Book of All the Dead*, which, incredibly long and erudite, is 'the most ambitious Dante film-work ever attempted.' Postmodernist in style and complexity, *The Book of All the Dead* traverses modernity and encapsulates both the tripartite cycle and the times of Dante's poem to become 'a twenty-years' cumulative, highly wrought segment serving the prospect of a postmodern hermeneutic cinema crossing over the historic chasm between the poet and us.'

From these essays, it can be seen that Dante's influence on cinema and television has been enormous. A perennial inspiration for actors, writers, producers, and directors, Dante remains one of the most enduring presences in the modern visual arts (Marcus, *Filmmaking by the Book*, passim). The Florentine poet is thus as much a force in the modern media as he is in modern literature, in short, an ongoing source of creative power, a power that is both pristinely ancient and innovatively new, as the broad range of essays in this volume bear ample witness.

Amilcare A. Iannucci
Toronto, June 2003

Bibliography

Bloom, Harold. *The Western Canon: The Books and School of the Ages*. New York: Harcourt Brace & Co., 1994.

Fiske, John. *Television Culture*. London: Methuen, 1987.

Gilbert, Sandra M. 'Shadows of Futurity: The Literary Imagination, the MLA, and the Twenty-First Century.' *PMLA* 112 (1997): 370–9.

Havely, Nick. 'Introduction: Dante's Afterlife, 1321–1997.' *Dante's Modern Afterlife: Reception and Response from Blake to Heaney*. Ed. Nick Havely. New York: St Martin's Press, 1998. 1–14.

Iannucci, Amilcare A. 'Dante Produces Television.' *Lectura Dantis* 13 (1993): 32–46.

– 'Dante, Television and Education.' *Quaderni d'Italianistica* 10 (1989): 1–33.

– 'The Presence of Italian Literature (Old and New) Abroad in the Twentieth Century.' *Italian Studies in North America*. Ed. Massimo Ciavolella and Amilcare A. Iannucci. Ottawa: Dovehouse Editions, 1994. 17–54.

Marcus, Millicent. *Filmmaking by the Book: Italian Cinema and Literary Adaptation*. Baltimore: Johns Hopkins University Press, 1993.

McDougal, Stuart Y. 'Preface.' *Dante among the Moderns*. Ed. Stuart Y. McDougal. Chapel Hill: University of North Carolina Press, 1985. ix–xiii.

Vickers, Nancy J. 'Dante in the Video Decade.' *Dante Now: Current Trends in Dante Studies*. Ed. Theodore J. Cachey, Jr. Notre Dame: University of Notre Dame Press, 1995. 263–76.

DANTE, CINEMA, AND TELEVISION

Dante and Hollywood

AMILCARE A. IANNUCCI

The influence of Dante has continued to demonstrate rare staying power to the present day. In the literary world that influence is pre-eminent. In 1929 T.S. Eliot declared that 'Dante and Shakespeare divide the modern world between them' (51), and in his preface to *Dante among the Moderns*, Stuart Y. McDougal adds, some sixty years later, that 'Dante's impact on the major writers of the modern world has far exceeded that of Shakespeare' (ix). Such influence has bestowed upon Dante the status of cultural icon, and he is regarded by cultural commentators, such as Harold Bloom (46), as the very heart, along with Shakespeare, of the Western Canon. Moreover, Dante continues to exert his influence in academic circles, where he is an object of research, teaching, commentary, and criticism and where manifold editions and studies of his works proliferate. At the same time, however, Dante, to borrow a line from Hollywood production parlance, has made 'the cross-over.' For he has also migrated from these literary, cultural, and academic niches to the outside world and has deeply affected the educated and non-educated general public. Today, for example, he contributes greatly to all forms of popular entertainment. Casual readings and performances of his works abound, and strict and free adaptations thrive in almost every popular medium imaginable, from cinema to song. Finally, his very name and image, as well as scenes and characters from his works, have become instantly recognizable and are used commercially for every conceivable mass-marketing purpose, even for toiletries (in the late 1940s, an Italian laxative was named Beatrice, this on a totally errant reading of Beatrice's speech to Virgil in *Inferno* 2.70: 'I' son Beatrice che ti faccio andare' [For I am Beatrice who makes you go]). In short, the apt summary of Michael Bristol on the popular appeal of Shakespeare (3) may also be extended to Dante: he has hit the big time.

What accounts for the staying power and the broad popular appeal of Dante? First, there is a timelessness to Dante's works. By timeless I do not mean a vague and romantic notion of Dante's immortality. Rather, I wish to suggest that Dante's works, like all other great works of art, have enjoyed and continue to enjoy a sustained cultural afterlife. They share, to employ a phrase from Mikhail Bakhtin, a macro-temporality that has allowed them to enter the *longue durée* and to enjoy a gradual coming-into-being which continues in our present day. Secondly, Dante's works possess a universality, not in any kind of an abstract sense, but in a concrete historical one. Just as Dante created his world out of dialogue with all of the voices which had preceded him, so Dante continues to engage in dialogue with the whole of human culture, seen as a complex aggregate of alterity and outsidedness.[1] As such, Dante's work possesses incredible potential to generate new meanings. Thirdly, there is a moral or ethical dimension to Dante's works which allows readers, in ongoing dialogue, to grasp principles of practical morality, that is, a sense of the enterprise of being human. Fourthly, what makes the preceding qualities possible is the dynamic nature of Dante's work. For the *Commedia* is polysemous in nature, and this polysemy allows it to be read in a host of different ways and to speak to audiences that differ socially, culturally, and historically – from the illiterate to the most educated and pedantic (Iannucci, 'Dante, Television and Education' 7–8; Iannucci, 'Dante Produces Television' 34–5). Thus the *Commedia* subsumes the categories of readerly/writerly (Barthes) and closed/open (Eco) text, appealing to both general reader and discerning critic alike. In fact, the *Comedy* is more like what John Fiske calls, with specific reference to television, a 'producerly text' (95), that is, one which 'combines the televisual characteristics of a writerly text with the easy accessibility of the readerly.' It is this 'producerly' quality, this never-ending potential of the text to enable, that has allowed it to endure and to reach the largest possible audience. Moreover, it is this same quality that has allowed the *Comedy* to become the perennial inspiration of myriad artists who have reworked the text, at both the popular and avant-garde levels, in almost every artistic form, from medieval paintings and miniatures down to contemporary drama and visual arts.

It is to Dante's influence on the modern visual arts, especially cinema, that I now wish to turn. The extent of Dante's influence on cinema is uncanny, just as uncanny as the influence of Shakespeare on this same art form. At first glance, it would seem that Shakespeare far outweighs Dante in this regard. It is estimated that over 40 sound films have been made of Shakespeare's plays and some 400 silent films on Shakespearian subjects (Jackson 2). Dante seemingly pails into insignificance by comparison. But we must remember that with Shakespeare we have an extensive corpus of plays, which have been filmed more or less as is, while with Dante there is really only one filmable text, the *Commedia*, although his *Vita Nuova* has inspired a surprising number of films. Indeed, the impact of Dante on cinema throughout both the silent and sound periods is enormous. This is true not only of Italian cinema but also of other national cinemas. In the remainder of this paper, I wish to focus on one such national cinema, Hollywood. In so doing, I want to canvass both the silent and sound periods and use representative films of these eras to illustrate the extent of Dantean inspiration, which runs the gamut from outright and holistic appropriation to appropriation of a far more allusive nature. To be sure, not all of these films are great; some, in fact, are less than stellar. My concern, however, is not artistic merit *per se*, but the level of engagement with Dante's text, whether that engagement is direct or mediated.

By and large, the silent film period was given over to wholesale appropriation of Dante. These early films tended to concentrate not only on the *Inferno* as a whole, but also on select episodes, the favourite being Dante's tale of Francesca da Rimini. Three select silent films are representative of these tendencies. The first, and earliest Dante film, albeit not a product of Hollywood west but Hollywood east, was driven by the Francesca story. The New York Vitagraph Company, from its foundation in 1897 until 1925, was one of the most dominant and creative forces of the young American film industry. It churned out scores of popular one and two reelers of between fifty to a hundred feet, which ran the gamut from propaganda to slapstick comedy. A staple of the Vitagraph film output, especially in the years 1907–10, was the so-called 'quality' film that promoted respectable culture and therefore created a climate in which the newly invented cinema might be considered an art form in and of itself (cf. Uricchio and Pearson 48–9).[2] Devoted to historical, biblical, and literary subjects, the 'quality' films included, among many others, such filmic vehicles as *Washington under the American Flag* (1909), *The Life Drama of Napoleon Bonaparte and the Empress Josephine* (1909), *The Life of Moses* (1909), Shakespeare's *Julius Caesar* (1908), and Dante's *Francesca da Rimini* (1907).

Francesca da Rimini or *The Two Brothers* was directed by William B. Ramous and has a running time of about ten minutes. The film is preceded by the following synopsis: 'Lanciotto, a hunchback, is betrothed and wedded to Francesca. Being called to the wars, he leaves his bride in the care of Paolo his brother.' The action of the film then unfolds in seven parts: the hunchback is betrothed to Francesca and sends Paolo to fetch her; Paolo bears his brother's message and brings Francesca to Lanciotto; Francesca shows deep repugnance on meeting Lanciotto; the wedding follows and Lanciotto is immediately called to war; Paolo and Francesca celebrate their love; the fool brings news of the lovers to Lanciotto; the hunchback returns and exacts his revenge. These parts are captured by fifteen shots, thirteen in long-shot and two close-ups of the locket containing Francesca's picture. All of the shots were executed at Vitagraph's Flatbush studio and in the open, most probably in New York's Central Park.

The film shows obvious congruences with the many popular theatrical treatments of the Francesca story during the same period, four different theatrical versions of Francesca playing in 1901 and 1902 alone, in London, Paris, and New York. Moreover, there are strong similarities between the Vitagraph film and the American theatrical presentation of the Francesca story, which was originally written by George H. Boker in 1855, but which was revived in 1882 by Lawrence Barrett and again in 1901 by Otis Skinner. For, like Boker's play, the film develops certain key dramatic concepts, such as the deformity of Lanciotto, which drives the tragic pathos of the protagonist and lends human depth to a tortured soul, ugly on the outside but with a heart yearning for love. Moreover, the film was clearly inspired by the hand-created and -painted sets of the Boker play, especially the revivals of 1882 and 1901.

The second film is from Hollywood west, the product of Fox Film Corporation. *Dante's Inferno* of 1924 was directed by Henry Otto. It is unique among American silent films in that it attempts to stage the entire Dantean *Inferno* according to the illustrations of Doré, albeit in selected scenes. These scenes, however, reveal the main concern of the film, which is morality. For the film is not so much interested in the Dantean material for its own sake, but rather in employing it as a frame to contain the unfolding of the film and to lend a moralistic purpose to the storyline. The story is contemporary and concerns the unscrupulous workings of one Mortimer Judd, a millionaire who is responsible for the financial ruin of Eugene Craig. Craig pens his own curse to a

Poster for Henry Otto's *Dante's Inferno* (1924).

copy of the *Inferno* ('If there is Hell, this, my curse will take you there') and sends it to Judd, who accordingly takes up reading it and so enters into a lengthy dream at the centre of which is the Dantean vision of Hell. Here the journey through the underworld is telescoped into select scenes. We have the prologue, the crossing of the Acheron, the encounter with Minos, the struggle with the forces of darkness before the City of Dis, and the presentation of various 'tormented souls which invoke a second death,' especially, in terms of the film's thematic thrust, the three most malicious categories of sinners, the avaricious and the prodigal condemned to roll their heavy weights, the fraudulent and the deceitful, who are plunged into the boiling pitch, and the suicides transformed into lifeless trees. Everything associated with the underworld journey – the incredible sets, the menacing demons, the towering mass of Minos, the horrible punishments, the categories of sinners and their resultant doom – everything, in short, that is Dantean material is here evoked for a moralistic purpose. For all is to remind the millionaire that the path of his wicked ways will lead to horrible perdition and to prepare for his ultimate conversion. The closing scenes of the movie not only detail the protagonist's conversion but also permit the director to make his moral point, a point which he emphasizes in the closing caption of the film. In addition to its appropriate moral and happy ending, the movie, no doubt, also owed its mass popular appeal to the astonishing special effects which Dante's text conjures up.

The third silent film, also produced by Fox, is a feature length film of the Francesca story, *Drums of Love*. The film was directed by D.W. Griffith and appeared in 1928. Griffith wields a free hand in adapting the Dantean tale, transposing the setting to South America and unfolding his version against the petty squabbles of South American states. Griffith's tale is of two South Americans, the lame hunchback Duke Dom Cathos de Alvia and his brother Count Leonardo de Alvia. They share a special bond and at their father's death swear to preserve with their lives the honour of the house of Alvia. After inflicting a crucial defeat on the forces of his arch-enemy, the Duke of Grenada, Dom Cathos accepts a marriage proposal with Emanuela, the Duke's daughter, and sends his brother to retrieve her. At the betrothal ceremony, Emanuela and Leonardo fall instantly in love. Cathos weds his bride and summarily leaves her to deal with sedition in one of his domains, entrusting Leonardo with the task of guarding his wife. The latter two enter into a rather erotic, drawn-out, and desultory affair. They waver back and forth between doing the right thing and satisfying their passion. A particularly telling scene is the one in which Emanuela is reading from Tennyson's *Camelot* (i.e., *The Idylls of the King*) and becomes transfixed by her love for Leonardo ('and knew full well / how ill that love / and yet that love / how deep'), a scene which recalls Dante's account of the lovers' first kiss during their reading of the romance of Lancelot du Lac. In time, news of the affair is brought to Cathos by the fool, renamed Bopi, after Boker's Pepe, for the film. Cathos returns, and after spying on the lovers, surprises and kills them, reminding Emanuela that she has been unfaithful and Leonardo that he has brought dishonour on the house of Alvia and thereby broken his solemn vow. This tragic ending, however, left American preview audiences cold, and so, before the film's opening, Griffith was constrained to add another ending (Wagenknecht and Slide 231, Schickel 539–40, Martinelli 118) in which Cathos, after surprising the lovers, is killed by the fool and dies forgiving Emanuela and Leonardo and blessing their union. This second ending has conferred on the film the unique novelty of being a silent film in circulation with two distinct endings.

As with the Vitagraph *Francesca*, the material has been carefully reworked along the lines of earlier American dramatic treatment, especially that of George Boker. Thus, Cathos, the Lanciotto of Boker's play, is the driving catalyst for the film. It is his deformity, as in Boker's play, that is the dramatically controlling concept, the key to his character and his tortured soul. Moreover, the backdrop for the film is rooted in a strong awareness of the hollowness of many of society's norms, an awareness revealed in such scenes as Emanuela recoiling at the thought of marrying simply out of honour a man she has never seen, and Cathos, fumbling with his wardrobe, surrounded by obsequious tailors and servants who compliment him on his every improvement. Thus Griffith shares Boker's view of society's blindness and, like Boker, uses it as the background for a dramatic treatment of the Francesca material, which 'recognizes that callous society, not fate, was the agent of the tragedy' (Spiller 1002).

Although *Drums of Love* was produced during the period of Griffith's decline, the film displays many of the distinguishing marks of his towering genius. These include the lavishly produced opening battle scene, with a plethora of Griffith-type shots, especially the panoramic shot of the entire battleground and the truck-mounted camera closely following the charging cavalry; the interesting camera shots and angles which accompany such scenes as the betrothal ceremony; the famous Rembrandt lighting, as in the scene of Emanuela entering a darkened chamber, photographed from the front and backlit in her white wedding dress, with the brooding figure of Cathos, himself bathed in light, shuddering on the bed; and the use of inanimate objects to produce a code of visible hieroglyphs (Knight 31), such as the clay statuettes which the fool employs to re-enact the adultery. With these and many other features, Griffith in *Drums of Love* reminds us that, although *Birth of a Nation* and *Intolerance* are in the distant past, he can still demonstrate, even in this late melodrama, his right to be regarded as the father of film technique.

The sound period in Hollywood, with one notable exception, favours much more allusive appropriation of Dante. The exception is Harry Lachman's *Dante's Inferno* of 1935, yet another Fox film, which continues Otto's moralistic appropriation of Dantean material. It is a film notable for its blatant exploitation of Dante, for its terror-inducing sets, for the participation of Spencer Tracy in the lead role, and for the screen introduction of Rita Hayworth, who appears as one of the dancers under the name of Rita Casino. It amounts, in the words of the *New York Time*'s film critic A. Sennwald to a 'stirring if somewhat pointless spectacle' (1 Aug. 1935). The film, like Otto's, is a modern morality story which follows the life of the ruthlessly ambitious Jim Carter (Spencer Tracy). He inherits a fair-ground concession known as 'Dante's Inferno,' causes its eventual collapse (and the suicide of the building inspector whom he had bribed), goes free on perjured testimony, and turns his attention to establishing a floating pleasure palace, laden with sin and shameless revelry. But when the pleasure palace catches fire, Carter heroically saves as many passengers as he can, and he follows this heroic deed by the realization that money isn't everything. Once again, the Dantean material is not pursued here for its intrinsic high poetry, but for its significance as a popular moral inculcator. In this movie, as in Otto's, Dante's *Inferno* simply becomes the frame which holds in place the unfolding moral narrative, a narrative of unbridled capitalism eventually subdued and repentant. In this case, the horrors of Hell are staged with state-of-the-art special effects.

More allusive appropriation by Hollywood is practised throughout the sound era, extending from early films such as William Deterle's 1941 *The Devil and Daniel Webster*, in which the storyline is Faust but the special effects recall Dante's infernal realm, to Peter Hyams's 1999 *End of Days*, which pits an unlikely pilgrim in the guise of Arnold Schwarzenegger against a true Dantean Lucifer. This type of appropriation, however, has become much more common in contemporary films, that is, films since the 1970s, and is shared by numerous Hollywood directors as diverse as Martin Scorsese, Francis Ford Coppola, Alan Parker, Tim Burton, David Lynch, Adrian Lyne, and Vincent Ward, all of whom have employed Dantean ideas and images to drive their particular cinematic visions. Both Scorsese and Coppola have employed the Dantean journey through the underworld to serve as the backdrop to their visual treatment of a modern journey through Hell. Thus, Scorsese in *Mean Streets* (1973) and, especially, *Taxi Driver* (1976) has focused on infernal urban journeys, and Coppola in *Apocalypse Now* (1979) has fashioned the journey through the evil and surreal nether realms of the jungle to reach the devil incarnate, a story based primarily on Conrad but with a subtext provided by Dante. Similarly, Alan Parker has employed in *Angel Heart* (1987) the image of Dante's Lucifer to create an unforgettable cinematic demon who is responsible for the protagonist's serpentine journey through the gothic Hell of intrigue and crime. Moreover, Tim Burton in *Batman* (1989) has created a Dantean-like 'comic' pastiche of the great battle between good and evil, played out in a Gotham City that looks precariously like the visions of Hell conjured up by earlier cinematic pioneers. Likewise, David Lynch has made extensive use of Dante to structure his tale of his protagonist's descent into the hellish world of crime and sadomasochism in *Blue Velvet* (1986). Finally, Adrian Lyne has used Dantean material to shape his cinematic vision of the Hell of a disordered mind in *Jacob's Ladder* (1990), and Vincent Ward in *What Dreams May Come* (1998) has openly appropriated Dante and his world to create a visualization of his hero's quest through Hell to retrieve his wife from a brilliantly cinematic recreation of the Italian poet's wood of the suicides.

All such appropriation serves one of three ends. First, Dante is used to drive a film's plot, theme, or structure. We see this mode of appropriation front and centre in Taylor Hackford's *The Devil's Advocate* (1997), a film which borrows Dantean material so transparently that it borders on wholesale appropriation. The storyline of the film is straightforward and at its heart, as at the heart of the *Commedia*, is an elaborate courthouse vision experienced by one Kevin Lomax. He, a hotshot attorney from Gainesville, Florida, is hired by a prestigious New York law firm and given a series of cases which advance his career still further. But from the moment he arrives in New York, all is not well for Kevin and strange happenings beset him and, particularly, his wife, Mary Ann. Eventually, Kevin realizes that evil is ubiquitous at the law firm and that its owner is the incarnation of Satan himself. Kevin has truly become the devil's advocate, a position consonant with his status, revealed in the film's climatic sequence, as the devil's son. But Kevin does battle with his mentor and father and is thereby released from his clutches, taking us full circle back to the beginning of the opening vision.

Critics were quick to establish parallels between Hackford's version of Satan and that of the English poet John Milton. Certainly, it is true that not only does Hackford's Satan bear the name John Milton but he also, like his Miltonian counterpart, dominates much of the action, and, again as in Milton, is the best drawn of all the characters. The key to the delineation of Milton's Satan is his 'sense of injur'd merit' (*Paradise Lost* [*PL*] 1.98), a condition which, as C.S. Lewis wryly noted, 'we can all study in domestic animals, children, film-stars, politicians, or minor poets ...' (*Preface* 96). This 'sense of injur'd merit' is also the key to Hackford's Satan. A perverted, malevolent, and twisted creature, he is in full revolt against his maker. He is, exactly like Milton's Satan, 'Heav'n ruining from Heav'n' (*PL* 6.868), and all of his attendant characteristics follow accordingly. These characteristics are admirably brought to life by Al Pacino's over-the-top portrayal. Thus, Hackford's Satan, like Milton's, is an ever-present menace, totally insidious, always waiting for an opportunity, always staying close to human free action. A vainglorious braggart who maintains it is better to 'rule down here than serve in Heaven, Milton boasts, 'I've been underestimated from day one. You never think I was a master of the universe – I'm a surprise – they don't see me coming.' He thus is always looking for an opportunity to tempt, a clever liar who blames everything on God, whom he derides as an 'absentee landlord': in short, a deformed megalomaniac who believes he will outwit God and take over the world through the birth of his grandchild, the 'Anti-Christ.' But in a fitful reversal of fate, Satan's own son, Kevin, reeks his Oedipal revenge and denies his father his wish by killing himself.

This close connection between Milton and Hackford in the portrayal of Satan, though undeniable, is nevertheless submerged by the film's appropriation of Dante, with whom it has much more in common. The intimate connection between the movie and Dante, in fact, is made abundantly clear by the Warner Brothers web site for the film. There the title page has the *Inferno*'s inscription from the gate of Hell (*Inf.* 3.9), and inside, all of the credits for the film are arranged within a series of nine concentric circles with Lucifer at their base. Furthermore, the sharing between Hackford and Dante is apparent from the film itself on three important fronts.

First, there is the basic story, which is shaped by Hackford from Andrew Neiderman's humdrum novel into a journey of epic proportions. Thus, like the *Commedia*, the film starts in the *selva oscura* and proceeds through the depths of Hell. In the opening sequences, Kevin is pictured as professionally and spiritually lost. His legal track record of sixty-four wins and no losses is more important to him than the truth of the cases he chooses to defend. The story starts with Kevin defending a seedy pedophile whom he knows to be guilty. Worse still, as he later confesses, his perfect record is the result of improper conduct. Just as significantly, in the celebration scenes at the local bar which follow the trial, Kevin is portrayed as being in love with the good things of this life – fame, booze, money, and, above all else, sex – as the adulterous subplot, borrowed from the Francesca story, makes clear. He is thus ripe for temptation. Prior to his leaving, his mother, a preacher's daughter, reinforces this and warns him of the evil on which he is embarking. But Kevin pays no heed and soon he is involved in a job which for him is Heaven on earth, but which, in reality, is a living Hell. Thus, Kevin, like Dante the pilgrim, descends into Hell. But, without a guide and impervious to his wife's love, Kevin becomes a part of the devil's realm. For here Satan is everywhere, watching and waiting. Here, too, the good life is rampant. As Satan tells Kevin, 'Ha, that's our secret. We kill you with kindness.' Above all else, here evil is ubiquitous. The law firm of Milton, Chadwick, Waters has its fingers in every legal pie, victory is marked by success, and justice is of no concern. As Satan tells Kevin toward the close of the film, he has chosen law as his entry point into the world because there are so many lawyers. Legal evil has replaced the legal eagle, and this evil, in turn, spreads everywhere and tarnishes every character in the film, a fact reinforced by cameo appearances by Senator Alfonse D'Amato and Don King. Kevin freely participates in this Hell and succumbs to its pleasures. Although his wife realizes the enormity of the evil before Kevin does and wants to leave, Kevin cannot and so drags them both still deeper until he loses her for good and for bad. It is only her death that brings him to his senses and makes him resist the devil and all his trappings, thus breaking the hold that Satan has exerted on him in his domain and restoring him to right judgment.

Secondly, the film borrows much from Dante for its structural components. Thus, both the law firm of John Milton and his apartment building are figured as inverted Hells. Milton has his business office on the roof of a modern skyscraper. Surrounded by water which flows over the building's side, this domain recalls Lucifer's icy abode of Cocytus, which is at the very bottom of Hell's pit (*Inf.* 31–4). But now this domain is at the top, more in keeping with today's urban scene and Satan's tightening grip on his empire, the latter underscored by Milton's carefree tottering on the building's edge in front of a startled and nervous Kevin. Moreover, Milton's 5th Avenue luxury penthouse is at the top of an apartment building reserved for his close associates. The trappings of it are bare. Gigantic stone pillars bring to mind the towering giants of *Inferno* 31, and there is a huge fireplace with, of course, a permanently blazing fire. Behind his altar-like desk is a wall mural. This mural (reminiscent of Rodin's *Gates of Hell*) is at first indistinct, but in the closing battle between Milton and Kevin, it is transformed by Rick Greenberg's amazing visual effects to resemble the 'bufera infernale' of *Inferno* 5, in which lovers are storm-tossed and reach out to Kevin in order to entice him to become one with them. The structure, then, of Milton's office and home are steeped in Dante. His is a gaping pit of chaos (*Inf.* 4.7–8), a 'blind world' (*Inf.* 4.13) anchored firmly in him and in his ubiquitous appeal. His realm is that of a fallen creature of great stature (*Inf.* 34.28ff) who lords over his domain. Moreover, this universe is replete with darkness (all of the interior shots of Milton are filmed in muted light), eerie spectres and sounds (the scene leading up to Eddie Barzoon's murder is an excellent example), fiendish appearances and transformations, and grisly deeds of black magic, voodoo, and the occult. In short, Hackford has structured his picture of Hell from components largely drawn from Dante's *Commedia*.

Finally, the theme of the film is as Dantean as it is Miltonian, for it explores the close connections among Satan, the universality of evil, and free will. As Kevin comes to appreciate, Milton's hold on him is the result of his free participation. As Milton reminds Kevin, nothing can take place apart from human free will. Satan merely cooperates with the expression of that freedom. But once Satan is allowed to enter and once evil is chosen freely, the resultant slope is both downward and pernicious. In a speech recalling *Purgatorio* 10.124–5, Milton compares free will to butterflies' wings, which, as he says, 'once touched never get off the ground.'[3] Thus Kevin and Milton are locked in a deadly battle at the centre of which is free will. By choosing freely, even to the point of taking his own life and refusing to do the devil's work, Kevin not only thwarts Satan's plan but restores his own moral vision so that he can freely soar to his maker. Thus, free will is pivotal, and it is human free will that accounts for evil in the world. As Virgil reminds the pilgrim, 'if the present world has gone astray, / in you is the cause, in you it's to be sought' (*Purg.* 16.82–3). So Hackford reminds us all. Kevin Lomax is thus a character who is resolutely shaped by the Dantean theme of the all-important and all-pervasive doctrine of free will.

The second end of Dantean appropriation is to lend an overall mood to a particular film. One of the best examples of a Dantean mood film is David Fincher's 1996 *Seven*. The film details the investigation by a retiring detective and his novice replacement of a series of gruesome murders perpetrated by a fiendish serial killer. Early on, Dante is established as a relevant intertext, for the murders are being carried out according to a pattern of the seven deadly sins, each victim representing one sin. Dante's classification of sins in the *Purgatorio* is invoked repeatedly to provide an underlying explanation, and there is a scene near the beginning of the film in which the older detective photocopies a drawing of the Dantean classification of sins and sends it to his young apprentice. Outside of providing a schema for the murders, however, the *Purgatorio* does not figure pre-eminently in the film's story and mood. Rather, the story and the mood are resolutely hellish along Dantean lines. There is a sharp compartmentalization to the movie, with sets that are strongly claustrophobic and with movement within these closeted sets being largely up and down. Most scenes are of dark interiors in which light is absent, and pitch-black shadows are the norm, recalling the utter darkness of Dante's Hell as a place 'where no thing gleams' [ove non è che luca]. In addition, dank rain pervades almost every shot, and there are repeated references to the fetid smells of the rancid crime scenes, both details recalling Dante's infernal realm. Finally, as in Dante's Hell, unspeakable suffering is everywhere to be found. All of the murder victims, who are filmed in extreme graphic detail, are exposed to prolonged torture and appalling horrors. As an attending physician aptly remarks of one of the victims, 'He has experienced about as much pain and suffering as anyone I've encountered ... and he still has Hell to look forward to.' The overall mood is thus eerily sepulchral and infernal, and it is quite clear from the beginning, as one character remarks, that 'this isn't going to have a happy ending.' Moreover, the killer, chillingly portrayed by Kevin Spacey, is figured as Satan himself. The older detective says to his partner, 'If we catch John Doe and he turns out to be the devil, if he is Satan himself, then he might live up to our expectations.' As the movie progresses, John Doe becomes more and more the devil, until he is revealed in the film's closing sequence, whose tall electrical poles recall the giants of the lowest circle of Dante's Hell, as the incarnation of all evil, the self-appointed scourge of God, the agent of one final horrible and terrifying event. Astute critics responded to and summarized the overall eerie mood and impression that the above details create. Marc Savlov of the *Austin Chronicle* (www.auschron.com/film/pages/movies/658.html), for example, described the film as follows: 'Positively dripping with a soggy, oppressive atmosphere, the film is blanketed with a miasma of madness: the city itself is the enemy here, and the mysterious quarry only a symptom of a much more insatiable disease.' Nathaniel R. Atcheson (www.pyramid.net/natesmovies/seven.htm) confessed: 'I've never felt mood and atmosphere as strongly as I did in this film. This is the most darkly immersive and absorbing film I have ever seen. The music, the cinematography and the direction all work together in perfect compatibility to create this nameless, rainy city and the murky interiors of buildings within it.' I would suggest to you that this nameless city is none other than Dis and that Fincher has imbued it with all of the dark and desolate mood that is the hallmark of Dante's *Inferno*.

Thirdly, Dante is employed for comedic effect, the best example being Woody Allen's *Deconstructing Harry* (1998). Like the *Commedia*, *Deconstructing Harry* is made up of three interlocking biographical stories. Harry Block is a middle-aged writer who has gone through six psychiatrists, three wives, and numerous girlfriends and who in the present is experiencing a severe case of writer's block. Three separate biographical strands link this material together, as they do in the case of the *Commedia*. The first is Harry's love story. Like Dante, Harry is tormented by the memory of former love, and he is most cognizant of his many failures in the area of love, resorting to casual affairs and trysts with prostitutes. The second strand is Harry's exile. Here, however, unlike Dante, exile is not from one's native city but from one's beloved boyhood college in upper state New York. Harry, in fact, had been expelled many years ago for boyish pranks and is returning to his college to be honoured for his literary accomplishments. The final strand is the emergence of the artist. Like Dante, Harry muses on the meaning of his vicissitudes and comes to see that everything that has happened to him has happened to further one aim and one aim only, his growth as a writer. His literary career, therefore, is what makes sense of all the strands of his life.

These biographical connections aside, there is also a pivotal scene near the conclusion of the movie which highlights Allen's evident borrowing from the Italian poet. Mind you, as in all of Allen's borrowings, it is filtered through other influences of a more cinematic kind. In the scene, Allen dreams, or imagines, that he is sent to Hell, where he encounters his father and eventually meets Satan himself. This scene with its serio-comic encounter with death and judgment is first of all reminiscent of Ingmar Bergman. His *Wild Strawberries* (1957) is, obviously, the basis of Allen's tale, affording not only the plot (in Bergman, an elderly professor, Isak Borg, makes his way to his alma mater to receive an honorary degree and falls prey to a host of characters and memories which afford his 'deconstruction') but also most of the principal themes, such as self-discovery, memory, dreams, guilt, relationships, death, and salvation. In fact, the final scene in Allen recalls, albeit very comically, one of the most striking moments of *Wild Strawberries*, in which Isak dreams that he is walking through a desolate city and watching a funeral procession from which a corpse, again Isak, emerges and attempts to pull him into the afterlife. At the same time, the scene is also an evocation of Federico Fellini's *Otto e mezzo*. Like Fellini's Guido, Allen's Harry is involved in a journey of self-discovery, and, like Guido, Harry comes to realize that it is only art which makes ultimate sense of one's seemingly futile existence. Once again, the scene is a comic take on one in *Otto e mezzo* in which Guido faces an all-powerful judgment figure, a Roman Catholic cardinal, who keeps reminding him that 'outside the Church there is no salvation,' in much the same way that the devil, an all-powerful judgment figure, keeps reminding Harry that 'outside Hell there is no pleasure.' But though filtered, the scene is also an evocation, although of a most satiric kind, of the *Commedia*'s structure and theological import. For Harry descends to Hell in a freight elevator (perhaps a nod to Greenaway and Phillips' *A TV Dante*), the operator calling out floors in the manner of a department store employee ('floor five: subway muggers, aggressive panhandlers, and book critics'), and at the bottom encounters his father, whose fate in the afterlife is a comic send-up of the traditional Catholic belief that only Christians can enter Heaven, Hell being reserved for Jews, such as Harry's father. Moreover, his father celebrates his disbelief comically, preferring, as he pointedly says to his son, a Chinese dinner to Heaven. Thus, this scene, which is ultimately traceable to Dantesque concerns, is comically executed and accompanied by a wealth of other references, including Bergman, Fellini, Brignone (director of the silent classic satire *Maciste all'Inferno*, whose netherworld pleasure-prone and lascivious denizens populate Allen's Hell), the myth of Orpheus and Eurydice, Faust, Sartre, Lacan, and Heidegger. Dante is thus buried deep in the abyss of *Deconstructing Harry*, but his presence is unmistakable and a quip by one of the film's characters refers equally to Harry's and Dante's talent: 'He takes everyone's suffering and turns it into gold.'

Throughout the history of Hollywood, therefore, Dante has been a sustained and continued influence. He has contributed to filmic vehicles of every sort and has fed the imagination of countless directors who, once they enter Dante's world to retrieve a single detail, scene, or idea, often become ensnared in the web of interrelated references that his rich and varied parallel poetic universe provides. As a result, they wind up appropriating from Dante much more than they had probably originally intended, and the Dante intertext often overwhelms other obvious sources. This is true of the films I have discussed, certainly of the three I have privileged in the sound era. This overriding form of borrowing from Dante I like to call 'appropriation by metonymy.' In fine, myriad characters, scenes, themes, and structural elements from Dante's work have been given new cinematic life, and through the cinema his work is reaching an ever growing audience. Thus, in film, as in so many other areas, Dante has achieved rare star power. The new millennium thus bodes well for the Florentine poet, whose work continues to fulfil Cacciaguida's great prophecy as it provides 'sustaining nourishment' [vital nodrimento] to this century's pre-eminent visual art form.

Notes

1 This is an extension of T.S. Eliot's observation about the poet's universality, although he eschews that word and claims that Dante's work is more accessible to a foreigner and thus relatively 'easy to read': 'I merely affirm that the differences are such as to make Dante easier for a foreigner. Dante's advantages are not due to greater genius, but to the fact that he wrote when Europe was still more or less one' (*Dante* 13).

2 Frank Dyer (quoted in Uricchio and Pearson 48), the vice-president of the Motion Picture Patents Company, commented in 1910: 'The producing men ... realize [the potential for] the ultimate development of the art to a position of dignity and importance. When the works of Dickens and Victor Hugo, the poems of Browning, the plays of Shakespeare and stories from the Bible are used as a basis for moving pictures, no fair-minded man can deny that the art is being developed along the right lines.'

3 The text from *Purgatorio* 10 is part of a speech by Virgil: 'do you not know

that we are worms and born / to form the angelic butterfly that soars, / without defences, to confront His judgment?' In his commentary on John (1.13), Augustine uses a similar sentiment and offers the following interesting aside: 'All men who are born of the flesh, what are they if not worms? And from worms He makes angels.'

Bibliography

Bakhtin, Mikhail M. *The Dialogic Imagination.* Austin: University of Texas Press, 1981.
– *Speech Genres and Other Late Essays.* Ed. Caryl Emerson and Michael Holquist. Austin: University of Texas Press, 1986.
Barker, Arthur E., ed. *Milton.* New York: Oxford University Press, 1965.
Barthes, Roland. *S/Z.* Trans. Richard Miller. New York: Hill and Wang, 1974.
Baxter, John. *Woody Allen: A Biography.* London: HarperCollins, 1998.
Bloom, Harold. *The Western Canon: The Books and School of the Ages.* New York: Harcourt Brace & Co., 1994.
Bristol, Michael D. *Big-Time Shakespeare.* New York: Routledge, 1996.
Casadio, Gianfranco, ed. *Dante nel cinema.* Ravenna: Longo, 1996.
Daiches, David. *Milton: Paradise Lost.* London: Edward Arnold, 1983.
Danielson, Dennis, ed. *The Cambridge Companion to Milton.* Cambridge: Cambridge University Press, 1989.
Dollimore, Jonathan. *Radical Tragedy: Religion, Ideology and Power in the Drama of Shakespeare and His Contemporaries.* Brighton: Harvester Press, 1984.
Eco, Umberto. *The Role of the Reader.* Bloomington: Indiana University Press, 1979.
Eliot, T.S. *Dante.* London: Faber & Faber, 1929.
Fiske, John. *Television Culture.* London: Methuen, 1987.
Frye, Roland Mushat. *God, Man and Satan: Patterns of Christian Thought in 'Paradise Lost,' 'Pilgrim's Progress,' and the Great Theologians.* Princeton: Princeton University Press, 1960.
Gardner, Helen Louise. *In Defence of the Imagination.* Cambridge: Harvard University Press, 1982.
Hanford, James Holly. *A Milton Handbook.* New York: Appleton-Century-Crofts, Inc., 1961.
Hawkes, Terence. *Meaning by Shakespeare.* New York: Routledge, 1992.
Hirsch, Foster. *Love, Sex, Death and the Meaning of Life: Woody Allen's Comedy.* New York: McGraw-Hill, 1981.
Iannucci, Amilcare. 'Dante Produces Television.' *Lectura Dantis* 13 (1993): 32–46.

- 'Dante, Television and Education.' *Quaderni d'Italianistica*, 10 (1989): 1–33.
Jackson, Russell, ed. *The Cambridge Companion to Shakespeare on Film*. Cambridge: Cambridge University Press, 2000.
Jacobs, Diane. *The Magic of Woody Allen*. London: Robson Books, 1982.
Knight, Arthur. *The Liveliest Art: A Panoramic History of the Movies*. New York: New American Library, 1957.
Lewis, C.S. *A Preface to Paradise Lost*. New York: Oxford University Press, 1965.
Martinelli, Vittorio. 'Filmografia ragionata.' *Dante nel cinema*. Ed. Gianfranco Casadio. Ravenna: Longo, 1996. 103–19.
McDougal, Stuart Y., ed. *Dante among the Moderns*. Chapel Hill: University of North Carolina Press, 1985.
Schickel, Richard. *D.W. Griffith: An American Life*. New York: Simon and Schuster, 1984.
Sennwald, A. Review of *Dante's Inferno*, directed by Harry Lachman. *New York Times*, 1 August 1935.
Spiller, Robert E., et al., eds. *Literary History of the United States*. New York: Macmillan, 1974.
Uricchio, William, and Roberta E. Pearson. *Reframing Culture: The Case of the Vitagraph Quality Films*. Princeton: Princeton University Press, 1993.
Wagenknecht, Edward, and Anthony Slide. *The Films of D.W. Griffith*. New York: Crown Publishers, 1975.
Yacowar, Maurice. *Loser Take All: The Comic Art of Woody Allen*. New York: Frederick Ungar, 1979.

Early Cinema, *Dante's Inferno* of 1911, and the Origins of Italian Film Culture

JOHN P. WELLE

A national cinema is not a set of films which help to distinguish a nation from other nations, it is the chain of relations and exchanges which develop in connection with films, in a territory delineated by its economic and juridical policy.

– Pierre Sorlin, *Italian National Cinema*, 10

In describing the massive impact of film on the culture of the previous century, Raymond Williams observes:

Film was to become the central art form of the twentieth century, but it took a long time – longer in some nations and in some classes than in others – for this centrality to be recognised in relation to already established culture. From its marginal beginnings, within both the content and the institutions of popular culture, it made its way to a qualitatively different position: not only or even primarily because of its individual qualities as art, but mainly because of the radical change in the means of artistic production employed. In the early decades most cinema industries tried to move towards respectability within the terms of the established culture. (139–40)

In Italy, the cinema's movement from marginality toward cultural respectablity can perhaps best be understood by emphasizing the key role that the film *L'Inferno* (*Dante's Inferno*, 1911) played in gaining cultural prestige for the cinema among the country's traditional literary/cultural elite.

Directed by Francesco Bertolini and Adolfo Padovan for the Milano

Films Company, which had taken over an earlier Dante production begun in 1909 by the Saffi-Comerio Company,[1] *Dante's Inferno* helped prepare the way in Italy, the United States, and other countries for the multi-reel or feature film.[2] With its patina of high culture, this film constitutes an important example of 'film d'arte,' 'cultural up-lift,' or 'the cinema of quality'[3] and was the forerunner of such historical spectacles as *Quo vadis?* (1912), *Gli ultimi giorni di Pompei* (*The Last Days of Pompeii*, 1913), *Marcantonio e Cleopatra* (1913), *Giulio Cesare* (1914), and *Cabiria* (1914), the historical epic by Giovanni Pastrone with the collaboration of Gabriele D'Annunzio, a film which is considerded one of the highest achievements of silent film art. *Dante's Inferno* by Milano Films helped to establish the genre of the costume epic, which would propel the Italian film industry to international success in the years before the First World War. It was also one of many contemporary Italian films based on pre-existing literary texts. In this way, it foreshadows the importance that the interaction of film and literature would come to play in twentieth-century Italian culture.[4] As Gian Piero Brunetta asserts, 'Among all the histories of national cinemas that of the Italian cinema, along the entire arc of its development, is the most bound to the structures, models, and history of universal literature of all times.'[5]

Despite the remarkable flowering of scholarly and critical interest in silent cinema in past decades, films from the early period still seem strange from our current perspectives. Roberta Pearson explains why this is so:

> ... early film-makers tended to be quite self-conscious in their narrative style, presenting their films to the viewer as if they were carnival barkers touting their wares, rather than disguising their presence through cinematic conventions as their successors were to do. Unlike the omniscient narrators of realist novels and the Hollywood cinema, the early cinema restricted narrative to a single point of view. For this reason, the early cinema evoked a different relationship between the spectator and the screen, with viewers more interested in the cinema as visual spectacle than as story-teller. So striking is the emphasis upon spectacle during this period that many scholars have accepted Tom Gunning's distinction between the early cinema as a 'cinema of attractions' and the transitional cinema as a 'cinema of narrative integration' ... In the 'cinema of attractions,' the viewer created meaning not through the interpretation of cinematic conventions but through previously held information related to the pro-filmic event: ideas of spatial coherence; the unity of an event with a

recognizable beginning and end; and knowledge of the subject-matter. During the transitional period, films began to require the viewer to piece together a story predicated upon a knowledge of cinematic conventions. (17)

Within the terms outlined above, *Dante's Inferno* can be fruitfully situated on the cusp between what Gunning, along with André Gaudreault, has called the 'cinema of attractions' and the subsequent cinema of the 'transition toward narrative integration.' In fact, *Dante's Inferno* is perhaps best understood as a bridge between the early cinema of attractions and a cinema in transition toward classical film narration. Because this film is a compendium of the special effects and technical tricks characteristic of the early cinema influenced by Georges Méliès, I prefer to emphasize what comes before *Dante's Inferno* of 1911, rather than to read it in terms of what comes after. Respecting the format of the UCLA symposium – a general discussion of Dante at the cinema and on television for an audience of non-specialists – the following pages are synthetic in approach and seek to construct an historical context within which the Milano Films Company's Dante film of 1911 might be better appreciated (illus. 1). Because narratives of early Italian cinema are still relatively unfamiliar to non-specialists, I provide a brief overview of Italian silent film, followed by a synopsis of current critical work on the film itself. By way of conclusion, I point to the film's participation in a broader set of dynamics involving the interaction of film and literature, whose interrelationship has helped to establish the parameters of Italian film culture.

The Lumière brothers began the commercial history of film by showing the first moving pictures to a paying audience in Paris in December of 1895. Shortly thereafter, they took their 'cinématographe' to Italy and other European countries. In the spring of 1896, screenings were held in Milan, Rome, and Naples. In the southern capital, the first screenings were held at the most prestigious sites in the city, the Salone Margherita, for example, which had been open since 1890 in the lower reaches of the Galleria Umberto I.[6] The following newspaper announcement illustrates the cultural context of the new spectacle:

Questa sera riapertura del salone Margherita con programma completamente nuovo. Verrà esposto il Cinematografo Lumière, la più grande novità del secolo. Poi vi saranno: la famiglia Benedetti, acrobati icariani non plus ultra espressamente scritturati da Berlino. La coppia in miniatura

Illustration 1. Cover of a publicity pamphlet for Milano Films' *Inferno*.

Vargas Bisaccia reduce dal suo trionfale giro artistico in Russia, Spagna e Germania. L'étoile eccentrica francese Bloquelle, la baronessa Milford cantante tedesca, Hermand uomo serpente, la Belvalle canzonettista. In una parola, uno spettacolo attraentissimo. (Bernardini, *Cinema muto italiano* 1:31)

[This evening the reopening of Margherita Hall with a completely new program. The Lumière Cinematographe will be featured, the greatest novelty of the century. There will also be the Benedetti family, unparalleled flying acrobats expressly brought in from Berlin. The dwarf couple, the Vargas Bisaccia, recently returned from their triumphant artistic tour in Russia, Spain, and Germany. The eccentric French star Bloquelle, the German singer Baroness Milford, Hermand the snake man, Belvalle the cabaret singer. In a word, a most attractive spectacle.]

As this newspaper advertisement illustrates, the early cinema was primarily a curiosity, a scientific and technological marvel, which had closer associations with previous forms of spectacle, such as the magic lantern and the diorama, than with subsequent forms of visual narrative. As Aldo Bernardini observes,

Negli anni 1896–97, quando i fratelli Lumière di Lione ottennero i primi successi, realizzando film e organizzando pubbliche proiezioni a pagamento con il loro Cinématographe, lo spettacolo cinematografico aveva tutti i requisiti per diventare subito popolare, per trasformarsi in una specie di 'teatro dei poveri': si trattava infatti di un intrattenimento elementare, basato sull'immagine fotografica in movimento e quindi accessibile anche agli sprovveduti, agli analfabeti (che nel 1901 costituivano ancora quasi la metà della popolazione italiana); non durava più di mezz'ora e i suoi primi, ingenui raccontini risultavano immediatamente comprensibili a un pubblico che ritrovava sullo schermo personaggi e generi della narrativa popolare, gli stessi già ricorrenti nei Panorami, nei Diorami, negli spettacoli dei circhi e delle lanterne magiche. I fatti di cronaca rappresentati nei 'dal vero,' le suggestive vedute in movimento di Paesi lontani, esotici e sconosciuti, potevano facilmente colpire l'immaginazione popolare; così come risultava certamente affascinante per un pover'uomo poter assistere da un posto di prima fila alle cerimonie ufficiali, alle sfilate di re, regine, principi e capi di Stato, i rappresentanti di un mondo di ricchi e di potenti che il realismo dell'immagine cinematografica gli metteva per la prima volta a portata di sguardo. ('Industrializzazione' 22–3)

[In the years 1896–97, when the Lumière Brothers of Lyon obtained their first successes, making films and organizing public screenings for pay with their Cinématographe, the cinematic spectacle had all the requirements for becoming immediately popular, to transform itself into a kind of 'theatre of the poor': it was, in fact, an elementary entertainment, based on the photographic image in movement and therefore accessible also to those without means, to the illiterate (who in 1901 still constituted almost half of the Italian population); it didn't last more than a half hour and its first, naïve little stories were immediately comprehensible to a public that found again on the screen characters and genres of popular narrative, the same that were recurring in the Panoramas, in the Dioramas, in circus spectacles, and in the magic lantern shows. The events of daily chronicles represented in the 'films from life,' the suggestive views in movement of far-off countries, exotic and unknown, were easily able to strike the popular imagination; just as it was certainly fascinating for a poor man to be able to be present in a front-row seat at the official ceremonies, at the parades of kings, queens, princes, and heads of state, the representatives of a world of rich and powerful people that the realism of the cinematic image put before his gaze for the first time.]

In Italy, as in other European countries, films were shown at fairgrounds, in existing theatres, as well as in taverns, 'caffé-concerti,' beer halls, and other public spaces in the growing urban centres. The poet Gian Piero Lucini expresses the attitude of wonder and amazement toward the early cinema – which he encounters in a pavilion – that is typical of the period of the mobile exhibition sites in Italy:

Ma dentro al Paviglione, con maggior ragione, batterete le mani.
Vi mostrerò l'ultime scoperte della scienza:
ecco un cinematografo perfezionato e brevettato –
materia grigia, sensibile ai segni, simpatico e squisito
diaframma, a conservar la luce, i colori ed il moto.
Un teatro meccanico, dei quadri dissolventi,
proiettati nel vuoto, fatti rivivere, così, per giuoco;
cinematografo, cervello ed arte,
un'arte che si inganna, che riveste d'ogni preziosità
questa tua fragile perversità. (Verdone, *Cinema e letteratura* 125)

[But inside the Pavilion, with even greater reason, you will clap your
    hands.
I will show you the latest scientific discoveries:

Behold a cinema, perfected and patented –
raw matter, sensitive to signs, a friendly and exquisite
diaphragm, for conserving light, colours, and movement.
A mechanical theatre, dissolving pictures,
projected onto the void, brought back to life again, simply for fun;
cinema, both brain and art,
an art that is deceived, that covers with every preciousness
this fragile perversity of yours.]

In a similar fashion, Delio Tessa, a Milanese poet, film critic, and
would-be scriptwriter active in the 1930s, describes the mobile exhibition sites of the early cinema of attractions in his native Milan. His
recollections evoke the travelling film wagons of the early cinema before permanent film theatres were constructed:

A Milano i primi cinematografi io li ho ammirati alla Fiera di porta
Genova. Curiosità esotiche, arrivavano su quattro ruote coi serragli e con
le giostre. Uno di essi, il più modesto e il più a buon mercato, andava
ancora a manovella e ballava ch'era un piacere. Ma gli altri avevano le loro
belle macchine a vapore lucenti e fumanti che producevano l'energia
elettrica per la luce e per il resto. (120)

[In Milan I admired the first cinematographs at the Fair of Porta Genova.
Exotic curiosities, they arrived on four wheels with the animal cages and
the merry-go-rounds. One of them, the simplest and the most inexpensive,
was still cranked by hand and danced about in a funny manner. But the
others had their fine, steam-powered machines, shining and smoking,
which produced the electricity for the lights and all the rest.]

The period of mobile exhibition sites, 'i cinema ambulanti,' lasted in
Italy until around 1905, when permanent film theatres began to be
constructed in the major cities. In 1906, for example, Rome had twenty-
three cinemas, Naples boasted twenty-five, Turin nine, and Milan seven
(Bernardini, *Cinema muto italiano* 2:227–9). Aldo Bernardini explains the
transition from the early period of mobile exhibition sites to the establishment of permanent film theatres, in part, as the arrival on the scene
of a second generation of entrepreneurial film pioneers:

Le sale cinematografiche si aprirono al pubblico più largo quando alcuni
esercenti lungimiranti decisero di abbassare i prezzi d'ingresso (da 50 a
20–30 centesimi), preoccupandosi nello stesso tempo di aggiornare e di

migliorare le attrezzature delle sale e dei proiettori. Ne conseguì una rapida proliferazione delle sale stabili e quell'incremento della domanda di film e di apparecchi che rese possibile la nascita anche da noi delle prime Case di produzione. Questa importante svolta, decisiva per il rilancio e l'affermazione dello spettacolo cinematografico presso il pubblico più largo, si verificò negli anni tra il 1904 e il 1907, a partire dalle città del Centro-Sud (soprattutto Roma e Napoli), dove il tenore di vita era più basso e meno accentuate e virulente risultavano le lotte sociali.

Protagonisti di questa nuova fase di avvio delle attività cinematografiche furono alcuni pionieri di nuovo tipo, professionalmente preparati e dotati di uno spirito imprenditoriale che mancava ai cineasti del primissimo periodo. Produttori, realizzatori, commercianti, e a volte esercenti, questi pionieri della 'seconda generazione' ... ebbero il merito storico di creare le basi e le condizioni per lo sviluppo della cinematografia nazionale ... L'esempio di Roma determinò un analogo sviluppo dell'esercizio a Napoli, e via via, il fenomeno si allargò, negli anni tra il 1905 e il 1907, anche all'Italia del Nord, che vide la costituzione, a partire dal 1906, di società e iniziative sempre più numerose.

Il cinema poteva dunque ora contare su una clientela fissa, per lo più di estrazione popolare, che cominciava a frequentare con regolarità le sale di proiezione: anche perché analoghi miglioramenti stavano intervenendo a livello della produzione, con lo sviluppo del film di finzione, basato sui trucchi e su una vera e propria messa in scena, con la tendenza all'allungamento dei metraggi e quindi dei programmi di spettacolo, divenuti così vari da sapere accontentare tutti i gusti. ('Industrializzazione' 24)

[The film theatres opened to the larger public when some forward-looking exhibitors decided to lower the price of admission (from 50 to 20–30 cents), taking care at the same time to update and to improve the equipment in the theatres and the projectors. There followed a rapid proliferation of fixed film theatres, and that increase in the demand for film and for equipment also made possible the birth [in Italy] of the first production companies. This important turning point, decisive for the relaunching and the affirmation of the cinematic spectacle among the larger public, was confirmed in the years between 1904 and 1907, starting in the cities of the Center-South (above all Rome and Naples), where the tenor of life was lower and the social struggles were less accentuated and virulent.

The protagonists of this new phase of boosting cinematic activities were pioneers of a new type, professionally prepared and filled with an entrepreneurial spirit that was missing among the cineastes of the very first period. Producers, filmmakers, businessmen, and, at times, exhibitors, these pioneers of the 'second generation' ... had the historic merit of creating the bases and the conditions for the development of national cinematography ... Rome's example in the years between 1905 and 1907 gave rise to an analogous development in Naples, and in this way, the phenomenon spread also to Northern Italy, which saw the creation, starting in 1906, of ever more numerous companies and initiatives.

The cinema therefore could now count on a fixed clientele, of popular extraction for the most part, which began regularly to frequent the projection halls: also because analogous improvements were taking place at the level of production, with the development of fiction films, based on tricks and on a genuine *mise-en-scène*, with the tendency to increase the length of the films and therefore the film programs, which had become so varied as to appeal to all tastes.]

At this time, Italian literary intellectuals, including Edmondo De Amicis, Luigi Pirandello, and Giovanni Verga, among many others, began to take notice of the cinema (Càllari; Cardillo; Genovese and Gesù; Raya; Verdone, *Gli intellettuali*). In May of 1907, for example, Giovanni Papini attempted to explain the success of the cinema and reflected on its growing popular fascination. In an article entitled 'La filosofia del cinematografo' ('The Philosophy of the Cinematograph'), he provides a brilliant description of the modes and forms of consumption of early cinema in Italy:

> Da pochissimo tempo, in ogni grossa città d'Italia, assistiamo a una quasi miracolosa moltiplicazione di cinematografi.
>
> Nella sola città di cui sappia il numero preciso, in Firenze, ve ne sono già dodici, vale a dire uno per ogni diciottomila abitanti.
>
> I cinematografi, colla loro petulanza luminosa, coi loro grandiosi manifesti tricolori e quotidianamente rinnovati, colle loro rauche romanze dei loro fonografi, gli stanchi appelli delle loro orchestrine, i richiami stridenti dei loro boys rossovestiti, invadono le vie principali, scacciano i caffè, s'insediano dove già erano gli halls di un restaurant o le sale di un bigliardo, si associano ai bars, illuminano ad un tratto colla sfacciataggine delle lampade ad arco le misteriose piazze vecchie, e minacciano, a poco a poco, di spodestare i teatri, come le tranvie hanno spodestato le vetture pubbliche, come i giornali hanno spodestato i libri, e i bars hanno spodestato i caffè. (1328)

[In a very brief time span, in every large city in Italy, we are witnessing an almost miraculous multiplication of cinematographs.

In the only city of which I know the precise number, in Florence, there are already twelve, which is to say one for every eighteen thousand inhabitants.

The cinematographs with their luminous petulance, with their grand three-coloured posters, which change daily, with the raucous songs of their phonographs, the tired appeals of their small orchestras, the strident calls of their boys dressed in red, are invading the main thoroughfares, they are crushing the cafés, they are moving in where formerly there had been the halls of a restaurant or the rooms of a billiard parlour, they associate themselves with bars, they illuminate suddenly with the boldness of their electric lights the mysterious ancient squares, and they are threatening little by little to displace theatres, just as the streetcars have displaced public trams, as newspapers have displaced books, as bars have displaced cafés.]

Although Pierre Leprohon has argued that the Italian cinema did not experience an early period of disapproval and moral condemnation similar to that of the nickelodeon age in the United States,[7] Italian public officials and the ecclesiastical authorities were not unconcerned about the rapid growth of the cinemas. In 1907, for example, Giovanni Giolitti issued a circular enjoining local government prefects to begin to patrol the cinemas in the name of public morality (Bernardini, *Cinema muto* 2: 206–7). In 1909, Cardinal Pietro Gasparri, vicar of Rome, issued a decree forbidding Catholic priests to enter the cinemas of the Eternal City. Despite the high number of hagiographic films, biblical films, and films on the life of Christ, Cardinal Gasparri, invoking the authority of Pope Pius x, decreed: 'Uterque clerus prohibetur interesse publicis Kinematographis in Urbe' (Arioso et al. 11). This ban would be reissued in 1918 in the following terms: 'La proibizione assoluta al clero, così secolare come regolare, di assistere alle proiezioni che si svolgono nei pubblici cinematografi di Roma, anche se fossero di soggetto sacro, senza alcuna eccezione' [The clergy, whether secular or regular, are absolutely prohibited to be present at projections in the public cinemas of Rome, even those of a sacred nature, without any exception (Arioso et al. 11)].

The gradual transition from mobile exhibition sites to fixed theatres in Italy, as noted above, coincided with a similarly gradual transition toward longer films with a greater emphasis on narrative. In terms of exhibition, longer films meant that there would be fewer films screened during the day's programming. More people would need to be accommodated at a single showing. Consequently, film theatres were built that could seat as many as a thousand people. These cinemas had names like 'Splendor,' 'Eden,' and 'Fulgor.' In Venice the cinema Rossini resembled architecturally the famous Venetian theatre La Fenice. At Turin, il Ghersi was constructed; at Florence, il Gambrinus; at Genoa, l'Olimpia; and at Naples, l'Excelsior.[8]

Let us now turn to briefly consider aspects of film production in Italy between 1905 and 1911. In 1905, a decade after the Lumière brothers began making films in France, the first Italian film with a complex plot was produced by Filo Albertini: *La presa di Roma* (*The Capture of Rome*), an historical film celebrating the liberation of the Eternal City from papal control. By the time Italy began producing films in 1905, France, Germany, Britain, and Denmark had already developed flourishing film industries. After 1905, however, according to Paolo Cherchi Usai,

> the rate of production increased dramatically in Italy, so that for the four
> years preceding the First World War it took its place as one of the major
> powers of world cinema. In the period 1905–31 almost 10,000 films – of
> which roughly 1,500 have survived – were distributed by more than 500
> production companies ... the figures ... give a clear indication of the boom
> in this field in a country which, though densely populated (almost 33
> million in 1901) lagged behind the rest of Europe in terms of economic
> development ... In 1912 an average of three films a day were released
> (1,127 in total, admittedly many of them short ...) (123)

Three genres dominate the earliest period in Italian film history: (1) spectacle films based on historical and literary subjects; (2) documentaries; and (3) comedies. Historical subjects, such as that of *La presa di Roma* mentioned above, provided grist for the cinematic mill, particularly films dealing with the Risorgimento, but also with the Renaissance and Roman antiquity. These historical films, as well as the literary films which I will discuss below, constitute an important example of what Williams calls the film industry's 'move toward respectability within the terms of the established culture' (140).

A literary representation of the early Italian cinema, *Al cinematografo* (*At the Cinematograph*), by Gualtiero Fabbri, a novella of some forty pages, published in 1907, contains a reference to *La presa di Roma* which describes this proto-typical Italian historical film and the patriotic sentiments that it sought to arouse. *Al cinematografo* relates the story of a young intellectual, Gastone Fedi, who frequents the film screenings at an urban cinema for three consecutive evenings, falling in love with the cinema and with a certain young lady whom he meets there. After taking his seat, the narrator/protagonist describes the action as follows:

> Improvvisamente, non so per quale collettivo impulso, si fa un sepolcrale silenzio, poi un gran buio: il bottone elettrico, che toglie la luce, ha funzionato. E sul gran quadro, nel vasto campo della tela di *calicot*, appare vivamente illuminata dal projettore della *cabina*, e a lettere cubitali rossiccie, la scritta seguente: *La Presa di Roma*.
>
> Poi la scritta scompare, e, al suo posto, emerge nitidissimamente, con una grande vivezza di realtà, e con punto o pochi tremolii, la marziale figura del generale Carchidio, conte di Malavolta, quegli che, il 18 settembre 1870, è stato inviato dal generale Cadorna agli avamposti ... Questo il primo quadro, sparito il quale, fattasi la luce, e poi tornate le tenebre ... Ed è maravigliosa tanto che un mormorìo di ammirazione sfugge da ogni petto: E' *l'Alba del Venti Settembre al campo dei bersaglieri*. Ecco la livida aurora, ecco la brigata Modena accampata nella villa Bonacci, sulla via Nomentana, ed ecco il XII battaglione bersaglieri, che ne è parte, ancora tutto immerso nel sonno. Ad un tratto il trombettiere squilla l'allarmi: tutti i militi sorgono in piedi, e si vedono levare il campo. Essi comprendono che l'ora della battaglia è imminente, e al grido di *Viva l'Italia! ... Viva Roma! ...* si slanciano all'assalto. (Fabbri 17–18)

[Suddenly, for some unknown collective impulse, there was a tomb-like silence, then, total darkness: the electric switch, which turned off the light, did its work. And on the great frame, in the vast field of the *calicot* sheet, appeared vividly illuminated by the booth's projector, and in reddish cubed letters, the following text: *The Capture of Rome*.

Then the writing disappeared, and, in its place, emerged very clearly, with great vividness, and with no or only a few flickerings, the martial figure of General Carchidio, Count of Malavolta, he who, on September 18th, 1870, was sent by General Cadorna to the front lines ... This was the first frame, which disappeared, the light came back on, and then the darkness returned ... And it is so marvellous that a murmur of admiration escapes from every breast: It is *The Dawn of the Twentieth of September in the Camp of the Bersaglieri*. Here is the grey dawn, the Modena Brigade camped in Villa Bonacci, on the Via Nomentana, and here is the Twelfth Battalion of the Bersaglieri, which is part of it, still completely immersed in sleep. Suddenly the trumpeter sounds the alarm: all the soldiers jump to their feet, and the camp is seen rising. They understand that the hour of battle is imminent, and at the cry *'Long live Italy!'* ... *'Long live Rome!'* ... they throw themselves into the attack.]

After further describing the series of intertitles and moving images portraying this glorious (filmic) moment in modern Italian history, the writer seeks to capture the reactions of the spectators:

> A questo punto la commozione del pubblico, che assiste, è estrema. Un applauso prorompe spontaneo dal petto di ognuno. Gastone Fedi mormora convinto: – Perdiana! ... questo è spettacolo patriottico, moralissimo, educatore per eccellenza. (19)

> [At this point the excitement of the public which is present is extreme. Applause breaks out spontaneously from every breast. Gastone Fedi murmurs convincedly: – 'For goodness sakes! ... this is a spectacle that is patriotic, highly moral, and eminently educational.']

In addition to describing the screening of *La presa di Roma*, and to illustrating its didactic and moralizing purposes, *Al cinematografo* provides information about a typical program during the early period, including references to some twenty-four other films, which I will discuss briefly below. Perhaps most importantly, *Al cinematografo* offers precious evidence, albeit literary in nature, concerning early film audiences in Italy (Raffaelli 62–3).

In terms of film production, in addition to the costume spectacles, the early Italian cinema is characterized by a high number of non-fiction films. According to Cherchi Usai (124), Italian production companies 'developed an aggressive policy of documentary and real-life film-making, sending specialized film-makers to areas of natural beauty which had not yet been covered by Pathé, Éclair, and Gaumont, as well as to areas struck by natural disasters (such as Calabria and Sicily after the 1909 earthquake).' Once again, *Al cinematografo* illustrates the importance of this genre and includes references to such documentary films as *La caccia all'ippopotamo nell'Africa Centrale* (*Hunting for Hippopotamus in Central Africa*), *Canal grande* (*The Grand Canal*), *L'alcool engendre la tubercolosi* (*Alcohol Causes Tuberculosis*), *Lo sciopero* (*Strike, La grève*, Pathé, France, 1904), and *Vita proletaria* (*Proletarian Life*) (Raffaelli 68–9).

Professor Giusti, one of the characters whom Gastone Fedi meets in the course of the narrative, provides a long-winded theoretical dissertation on the nature of the early cinema. Celebrating film's capacity for realistic modes of representation, the professor expresses, in an exaggerated manner, the fascination inspired by the early non-fiction genre:

Anzi il Cinematografo è *realista* per eccellenza ... Oh! il Cinematografo! ... Ha mai pensato lei, signor Fedi, a questo splendido risultato edisoniano, in voga ora per tutto il mondo ... Che rivelazioni assolute e tutte esattissime! ... Per essa e con essa la commedia reale della vita, gli avvenimenti più importanti storici, le scoperte della scienza, le maraviglie dell'industria e del commercio, le gloriose bellezze dell'arte, quelle più riposte della natura e le meglio grandiose ... e mille altre cose ... ottengono realtà, valore, efficacia, risultato lodevolissimo educativo, morale e di progresso ... le meravigliose antichità di Grecia, di Roma, di Babilonia, dell'Assiria, dell'Egitto, del Messico, del Giappone, della Cina, delle Indie, eccetera, i costumi dei popoli, sì antichi che moderni, i ghiacciai dei poli, quelle zone iperboree non del tutto ancora rivelate, la loro fauna ... ne appaiono, o ne appariranno, davanti agli occhi inebbriati, in tutta la propria squisita realtà elettrizzante ... Il Cinematografo e l'arte sua ci riportano ai luoghi meno favoriti della sorte, a quei paesi scossi dalle convulsioni telluriche, o sismiche ... possiamo assistere alle desolanti scene delle inondazioni del Veneto e del disastro della Martinica, ai funesti effetti dei terremoti delle Calabrie, alla eruzione del Vesuvio, alla catastrofe distruttiva di S. Francisco ... E però, signor Fedi ... prevedo non lontano il giorno in cui la Cinematografia sarà parte integrale dell'insegnamento didattico, perché essa istruisce, moralizza, diletta. (Fabbri 47–9)

[On the contrary, the Cinematograph is eminently *realist* ... Oh! the Cinematograph! ... Have you ever thought, Mr Fedi, about this splendid Edisonian product, in fashion now in the whole world ... What absolute revelations and all so precise! ... Through it and with it the real comedy of life, the most important historical events, the discoveries of science, the marvels of industry and commerce, the glorious beauties of art, those most hidden of nature and the most grandiose ... and a thousand other things ... obtain reality, value, efficacy, an outcome laudatorily educational, moral, and progressive ... the marvellous antiquities of Greece, Rome, Babylon, Assyria, Egypt, Mexico, Japan, China, the Indies, etc., the customs of people, both ancient and modern, the polar glaciers, those hyperborean zones not yet completely discovered, their fauna ... they appear or will appear, beneath our inebriated eyes, in all of their exquisite electrifying reality ... The Cinematograph and its art take us back to the places less favoured by fortune, to those countries shaken by telluric or seismic convulsions ... we can witness the desolate scenes of the floods of the Veneto and of the Martinique disaster, the woeful effects of the Calabrian earthquakes, the eruption of Vesuvius, the destructive catastrophe of San Francisco ... And therefore, Mr Fedi ... I foresee not far off the day when the Cinematograph will be an integral part of didactic teaching, because it instructs, raises morals, and delights.]

The documentaries, travelogues, 'actualities,' that is, films of real events or 'film dal vero,' recounted here were an important international phenomenon of the early cinema. With regard to the travel genre, Charles Musser has shown that this form of documentary constituted 'one of the most popular and developed genres in early film' (cited by Gunning, 'The Whole World' 21).

Thirdly, the Italians developed successful comedies around such comic actors as Polidor, Fricot, and André Deed, to name only three of the many comics to achieve international followings. In the eight years between 1909 and 1917, Italian production companies created some 1,300 comedies (Robinson 109). Of this vast total, approximately 150 are known to survive today (Robinson 105). Discussing the comedians' attitudes of defiance and disrepect *vis-à-vis* the pieties of the official culture (the dialectical 'other' side of the process we have been tracing), Bernardini locates the comic genre within the context of Italian film history: 'Sometimes one has the impression that this genre provides a sort of free zone, emancipated from the bourgeois frustrations which are conversely punctiliously respected in the historical or dramatic films of the period, dominated as they are by moralism, the cult of patriotism, fine sentiments, respectability' (cited and translated by Robinson 111).

Similar in format to the costume epics with their interest in historical settings and famous characters, numerous short films based on literary and theatrical works were also created, derived, in part, from French models (Pathé founded Film d'arte italiana in 1909). These films were popular in Italy and abroad.[9] Canonical authors such as Dante, Tasso, and Manzoni were reduced to the ten-to-fifteen-minute format of these early films, as were texts by such popular writers as Carolina Invernizio, Eugene Sue, and Alexander Dumas. The Italian film industry's widespread borrowing from literature has been described by Gian Piero Brunetta as 'a migration of genres from literature to film' ('Migrazione' 83–90). Among the many works adapted to the screen, we note the following: five versions of Alessandro Manzoni's nineteenth-century novel *I promessi sposi* (*The Betrothed*), between 1908 and 1923, as well as other films based on the nineteenth-century historical novel; films derived from the epic tradition, including the *Iliad*, the *Odyssey*, *La Gerusalemme liberata* (*Jerusalem Delivered*), and the *Pilgrim's Progess* of John Bunyan; and even a film entitled *La cavallina storna* (*The Dappled Mare*), a film based on Giovanni Pascoli's poem of the same title.[10] Films derived from lyric opera were popular: *Rigoletto*, for example, and *Il trovatore*, to name but two. The works of Shakespeare were also reduced to this ten-minute format, and Italians produced short films based on *Romeo and Juliet*, *Macbeth*, *Othello*, and *Hamlet*.

Reflecting the importance of the 'historical/literary film' genre, and mirroring Dante's status as the national bard, the Italian film industry, between 1908 and 1912, produced no fewer than eleven films based on the *Divine Comedy*, on Dante's life, and on figures and scenes of Dantean inspiration.[11] Of these eleven films, *Dante's Inferno*, launched by Milano Films in 1911, is by far the most important and most influential. This film set a new standard for production quality and signifies the first serious artistic encounter between the nascent film industry and the Italian literary tradition. In this way, *Dante's Inferno* represents the apotheosis of the early Italian cinema's use of literary texts, and it established a number of records. It was the longest film yet made at its advertised length of 1,300 metres, and it was the most costly, at more than 100,000 lire (Costa 59–60). Its length, its cost, its innovative special effects, and its publicity campaign distinguish *L'Inferno* by Milano Films as the first true Italian colossal. It contributed significantly to a tendency toward multi-reel or feature length films. The passage from the short to the longer feature film, inaugurated by *Dante's Inferno*, helped to kick off the boom era of the Italian silent cinema and allowed film to compete favourably with the theatre for the first time as a spectacle worthy of the attention of the traditional literary/cultural elite.

L'Inferno was accompanied by an advertising campaign aimed at achieving high visibility for the new film product (Costa 59–60). Gustavo Lombardo, the future owner of the Titanus film production company and the producer of *L'Inferno*, also founded *Lux*, a weekly magazine devoted to films, entertainment, and culture (illus. 2). *Lux*, both before the debut of *Dante's Inferno* and after it began its run, published a number of articles about the film. On 16 October 1911, for example, four months before the film's debut, *Lux* published a parody of the opening stanzas of the *Divine Comedy*. Entitled 'La Divina Visione,' this poem brings Dante back to life to view the film that his poem had inspired. Here, the medieval poet's 'dark wood' is transformed into a film the-

Illustration 2. Cover of the film magazine *Lux* (October 1910), founded by Gustavo Lombardo.

atre, a trope that will be picked up by numerous other writers in the course of the century. The parody includes the following tercet of hendecasyllables, the traditional Italian line, in which Dante the poet testifies to the fidelity of the filmmaker's vision:

la Commedia interamente
io vidi riprodotta al naturale
come sgorgata m'era dalla mente.

[the Comedy in its entirety
I witnessed reproduced naturally
as it flowed from my mind.]

'La Divina Visione' even includes a parody of the notes at the bottom of the page which are prevalent in Italian scholarly editions. Although they are the words of Virgil in the original, in the text of the parody Dante affirms, 'Li parenti miei furon Lombardi' [My parents were Lombards]. As noted above, the film was produced by a certain Gustavo Lombardo. A note at the bottom of the page points out that Dante, in claiming that his relatives were Lombards, seeks to establish his family relationship to Gustavo Lombardo, so that, in good Italian fashion, he can enter the movie theatre without having to buy a ticket.

Prepared by a long and colourful advertising campaign (illus. 3), the film had its Neapolitan debut at the Regio Teatro Mercadante in the spring of 1911. Those attending included the dramatist Roberto Bracco, the novelist Matilde Serao, and the philosopher Benedetto Croce. Matilde Serao admits to having been impressed by the film and comments on its iconographic typology: 'For us, the film by the Milano Company of Dante's *Inferno* has rehabilitated the cinematograph ... And if Gustave Doré has written with the pencil of the draftsman the best graphic comment to the Divine Poem, this film has brought back to life Doré's work' (Serao cited by Bragaglia 16).

Dante's Inferno was also the subject of a lecture at the École des hautes études by Ricciotto Canudo, a poet and writer from Bari residing in Paris, who authored the first treatise on film aesthetics (Brunetta, *Storia del cinema* 144). The increased cultural status that this film gained for the cinema in Italy can be documented by the sympathetic response it prompted from Italian intellectuals, who also recognized the potential of the new medium to contribute to Italian cultural unification. As a reviewer wrote in an article from 1911, 'We judge the Dantean film to be

Illustration 3. Publicity poster for Milano Films' *Inferno*.

a work that will contribute mightily to the development of national culture and civil consciousness' (Brunetta, *Storia del cinema* 144). Another reviewer, Angelo Aliverti, whose opinions were quoted in *Lux* on 2 April 1911, makes explicit the early cinema's vast potential for constructing Italian national identity based on filmic adaptations of literary texts:

C'è dunque da rallegrarsi che con il film di Dante la cinematografia italiana, anzi milanese, dia il nobile esempio di volersi staccare dalle volgarità di cui tutti sono sazi ormai. Poichè è appunto in questa diffusio-ne insperata delle opere artistiche e letterarie in questo riavvicinamento dei capolavori della stirpe con l'anima popolare, che bisogna riconoscere presentire un fattore potente della coltura e della civiltà di domani. (3)

[It is encouraging, therefore, that with the Dante film Italian cinematogra-phy, Milanese actually, gives a noble example of wanting to distance itself from the vulgarities of which we are all sated by now. Because it is precisely in this unhoped for diffusion of artistic and literary works, in this reconciliation of the masterworks of the race with the popular spirit, that one must recognize the premonition of a potent factor of the culture and civilization of tomorrow.]

In recent decades, Italian film scholars have devoted considerable attention to *Dante's Inferno*. Aldo Bernardini, for example, has analysed the film's most prominent stylistic and technical characteristics ('I film dall'*Inferno*' 31). The original version of the film consists of three parts and fifty-four scenes, and illustrates the poem's major characters within an iconographical framework made popular by Gustave Doré. The film narrative begins in the dark wood and concludes with the requisite return to a vision of the stars. The trajectory is linear, the tone solemn. The characters are seen in declamatory poses. The main actors were chosen, by the way, for their physical resemblance to popular images of Dante and Virgil, as well as for their athletic ability: both men were accomplished mountain climbers, or 'alpinisti,' which was an impor-tant attribute given the numerous scenes of them scaling rocky slopes and descending dry creek beds. The film contains three flashbacks, veritable films within the film, one for each part: Paolo and Francesca, Pier delle Vigne, and Count Ugolino. This film constitutes 'a compen-dium of the best results, from a technical and stylistic point of view, reached by the international cinema in the first period of its development' (Bernardini, 'I film dall'*Inferno*' 31).

In fact, as indicated earlier, the mixture of stylistic and technical elements in this film makes it a kind of bridge between the earlier cinema of attractions and the transition toward narrative integration. Once again Bernardini sheds light on the isssue at hand:

> Il procedere per episodi quasi sempre autonomi gli uni dagli altri – imposto del resto anche dalle peripezie della lunga e travagliata lavorazione – sembra in apparenza non porsi in contraddizione con l'estetica del cortometraggio; e tuttavia la frequente rottura dell'identità tra scena e inquadratura – che era la regola nel cinema dei primi anni – con raccordi tra le scene e movimenti interni all'inquadratura, e soprattutto l'ampiezza e la coerenza della concezione strutturale, ne fanno davvero un primo, importante, significativo ed esemplare saggio di quello che il cinema stava diventando, entrando nella nuova, inedita dimensione del lungometraggio. ('I film dall'*Inferno*' 31)

> [The proceeding by episodes almost always autonomous one from another – imposed, by the way, by the vicissitudes of the long and troublesome work period – seems at the outset to not place the film in opposition to the aesthetics of the one-reel film; and therefore the frequent rupture of identity between the scene and the frame – which was the norm in the early cinema. The bridges between scenes and movements within the shot, and above all the breadth and the coherence of the conceptual structure, really make this film a first, important, significant, and exemplary sample of that which the cinema was becoming, entering into the new, uncharted dimension of the multi-reel film.]

While the innovative relationship between scene and shot makes this film a key text for understanding the transition toward more developed narrative, it also shares a great deal, as Bernardini points out, with the preceding one-reel format of the cinema of attractions:

> In generale si può dire che, dal punto di vista tecnico, l'*Inferno* sia una antologia degli effetti speciali, dei trucchi più noti e sperimentati usciti da quello straordinario laboratorio che era stato nei primi anni del secolo lo studio di Georges Méliès: trucchi che il 'direttore tecnico' Emilio Ronsardo ha saputo padroneggiare nella maggior parte dei casi con ottimo mestiere.

Tutto il film è costellato di doppie (e perfino quadruple) esposizioni, di sovrimpressioni per ottenere l'apparizione o la scomparsa di personaggi ... o le trasformazioni a vista di uomini in animali e viceversa; e non mancano numeri da circo, diavoli e personaggi che arrivano e partono (volando sospesi a cordi non sempre del tutto invisibili) e l'impiego di fondali neri per scomporre l'anatomia dei corpi ... Il faccione di Lucifero che mastica Giuda, verso la fine, può far ricordare quello grottesco della Luna nel *Voyage dans la lune* (1902) di Méliès. ('I film dall'*Inferno*' 32)

[In general, one can say that, from a technical point of view, the *Inferno* is an anthology of special effects, of the most noted and tested tricks emanating from that extraordinary laboratory of the first years of the century that was the studio of Georges Méliès: tricks that the 'technical director' Emilio Ronsardo knew how to pull off in most cases with excellent skill. The whole film is spangled with double (and even quadruple) exposures, with superimpositions to obtain the appearance and the disappearance of characters ... or transformations before the naked eye of men into animals and vice versa; and the film is not lacking in circus acts, devils, and characters that come and go (flying suspended on ropes that are not always completely invisible) and the use of dark backgrounds to decompose the anatomy of bodies ... The large face of Lucifer chewing Judas, toward the end, may bring to mind that grotesque face of the Moon in the *Trip to the Moon* (1902) by Méliès.]

To summarize, then, *Dante's Inferno* played a key role in gaining greater cultural prestige for the nascent film industry and began an important season of expansion in film production, culminating in the so-called 'golden age of Italian silent film' between 1912 and 1914.[12] Stylistically, the film is replete with the tricks and special effects characteristic of the earlier cinema of attractions, while it also begins to experiment with the narrative elements made possible by the multi-reel format.

Dante's Inferno of 1911 reveals a fledgling film industry seeking commercial success by linking itself to a prestigious literary tradition dating back to the Middle Ages. Moreover, Dante had been constructed during the movement for Italian independence and national unification in the later nineteenth century as Italy's national poet.[13] Consequently, as I have argued elsewhere ('Dante in the Cinematic Mode'), the high number of Dante films produced in Italy during the silent period testifies to Dante's role in the on-going process of constructing an Italian national identity, however problematic.

To be sure, because Italian national unification, as is well known, was literary before it was political, the 'high' literary tradition has played a significant role in attempts to create an Italian national identity. It is not surprising, therefore, that the Italian cinema, as we noted at the outset, would be characterized, throughout its entire development, by a remarkable number of filmic adaptations of literary texts. No less significant, although an area of cultural history still in need of further exploration, is the salient fact that Italian literary intellectuals have collaborated extensively with the film industry. According to Brunetta,

> Una collaborazione tra il cinema ed i letterati ... costituisce uno dei caratteri più evidenti e continui di tutta la storia del cinema italiano dalle origini ad oggi. Il nostro, fin dall'inizio, è un cinema che ha delle ambizioni colte e che si propone un certo fine di 'promozione culturale.' (*Intellettuali cinema e propaganda* 19)

> [Collaboration between the cinema and literary intellectuals ... constitutes one of the most evident and continuous characteristics of the Italian cinema from the origins until today. Ours, since the beginning, is a cinema that has learned ambitions and which proposes for itself a certain objective of 'cultural promotion.']

The Italian cinema's perennial project of 'cultural promotion' is evident even during the early period. Gualtiero Fabbri's *Al cinematografo*, for example, was commissioned to draw a bourgeois audience to the new film theatres.[14] For his part, Gustavo Lombardo, by bringing *Dante's Inferno* to the moving picture screen, contributed to a wider appreciation of the cinema by Italian literary intellectuals while promoting a humanistic image of Italian culture both at home and throughout the industrialized world. Finally, Dante's 'authorial' presence in the cinema of 1911 can be said to foreshadow that of Gabriele D'Annunzio, whose collaboration with Giovanni Pastrone on *Cabiria* of 1914 would help garner further prestige for the film industry, and would help attract other Italian literary intellectuals to the cinema.

In addition to the Italian cinema's abiding interest in filmic adaptations of literary texts, and to the extensive collaboration provided by literary intellectuals, Italian film culture has been characterized by a third (literary) element: the production of a distinguished body of writing about cinema. As Pierre Leprohon has observed,

... the Italian cinema was the first to give rise to theoretical and critical studies ... From the outset, therefore (and throughout its career), the Italian cinema was defined, encouraged and guided by a particularly numerous and active band of critics ... The first film criticism in the Italian press began appearing as early as 1910 ... No other country can boast as large an output of *cinema literature*: and books and magazines on the subject still abound in Italy today. (15, emphasis added)

Leprohon's point about Italian film culture developing a strong tendency to produce written forms about the cinema merits emphasis. The literary texts that we have examined in this essay – Lucini's poem on fairgrounds cinema, Tessa's recollections of the early cinema in Milan, Papini's article on the first film theatres, and Fabbri's novella *Al cinematografo* – can all be considered forms of what Leprohon calls 'cinema literature.'

It should be pointed out, however, that while Leprohon gives the year 1910 as the beginning of film criticism in Italy, already as early as 1907, the Italian publishing world began to produce a significant number of magazines and journals devoted to cinema, and 1908 is generally considered to mark the appearance of the first regular column in a daily newspaper devoted to film (Micciché 10; Turconi, *La stampa*). As Davide Turconi observes,

La stampa cinematografica italiana è indubbiamente una tra le più fertili e longeve. I primi periodici di cinema iniziano in Italia nel 1907, ossia nel medesimo anno in cui negli Stati Uniti inizia la pubblicazione di *The Moving Picture World*, la prima, e per anni la più importante, rivista di cinema del periodo muto. ('Prefazione' viii)

[The Italian cinematic press is undoubtedly one of the most fertile and long-standing. The first film periodicals begin in Italy in 1907, or in the same year in which in the United States begins the publication of *The Moving Picture World*, the first, and for years the most important, film journal in the silent period.]

Between 1907 and 1920, Italy would produce no fewer than one hundred new film journals, many of which folded after a year or two, with a declared circulation between 30,000 and 50,000 copies. Turin, Milan, Rome, and Naples were the chief centres of these periodicals, with

Rome being the most active, where some forty film journals were published during this period alone (Micciché 13–14). While many of these publications can be described as trade journals, it is also true that many of them contain attractive design, photographs, and graphic work; and some of them feature the collaboration of important literary intellectuals, directors, and cultural figures. *In penombra*, for example, published between 1917 and 1919, provided a forum for such writers as Roberto Bracco, Lucio D'Ambra, Fausto Maria Martini, Luigi Pirandello, Antonio Baldini, Rosso Di San Secondo, Salvatore Di Giacomo, Luigi Chiarelli, Sebastiano A. Luciani, Silvio D'Amico, and Ugo Falena (Turconi, 'Prefazione' viii).

With his use of the term 'cinema literature,' cited above, Leprohon seems primarily to have in mind film criticism, film theory, and popular forms of writing about film: what Italians have come to call 'il cinema scritto.' We might add to these forms of 'written cinema,' which have proliferated through a remarkable appetite for film journals in Italy, an extensive and distinguished corpus of Italian literary texts dealing with cinema, and, in the later decades of the twentieth century, television. From Gualtiero Fabbri's *Al cinematografo* to Luigi Pirandello's film-novel *Si gira! Quaderni di Serafino Gubbio operatore* (*Shoot! Notebooks of Serafino Gubbio Cameraman*), from Carlo Emilio Gadda's short story 'Cinema' to Mario Soldati's novel *Ventiquattro ore in uno studio cinematografico* (*Twenty-Four Hours in a Film Studio*), from Cesare Zavattini's play *Come nasce un soggetto cinematografico* (*How a Film Subject Is Born*) to Andrea Zanzotto's film-poem in Veneto dialect *Filò per il Casanova di Fellini* (*Peasants Wake for Fellini's Casanova*), Italian poets, writers, and dramatists have sought to analyse, to circumscribe, to celebrate, and to contest the power of the moving image. All of these texts, and many others, point to the centrality in Italian culture of the interaction of film and literature over the course of the twentieth century.

Within this broad framework, the literary representations of early cinema examined in this essay can be seen to work hand in hand with such high-culture literary films as *Dante's Inferno* to establish – already in the beginning decades of this century – a set of dynamics whose import in Italian cultural history has yet to be fully examined. It is precisely through greater attention to what Sorlin calls 'the chain of relations and exchanges which develop in connection with films' (10) that we can arrive at a greater knowledge of the historical development of a 'national' film culture in Italy.

Notes

1 Bragaglia (15) provides the following information regarding the production dates of *Dante's Inferno* by Milano Films: 'Dante returns to the screen
   in ... 1909, when in October, at the I Concorso Cinematografico di Milano
   (First Milanese Film Competition) the Saffi-Comerio Company presents
   Saggi dell'Inferno dantesco (*Scenes from Dante's Inferno*). They are part of a
   longer film that the Milanese company had started working on and that
   would be finished only in 1911 (at that time the Saffi-Comerio Company
   would be transformed into Milano Films).' All translations in this essay,
   unless otherwise noted, are my own.
2 Uricchio and Pearson describe the situation from the point of view of the
   U.S. film industry as follows: 'Although on-going research has substan-
   tially complicated our understanding of the emergence of the feature film,
   foreign imports, especially spectacular Italian high-culture subjects, still
   figure prominently in the story of the transition from single reeler to multi-
   reeler. Both Tino Balio and Kristin Thompson point to the 1911 American
   release of the five-reel *Dante's Inferno* as the first of a string of multi-reel
   high-culture films, many ... of Italian origin' ('Italian Spectacle' 95).
3 For a detailed study of the production and reception in the United States
   of the Vitagraph 'quality films,' produced between 1907 and 1910, including *Francesca di Rimini*, see Uricchio and Pearson, *Reframing Culture*.
4 For an historical overview of film and literary interactions in Italian
   culture, see: Bragaglia; Brunetta, *Forma e parola, Letteratura e cinema*, and
   'Letteratura e cinema'; Welle, 'Introduction'; and Marcus.
5 Brunetta as cited and translated by Marcus (2). In *Filmmaking by the Book*,
   Millicent Marcus discusses theoretical aspects of film adaptation, provides
   a brief chronology of adaptation in Italy, and analyses ten post–Second
   World War Italian films based on literary texts.
6 On the exhibition sites of early Neapolitan cinema, see Bruno.
7 'The discredit attached to the early cinema in other countries was non-
   existent in Italy, where the cinema attracted attention from the élite at a
   much earlier stage' (Leprohon 15).
8 On the Italian cinema's transition from being primarily a spectacle for the
   subaltern classes toward its establishment as a form of bourgeois entertainment, see Bernardini, 'Industrializzazione.' On the early film theatres,
   see also Brunetta, *Buio in sala.*
9 See Bragaglia for an exhaustive chronicle of the Italian cinema's use of
   literary texts from its origins through 1990.
10 For information on the films produced in Italy between 1905 and 1931, see

the filmography published in twenty-one volumes by Aldo Bernardini and Vittorio Martinelli.

11 These films, according to Prolo (117–84), include *Pia dei Tolomei* (Cines, Rome, Mario Caserini, 1908); *Francesca da Rimini* (Comerio, Milan, 1908); *Il conte Ugolino* (Itala Film, Turin, 1909), *L'Inferno da La Divina Commedia di Dante Alighieri*, directed by Francesco Bertolini and Adolfo Padovan, with Giuseppe de Liguoro as chief actor (1909, Milano Films, Milan, 1,000 metres); *L'Inferno dalla Divina Commedia di D. Alighieri* (1910, Helios Film, Velletri, 400 metres); *Il Conte Ugolino* (Itala Film, Turin, 1910 [a reissue of the 1909 film by the same name]); *Il Purgatorio* (Ambrosio Films, Turin, 1911); *Guido Cavalcanti* (Cines, Rome, 1911); *Il Purgatorio dalla Divina Commedia di D. Alighieri* (Helios Films, Velletri, 1911); *Il Paradiso dalla Divina Commedia di D. Alighieri* (Psiche Film, Albano Laziale, 1911, 660 metres); *Dante e Beatrice* (Ambrosio, Turin, 1912).

12 Brunetta describes the expansion of the Italian film industry in these terms: 'The years between 1912 and 1914 mark therefore the great expansion and consolidation of the structures: the Italian industry enjoys its maximum splendour and success in the United States, but it also enters triumphantly into Great Britain, Argentina, Russia, Switzerland, France' ('La nascita' 22–3).

13 In characterizing the use of Dante during the Risorgimento, Adrian Lyttelton writes: 'In the age of nationalism, poets enjoyed a peculiarly privileged role as the guardians and even creators of national identity. Nowhere was this more true than in Italy. After all, Dante was the founding father of the Italian language. The diffusion of the Italian language had been the work of a literary and humanistic elite, unassisted by a powerful central state, as in France, or by a vernacular reformation, as in Germany. Dante and the other great poets of the past were elevated to the status of patron saints in the national revolutionary cult' (72).

14 Pietro Tonini, who established one of Italy's first film journals, *Rivista fono-cinematografica e degli automatici, istrumenti pneumatici e affini*, in 1907 (Redi 5), was largely responsible for the success of Fabbri's novella. The owner of the Cinematografo Marconi in Milan, Tonini was constantly looking for ways to draw spectators into his film theatre. He was particularly concerned to draw an older crowd and one more socially elevated. At the beginning of 1907, he organized a contest for the best short story dealing with cinema. He offered a prize of 200 lire and publication of the winning story. He declared Fabbri's story, *Al cinematografo*, the winner and published it in March of 1907. The story had a marvellous distribution, thanks to Tonini, who marketed the slim volume to other owners of film theatres,

and sales reached the milestone of forty thousand copies by 1926. Fabbri
also collaborated for a period on the journal (Raffaelli 60–1).

Bibliography

Aliverti, Angelo. 'Il successo della "Divina Comedia" della "Milano Films."'
    Lux [Naples], 2 April 1911, pp. 1–3.
Arioso, Mario, Giuseppe Cereda, and Franco Iseppi. *Cinema e cattolici in Italia.*
    Milano: Editrice Massimo, 1974.
Bernardini, Aldo. *Cinema muto italiano. I. Ambiente, spettacoli e spettatori
    (1896–1904).* Bari: Laterza, 1980.
– *Cinema muto italiano. II. Industria e organizzazione dello spettacolo (1905–1909).*
    Bari: Laterza, 1981.
– *Cinema muto italiano. III. Arte, divismo e mercato (1910–1914).* Bari: Laterza,
    1982.
– 'I film dall'*Inferno* dantesco nel cinema muto italiano.' *Dante nel cinema.* Ed.
     Gianfranco Casadio. Ravenna: Longo, 1996. 29–33.
– 'Industrializzazione e classi sociali.' *Sperduto nel buio: Il cinema italiano muto
    e il suo tempo (1905–1930).* Ed. Renzo Renzi. Bologna: Cappelli editore, 1991.
    22–33.
Bernardini, Aldo, and Vittorio Martinelli. *Il cinema muto italiano, 1905–1931.*
    21 vols. Torino: Nuova ERI, 1991–6.
Bragaglia, Cristina. *Il piacere del racconto: Narrativa italiana e cinema (1895–
    1990).* Firenze: La Nuova Italia, 1993.
Brunetta, Gian Piero. *Buio in sala: Cent'anni di passioni dello spettatore
    cinematografico.* Venezia: Marsilio, 1989.
– *Forma e parola nel cinema.* Padova: Liviana, 1970.
– *Intellettuali cinema e propaganda tra le due guerre.* Bologna: Patron, 1972.
– 'Letteratura e cinema: Da un rapporto di subalternità ad uno di prevalenza.'
    Cinema e letteratura in Italia: Attualità di un dialogo. Lugano: Cenobio, 1983.
– 'La migrazione dei generi dalla biblioteca alla filmoteca dell'italiano.' *Italian
    Quarterly* 21 (Summer 1980): 83–90.
– 'La nascita dell'industria cinematografica in Italia.' *C'era il Cinema. L'Italia al
    cinema tra Otto e Novecento. Reggio Emilia, 1896–1915.* Ed. Flavia De Lucis.
    Comune di Reggio Emilia: Edizioni Panini, 1983. 22–3.
– *Storia del cinema italiano, 1895–1945.* Roma: Editori riuniti, 1979.
– ed. *Letteratura e cinema.* Bologna: Zanichelli, 1976.
Bruno, Giuliana. *Streetwalking on a Ruined Map: Cultural Theory and the City
    Films of Elvira Notari.* Princeton: Princeton University Press, 1993.

Càllari, Francesco. *Pirandello e il cinema*. Venezia: Marsilio, 1991.
Cardillo, Massimo. *Tra le quinte del cinematografo: Cinema, cultura e società in Italia 1900–1937*. Bari: Edizioni Dedalo, 1987.
Cherchi Usai, Paolo. 'Italy: Spectacle and Melodrama.' *The Oxford History of World Cinema*. Ed. Geoffrey Nowell-Smith. Oxford: Oxford University Press, 1996. 123–30.
Costa, Antonio. 'Dante, D'Annunzio, Pirandello.' *Sperduto nel buio: Il cinema italiano muto e il suo tempo (1905–1930)*. Ed. Renzo Renzi. Bologna: Cappelli editore, 1991. 59–69.
Fabbri, Gualtiero. *Al cinematografo*. 1907. Ed. Sergio Raffaelli. Roma: Associazione italiana per le ricerche di storia del cinema, 1993.
Gadda, Carlo Emilio. 'Cinema.' *La madonna dei filosofi*. Torino: Einaudi, 1973. 59–82.
Genovese, Nino, and Sebastiano Gesù, eds. *Verga e il cinema. Con un testo di Gesualdo Bufalino e una sceneggiatura inedita di Cavalleria rusticana*. Catania: Giuseppe Maimone Editore, 1996.
Gunning, Tom. '"Now You See It, Now You Don't": The Temporality of the Cinema of Attractions.' *Silent Film*. Ed. Richard Abel. New Brunswick: Rutgers University Press, 1996. 71–84.
– '"The Whole World within Reach": Travel Images without Borders.' *Cinéma sans frontières 1896–1918. Images across Borders*. Ed. Roland Cosandey and François Albera. Québec: Nuit Blanche Editeur, 1995. 21–36.
Leprohon, Pierre. *The Italian Cinema*. Trans. Roger Greaves and Oliver Stallybrass. New York: Praeger, 1972.
Lyttelton, Adrian. 'The National Question in Italy.' *The National Question in Europe in Historical Context*. Ed. Mikulás Teich and Roy Porter. Cambridge: Cambridge University Press, 1993. 63–105.
Marcus, Millicent. *Filmmaking by the Book: Italian Cinema and Literary Adaptation*. Baltimore: Johns Hopkins University Press, 1993.
Micciché, Lino, ed. *Tra una film e l'altra: Materiali sul cinema muto italiano 1907–1920*. Venezia: Marsilio, 1980.
Papini, Giovanni. 'La filosofia del cinematografo.' *Prose morali*. Vol. 7. Milano: Mondadori, 1959. 1328–31.
Pearson, Roberta. 'Early Cinema.' *The Oxford History of World Cinema*. Ed. Geoffrey Nowell-Smith. Oxford: Oxford University Press, 1996. 13–23.
Pirandello, Luigi. *Si gira! Quaderni di Serafino Gubbio operatore*. 1915. Milano: Mondadori, 1954.
Prolo, Maria A. *Storia del cinema muto italiano (1896–1915)*. Milano: Poligono, 1951.
Raffaelli, Sergio. 'Un pioniere.' *Al cinematografo*, by Gualtiero Fabbri. Ed. S.

Raffaelli. Roma: Associazione italiana per le ricerche di storia del cinema,
1993. 53–69.

Raya, Gino. *Verga e il cinema*. Roma: Herder Editore, 1984.

Redi, Riccardo, ed. *Cinema scritto: Il catalogo delle riviste italiane di cinema 1907–
1944*. Roma: Associazione italiana per le ricerche di storia del cinema, 1992.

Robinson, David. 'The Italian Comedy.' *Sight and Sound* 55.2 (Spring 1986):
105–12.

Soldati, Mario (under the pseudonym Franco Pallavera). *Ventiquattro ore in
uno studio cinematografico*. 1935. 2nd ed. Palermo: Sellerio, 1985.

Sorlin, Pierre. *Italian National Cinema*. London and New York: Routledge, 1996.

Tessa, Delio. *Ore di città*. Ed. Dante Isella. Torino: Einaudi, 1988.

Turconi, Davide. 'Prefazione.' *Cinema scritto: Il catalogo delle riviste italiane di
cinema 1907–1944*. Ed. Riccardo Redi. Roma: Associazione italiana per le
ricerche di storia del cinema, 1992. vii–ix.

– *La stampa cinematografica in Italia e negli Stati Uniti dalle origini al 1930*.
Quaderni di documentazione, no. 2, Amministrazione provinciale di Pavia,
September 1977.

Uricchio, William, and Roberta E. Pearson. 'Italian Spectacle and the U.S.
Market.' *Cinéma sans frontières 1896–1918. Images across Borders*. Ed. Roland
Cosandey and François Albera. Québec: Nuit Blanche Editeur, 1995. 95–105.

– *Reframing Culture: The Case of the Vitagraph Quality Films*. Princeton:
Princeton UP, 1993.

Verdone, Mario. *Gli intellettuali e il cinema*. 1952. Rpt. Roma: Bulzoni, 1982.

– ed. *Cinema e letteratura del futurismo*. 1968. 2nd. ed. Rovereto: Manfrini, 1990.

Welle, John P. 'Dante in the Cinematic Mode: An Historical Survey of Dante
Movies.' *Dante's 'Inferno': The Indiana Critical Edition*. Ed. and trans. Mark
Musa. Bloomington: Indiana University Press, 1995. 381–95.

– 'Introduction. From Pastrone to Calvino: New Perspectives on Italian Film
and Literature.' *Annali d'Italianistica* 6 (1988): 4–17.

Williams, Raymond. *What I Came to Say*. London: Hutchinson Radius, 1989.

Zanzotto, Andrea. *Peasants Wake for Fellini's Casanova and Other Poems*. Ed. and
trans. John P. Welle and Ruth Feldman. Urbana and Chicago: University of
Illinois Press, 1997.

Zavattini, Cesare. *Come nasce un soggetto cinematografico*. Milano: Bompiani,
1959.

The Helios-Psiche Dante Trilogy

VITTORIA COLONNESE BENNI

'The audacity of the cinema is opening up boundless new horizons,' enthused Giulio Capra-Boscarini (3), with high expectations of film versions of the Florentine poet's *Purgatory* and *Paradise*. And they would arrive soon enough, although they would not come from the producer of the 1911 colossal version of the *Inferno*, Milano Films. Instead, they would emerge from what we can only call a black hole in the history of cinema – a black hole surrounded by a penumbra of mystery.

On 25 October 1980 *La Torre*, a local paper in Velletri in the Alban Hills south of Rome with a certain interest in the movies, published a short article by Vittorio Martinelli on Helios Films, whose very first production had been a 1900 documentary on the Pontine Marshes (not far from Velletri). The documentary was then bought by Frieda Klug, a pioneer movie entrepreneur based in Turin, and distributed successfully in Europe. An odd postscript closes Martinelli's article:

L'estensore di questa nota, che sta curando uno studio sul cinema muto italiano, sarà grato a chiunque, in possesso di notizie, documenti, fotografie o altro, sulla Volsca, la Helios e le Psiche Film di Albano Laziale vorrà mettersi in comunicazione con lo scrivente.

[The writer of this note is preparing a study on Italian silent movies and would be grateful to hear from anyone who has information, documentation, photographs, or anything else on the Volsca, Helios, and Psiche Films of Albano Laziale.]

The dearth of information on these early film studios and their output has been a constant in my research into silent Italian cinema and has been attested by many of those most familiar with the subject area. Thus, Martinelli, above and elsewhere, has drawn attention to the many black holes that still plague, and perhaps will forever plague, the history of silent cinema, considering that only about 20 per cent of Italian production has survived. In similar fashion, Roberto Zaccagnini, cinephile and publisher in Velletri, highlighted the missing films of Helios still further when he offered me a small but important piece of information, mentioned in passing. 'At home we often spoke of that movie of the *Inferno*, because it was filmed, at least in part, in an old quarry on the Appian Way, almost right across from the railway station, a quarry that had belonged to my grandfather and where my father too had worked.' Moreover, eminent film historian Aldo Bernardini has repeatedly documented scores of *lacunae* in Italian silent cinema and has made it his life's work to fill in many of the missing links. In a project sponsored by ANICA,[1] Bernardini, with the help of Gennaro Bruni, data entry manager and coordinator, is producing the first computerized archive of Italian cinema, and, with amazing patience, he has managed to save relevant pieces of information on Helios and Psiche Films which amply supplement what Martinelli had already written on Helios Films almost two decades ago:

> Si trattava forse di una società di fatto: mancano dettagli sulla sua costituzione e sui suoi assetti. Le prime notizie risalgono all'aprile-maggio 1909 ... mancano tuttavia notizie sui suoi fondatori ... Nel 1910 si ha notizia che il suo stabilimento viene ingrandito ... ma è il 1911 l'anno di maggiore attività della Casa che trova il momento di maggiore notorietà girando in fretta e furia e facendo uscire in gennaio una propria versione (400 m.) dell' Inferno dantesco ... Lo 'scoop' della piccola Casa di Velletri viene ancor più valorizzato dal fatto che essa riesce a far girare alla stessa equipe anche una propria versione del Purgatorio dantesco di ben 700 metri ... Nel luglio 1911 la Helios in Francia fa capo a Félix Brochier di Marsiglia che, per lanciare i film danteschi prende un'originale iniziativa: invierà gratuitamente a ogni esercente che noleggi il film una copia dell'opera di Dante (400 pagine, in francese) perché possa verificarne la conformità all'originale.[2]

> [Perhaps it was a real company, but we know nothing about its articles of incorporation and assets. The first facts go back to April-May 1909 ... but we don't know who its founders were ... We know that in 1910 the studios were expanded ... but 1911 was the major year of activities of the studio, which reached its pinnacle of fame by filming in great haste for January

release its own version (400 m.) of Dante's *Inferno* ... The coup by the small Velletri studio is enhanced by the fact that, with the same cast, it managed to film its own version of Dante's *Purgatory*, no less than 700 metres long ... By July 1911, Helios was headed in France by Félix Brochier of Marseilles, who took an original step to launch the Dante films: he sends every movie theatre owner who books the film a free copy of Dante's work (400 pages, in French), so that they can check for themselves how close it is to the original text.]

Bernardini has collected much more information on Helios, but nothing to do with the Dantean productions. Surrounding them an air of mystery persists for two reasons: (a) Helios Films, after two film productions in 1915, ceased to exist, although it continued to be known as a company; (b) in July 1911, a few kilometres away from Velletri, Psiche Films of Albano Laziale was born and in January 1912 produced its first film, *Paradise*, 700 metres long, the same length as Helios's *Purgatory*:

La Psiche, grazie a questa prima realizzazione di regista ignoto (ma per la quale Armando Brunero, uno dei soci fondatori, ex collaboratore della Helios ottiene la collaborazione come soggettista e sceneggiatore di Giovanni Pettine, titolare di un'altra piccola società cinematografica) trova subito accesso al mercato nazionale e internazionale: in Inghilterra è distribuito da una società che dalla denominazione – The Paradise Film Co. – sembra creata appositamente per l'occasione; in Francia arriva grazie a Frieda Klug; mentre negli Stati Uniti il Purgatorio della Helios e il Paradiso della Psiche vengono distribuiti insieme, per una lunghezza di 4 bobine, dalla Superior Feature Film Co. di New York.[3]

[On the basis of this first production by an unknown director (but for which Armando Brunero, one of Psiche's founders, previously involved in Helios, enlisted Giovanni Pettine, owner of another small film company, as script and screenplay writer), Psiche Films finds immediate access to national and international markets. In England the film is distributed by a company – The Paradise Film Co. – apparently created for the occasion. Frieda Klug introduces the film to France, while in the United States Helios's *Purgatory* and Psiche's *Paradise* are distributed together as a four-reel feature by the Superior Feature Film Co. of New York.]

Bernardini's research on Psiche has produced many other facts. Thus, by September 1912, Brunero had already left for Rome to set up Brunero Film, and the last traces of the Alban Hills film company date from

16 January 1916, when, in the face of financial difficulties (caused in part by the First World War), the board of directors decided to reduce the share capital by 85 per cent, without dissolving the company. Nothing more is known after that.

My research, however, has yielded still further information. In 1911 and 1912, the specialized press advertised *Purgatory* and *Paradise* as if they were a single work by Helios Films, and also the three *cantiche* package, including Helios's *Inferno*, for a total likely length of about 1,800 metres, a true 'super feature film' for those years, which apparently was received quite well in America. *The Moving Picture World* of 6 April 1912 has this to say about *Purgatory* and *Paradise*:

> At the beginning of *Purgatory* we see Dante and Virgil leaving the shades of the lower regions ... Dante and Virgil pass from sphere to sphere in the *Purgatory*, and while there accost numerous spirits known to the author of the *Divine Comedy*. The scenes are quite exquisite in many instances. Several of them are imposing in the extreme and are superior in comparison to some of the scenes of the Milano version of Dante's *Inferno* ...
>
> The *Purgatory* pictures flash back frequently to scenes upon earth for the purpose of telling an anecdote pertaining to the life of one of the spirits, to illustrate the story which the spirit is relating to Dante at the time. These spirits and anecdotes belong, of course, to certain definite periods of Italian history which cannot be dealt with at this time. But such as there are of them are fairly well done ... In the scenes of *Paradise* there is a most radical change; so much of a change, in fact, that we can scarcely credit the *Paradise* picture as having been made by the same producer that directed the *Purgatory* picture. This may be explained in a measure by remembering that in producing such a work as the *Purgatory*, the director is enabled to use scenes of earth as very suitable backgrounds, but in a reproduction of Heaven, the scenes call for studio finesse of the highest order, plus imagination without limit. Any pictured version of Heaven is one which might cause the ablest producer to pause and consider the overwhelming magnitude of such a task. But the producers of this picture have faced their task with boldness that must be admired. Feeling sure of their ability they have gone ahead in no uncertain manner in giving us glimpses of Heaven, which are far different from any imaginings we may have had on the subject. 'Mid rolling clouds we see the divine Beatrice welcome Dante to the realm of perpetual joy, and, under her tender guidance, to him is revealed the great glory of the hereafter. It would be impossible to describe in detail the many changing glimpses that we are accorded of this delightful place of abode. Needless to say the manufac-

turers have spared themselves no pains and have successfully rendered visual pictures from Dante's inspired description.

I have quoted this description at length because it is, in fact, one of the few contemporary records which describe Helios and Psiche productions. Most experts know little of Helios's *Inferno*, while the *Purgatory* is not to be found and the *Paradise* is very difficult to describe in detail, as the American periodical indicates. Of the *Inferno*, Bernardini writes as follows:

L'opera della Helios, secondo il giudizio di qualche critico straniero d'epoca e di qualche storico, era meno abborracciata di quanto si potesse supporre: aveva una sua dignità espressiva e riusciva a divulgare il poema dantesco senza eccessive cadute di gusto e di misura. ('I film dall'*Inferno*' 33)

[In the opinion of several foreign critics of the times and of some historians, Helios's film was less botched than one would have supposed: it showed a certain expressive dignity and managed to popularize Dante's poem without too many slips into bad taste or exaggeration.]

Going on to speak of the *Purgatory* and *Paradise*, Bernardini adds that 'unfortunately we cannot speak of these two episodes of Dantean cinema with full knowledge of the facts, since we have not seen them' (33). These movies, then, constitute another black hole in the history of early Italian cinema, so much so that they even elude a researcher of Bernardini's stature.

In my own research, I have been able to screen a film which, together with Milano Films' *Inferno* (on which see Bernardini, 'L'*Inferno* della Milano-Films'; Iannucci; Welle), has provided me with a partial but sufficiently extended glimpse into the history of Italian and world cinema. The film is a 700–metre copy of the third and fourth part of the four-reel feature distributed in the United States in 1912 under the title *Purgatory and Paradise*. The footage opens with the title '*Purgatory and Paradise, Part 3*,' followed by a caption which situates the first scene, immediately following, still in Purgatory, in Eden. The subtitle, in large characters, reads:

BEATRICE ORDERS MATELDA TO PURIFY DANTE IN THE WATERS OF THE EUNOË BEFORE MOUNTING TO PARADISE. (*Purg. XXXIII*)

I was able to count fifteen captions, including the preceding one, all in the same large characters, which I transcribe here directly from the film, having been unable to find them reproduced in any existing text. Twelve 'poetic' lines appear in italics in the film to complement the captions:

The poet ascends from the Paradise on earth to the sphere of fire.

Beatrice was standing with her eyes all fixed upon the eternal wheels, and I fixed my sight, removed from there above, on her.

The poet meets Piccarda de Donati in the Moon.

To the world I was a virgin sister, and if the memory be rightly scorched, my greater beauty will not hide me from thee but thou wilt know me again for Piccarda ...

Dante flies through the sphere of Mercury and speaks to Justinian.

Caesar I was, and am Justinian, who, by will of the Prince of Love which I now feel, withdrew from out the Laws excess and inefficiency.

Charles Martel appears in the stars of Venus and explains how the wicked rulers lit the Sicilian Vesper.

... would yet have looked to have its Kings sprung through me from Charles and Rudolph, had not ill lordship which doth ever cut the hearth of subject peoples, moved Parlermo to shriek out: Die, Die.

Dante speaks to Cunizza da Romano, the sister of the tyrant Ezzelino and to Folchetto of Marseilles. Folchetto shows Dante the soul of Raab who favoured the Jews in the defeat of the Holy Land.

In the sun he meets St. Thomas of Aquinas who speaks of the life of St. Francis.

From her bosom the illustrious soul willed to depart, turning to its own real, and for its body would no other bier.

The poet passes through two circles of vivid light.

The souls of the blessed form a shining cross in the sky of Mars.

Here my memory doth outrun my wit, for that cross so flashed forth Christ I may not find example worthy.

Cacciaguida, the great grandfather of Dante, tells how he fought for Christ in the Second Holy War.

There by that foul folk was I unswathed of the deceitful world, whose love befouleth many a soul, and came from martyrdom unto this peace.

The light from the souls form words of warning and the design of an eagle.

So did (and so did I uplift my brow) the blessed image, which plied its wing driven by so many counsels.

In the sky of Saturn, the souls pass up and down a very high staircase.

I saw moreover, descend upon the steps so many splendors that methought every light which shineth in the heaven had been thence poured down.

The sky of the fixed stars: St. Peter, St. James and St. John question Dante on faith, hope and charity.

'Good Christian, speak, and manifest thyself: what thing is faith?' Whereat I lifted up my brow upon that light whence breathed forth this word.

God is reflected in splendor surrounded by Angels and Cherubim.

A point I saw which rayed forth light so keen needs must the vision that if flameth on be closed because of its strong poignancy.

The poet sees the glorious Mother of God in the empyreal sky.

I saw there smiling to their sports and to their songs a beauty which was gladness in the eyes of all the other saints.

The alternation of captions in capital letters, verses in italics, and images create a film rhythm and language which strike me as being close to those of Milano Films' *Inferno* (on which see Brunetta, *Storia del cinema italiano* 157).

As it is impossible to screen an Italian version, I reproduce here the Italian captions as they appeared in *L'Illustrazione cinematografica* of Milan when the film was released:

Dal Paradiso terrestre il poeta ascende alla sfera di fuoco. / Beatrice tutta nell'eterne ruote fissa con occhi stava, ed io in Lei Le luci fisse ...

Nella luna si mostra al Poeta Piccarda de' Donati. / ... Io son Piccarda, Che, posta qui con questi altri beati, Beata son nella sfera più tarda.

Dante trasvola nella sfera di Mercurio e parla con Giustiniano. / Cesare fui e San Giustiniano.

Nella stella di Venere si manifesta Carlo Martello che spiega come la mala Signoria fe' divampare i Vespri Siciliani. / Mosso Palermo a gridar : «Mora, mora.»

Dante parla a Cunizza da Romano, sorella del Tiranno Ezzelino, ed a Folchetto di Marsiglia che gli mostra Raab che favorì gli Ebrei nel conquistare la Terra Santa. / Cunizza fui chiamata; e qui refulgo, Perché mi vinse il lume d'esta stella, Ma lietamente a me medesima indulgo.

Nel sole si manifesta S. Tommaso d'Aquino che parla divinamente della vita di S. Francesco. / ... l'anima preclara Muover si volle, tornando al suo regno; ed al suo corpo non volle altra bara.

Il Poeta attraversa due cerchi di vivissime luci. / ... di quelle sempiterne rose Volgeansi circa noi le due ghirlande.

Nel cielo di Marte i Beati splendono disposti in forma di Croce. / Qui vince la memoria mia lo ingegno; Che quella croce lampeggiava Cristo.

Cacciaguida trisavolo di Dante narra come morisse combattendo pel sepolcro di Cristo nella seconda Crociata. / Quivi fu'io da quella gente turpa Disviluppato dal mondo fallace.

In Giove le luci si atteggiano in modo da disegnar parole ammonitrici, e si compongono a forma di Aquila. / Parea dinanzi a me con l'ale aperte La bella immagine.

Nel cielo di Saturno le anime percorrono un'altissima scala. / Di color d'Oro, in che raggio traluce, Vid'io uno scaleo eretto in suso.

Nel cielo delle stelle fisse, S. Pietro, S. Jacopo e S. Giovanni interrogano Dante sulla Fede, Speranza e Carità. / Di,' buon Cristiano, fatti manifesto: Fede che è?

Dio è raffigurato in un punto risplendente circondato d'Angeli e Cherubini. / Un punto vidi che raggiava lume acuto sì, che il viso ch'egli affuoca/Chiuder conviensi per lo forte acume.

Nell'Empireo vede il Poeta la gloriosa Madre di Dio. / ... una bellezza, che letizia Era negli occhi a tutti gli altri santi. (Bernardini and Martinelli 55)

These captions were republished recently in a special issue of *Bianco e Nero* and referenced as 'a series of verses with which Psiche Films expounded the content of its film.' A comparison of the captions transcribed from the American copy with those published by *Bianco e Nero* reveals that what we have here are the subtitles of the original Italian version. This is a small but interesting piece of new information which can help in the reconstruction of the Psiche *Paradise*.

Let us return to the images. The cinematic language of the opening scene, featuring Matelda and 'terrestrial' flashbacks (the death of Cacciaguida, Raab hiding the Jews, the Sicilian Vespers evoked by Carlo Martello, the death of Saint Francis), offers a sharp contrast with the rest of the film. They are, then, crucial scenes which provide an insight, however approximate, into the films (*Inferno* and *Purgatory*, by Helios Films) which I have not been able to see. It is true that *Paradise* was produced by Psiche Films but, considering that the two studios were closely linked and that the three *cantiche* were distributed and shown as a single work, there could not have been a great stylistic difference between the 'non-heavenly' scenes; nor could there have been much of a difference between the 'less terrestrial' scenes of the *Purgatory* and the 'more heavenly' ones of *Paradise*.

Opinions on these three films vary widely. We have already noted the views of an important contemporary source (*The Moving Picture World*) and the cautious appraisal of Bernardini. Of the three, Helios's *Inferno*, as Martinelli has remarked to me, was 'a short controversial work, more deserving than anybody has ever said.' Roberto Paolella, the first great Italian movie historian and teacher of Martinelli, offers the following amusing anecdote about the film:

> ... un altro Inferno appare l'anno appresso, a cura della Helios Films di Velletri, ridotto a metri 400: dove a un certo punto si vede pure Taide, interamente nuda e che accoccolata sulle natiche trema miseramente di freddo, fin quando interviene la questura a toglierla da questa incomoda posizione. (82)

> [... the year after another *Inferno* appears, by Helios Films of Velletri, cut to 400 metres, in which, at a certain point, you even get to see Thais, completely naked, squatting and shivering, until the police intervene to help her out of that uncomfortable position.]

This short aside, though a bit imprecise and certainly colourful, is nonetheless significant. It is imprecise because 'the year after' was in fact two months before the Milano film opened in Naples. The Helios *Inferno*, therefore, actually came out before the much heralded Milano film. But Paolella, a true pioneer, was writing in 1956, long before he could profit from the recent boom in research on the early history of Italian cinema. The reference to Thais being taken away by the police is colourful, and likewise significant, since she obviously caused a stir, something confirmed by the non-existence of a 'censor's certificate' which many other films of the times carry (Bernardini and Martinelli 247). We do not know whether Paolella had seen this *Inferno*, also known as *Visions of Inferno*, but he must have found the information about Thais and the police raid in some contemporary source. Let us examine, therefore, these sources, especially reviews, in order to ferret out more thoroughly the prevailing opinions of the time.

In Italy, the leading cine magazine, *Lux*, which had been founded by Gustavo Lombardo and which was to play an important role in the publicity launch of Milano Films' *Inferno*, penned a decidedly negative review:

Tutto il nostro buon volere – come sicuramente quello del pubblico – si è infranto contro l'indecente mistificazione, contro la profanazione più sfacciata e volgare della più grande opera umana e del più squisito e maggior poeta italico ... Il film tenta di riprodurre l'Inferno quale è descritto nel poetico racconto di Dante. Ma, a parte le frequenti e innumerevoli omissioni, quali, per esempio, il Limbo, Cerbero e i golosi, lo Stige, l'episodio di Filippo Argenti ..., ecc. ecc., tutti gli episodi e gli ambienti che vi sono riprodotti appariscono falsati, impiccioliti, talvolta anche pervasi di balorda comicità, sì da venire spontaneamente la voglia di domandarsi se la spettabile casa di Velletri non abbia voluto offrirci una mal riuscita parodia ... Ed infatti il film comincia col presentare un Dante ... diciamo così, cretino. Minuscolo, dal viso terribilmente e comicamente truccato fino a lasciar vedere anche sulla tela le enormi rughe dipinte ... (Bernardini and Martinelli 248)

[All our good will – and surely that of the public – was dispelled by the indecent and deliberate misinterpretation, by the most brazen and vulgar desecration of the greatest human work and of the most refined and important Italian poet. The film tries to reproduce the *Inferno* as it is described in the poetic narrative by Dante. Leaving aside the frequent and innumerable omissions, such as, for example, Limbo, Cerberus, Styx, the Filippo Argenti episode ..., etc. etc., all the episodes and surroundings there reproduced appear counterfeit, reduced, even at times infused with a wicked sense of humour, so much so that the question arises whether the reputable Velletri studio had rather wanted to offer us a botched parody ...

In fact, the film begins by presenting – how can we put it – a rather idiotic Dante, diminutive, with a face heavily and so comically made up that the enormous wrinkles come through as painted even on the screen ...]

Elsewhere, however, the reviews were far more favourable. *La Cine-Fono e La Rivista Fono-Cinematografica*, for example, commented as follows:

La Helios ha un solo torto, quello di aver voluto sfruttare intempestivamente l' Inferno, già annunziato da tempo dalla Milano Films. Il lavoro presentato sotto questa cattiva luce, non ottenne il successo che specie alcuni quadri si sarebbero meritati ... Alcuni quadri dell'*Inferno* sono una vera affermazione e convincono che la giovane casa italiana non era impari all'aspro cimento impostosi. (Bernardini and Martinelli 249)

[The only fault of Helios Films was its desire to capitalize in an untimely manner on the *Inferno* announced for some time by Milano Films. Cast thus under a bad light, the film did not obtain the success which some scenes would have especially deserved ... Some scenes of the *Inferno* are a real accomplishment and attest that the young Italian studio was not unequal to the difficult task it took upon itself.]

Moreover, on 30 January 1911, the correspondent for *Vita Cinematografica* wrote from Bari:

In questi giorni suscita grande interesse l'Inferno dell'Helios. Tanto che se ne chiese con insistenza una ripetizione, alla quale il proprietario (del cinema Lux) acconsentì, appagando il desiderio di tutti. (Bernardini and Martinelli 249)

[These days Helios Films' *Inferno* has excited great interest. So much so that there was an insistent request that it be held over, to which request the owner (of the Lux theatre) agreed, thus satisfying everybody's wishes.]

And on the same date the film periodical *Arte y Cinematografía* of Madrid carried the following:

Hemos visto proyectada la conta editada por la casa Helios, y, en verdad, nos ha satisfecho. Hemos visto vivido lo que por nuestra mente pasó ya hace años. Sin necesidad de leer los subtítulos, hemos ido reconociendo uno a uno los Círculos del fantástico viaje ... Y, al admirarlos, nos hemos fijado en su preparación y ejecución. La casa editora ha querido hacer con ella un alarde de recursos y lo ha logrado. Tiene escenas en las que se ha alcanzado un grado tal de realidad, que supera, acaso, a cuanto se esperara. En ejecución hemos visto escenas en conjunto muy ajustadas, y figuras de primer término muy bien interpretadas. Es el *summum*? No lo afirmamos. Es un éxito? No lo negaremos ... (Bernardini and Martinelli 250)

[We have seen the narrative produced by the Helios studios and we were frankly satisfied. We have seen in images what for years had been only in our mind. Without having to read the subtitles, we recognized one by one the Circles of the fantastic voyage. In admiring them, we have particularly noted the script and the execution. The studio wanted to turn the film into a showcase of special effects and has succeeded. There are scenes in which such a high degree of realism is reached that it surpasses all expectations. We have seen scenes very well produced and known characters very well interpreted. Is this the best of the best? We would not go so far as to say that. Is it a success? That, we do not deny ...]

But when the movie crossed the Atlantic, the negative evaluation expressed in *Lux* held sway. This is not surprising, given the fact that the publicity campaign launching Milano Films' *Inferno* in the United States had included a warning to the American public to 'beware of fraud,' that is, to be on guard for a shoddy imitation of Milano Films' monumental film, an obvious allusion to the Helios *Inferno*. This notion that the latter film is greatly inferior to Milano Films' epic becomes the main thrust of Stephen Bush's extremely negative review of the Helios *Inferno* in *The Moving Picture World* of 6 January 1912:

This work is a base and clumsy imitation of the magnificent product of the Milano Films Company. All the great and striking features of the original creation are omitted entirely. With two exceptions every scene has been 'borrowed' from the Milano Films Company and invariably spoiled in the 'borrowing.' There is no pretense of art; the thing is evidently a very hurried effort to give a very cheap edition of the marvelous original ... Nothing could be cheaper than the opening scenes in the Helios make. The title boldly promises us the sight of the wild beasts that bar the path of the poet toward the summit, but there is no performance on the screen. This petty swindle well characterizes the spirit of the whole production ... The imitation leaves out the City of Dis entirely, not a trace in the Helios

Advertisement for Milano Films' *Inferno* in the *New York Dramatic Mirror* (1911).

make of the journey through the Stygian lake, the tower on the shores of Dis ... (Bernardini and Martinelli 250)

Still, Bush is forced to admit that the Helios movie contained more scenes than he was able to view and that 'it appears to have been reduced in size after it came to this country' (Bernardini and Martinelli 250). Once again, therefore, the state of incomplete information rears its ugly head. But on the basis of this documentary evidence, it would appear that the Helios *Inferno* was not as shoddy and irrelevant as some critics maintain, considering that it was discussed for over a year from Bari to Madrid to New York, and many of these discussions were positive.

We have already discussed how enthusiastically *Purgatory* and *Paradise* were at first received in America by *The Moving Picture World* of 6 April 1912. But the *Moving Picture* article tells us hardly anything about the contents of *Purgatory*. On the other hand, Martinelli writes:

Giuseppe Berardi, che ne è il factotum, se ne assume, coadiuvato dall'operatore Arturo Busnengo, sia la regia che l'interpretazione di Dante mentre ad Armando Novi viene affidato il ruolo di Virgilio. In effetti, libro alla mano, Berardi racconta di come Dante e Virgilio, dopo aver incontrato Catone Uticense, giungano in barca sulle rive del Purgatorio; ed in una serie di lever de rideau appaiono il poeta mantovano Sordello, i principi che ritardarono il pentimento dei loro peccati fino al punto di morte, una donna senese uccisa dal marito, ed altri. Il clou di questo viaggio, a giudizio di tutti i recensori, è il sogno di Dante, il quale, per toccare i vari gironi, si vede trasportato da un'aquila d'oro. L'effetto, per l'epoca ancora inusitato, venne realizzato con molta cura da Busnengo, con l'aiuto di Ferdinando Politi, che curava le riprese del film ... Ne Il Purgatorio, lungo i settecento metri della proiezione ed in successione rapida ... si susseguono i superbi, gli accidiosi, gli iracondi, gli avari, i golosi, i lussuriosi ... Dopo le fiamme del settimo girone, i Poeti entrano nel Paradiso terrestre e, dopo l'incontro con Matilde, Contessa di Toscana, altro prodigio, il carro trionfale tirato da un grifone, con le sette donne rappresentanti altrettante virtù, e quindi, l'apparizione di Beatrice. Il film termina con Dante che si immerge nelle acque lustrali dell'Eunoé, che lo purificano, preparandolo, come recita l'ultima didascalia 'a salire sulle stelle.' (109)

[Giuseppe Berardi, who is the jack of all trades in the production, assumes both the role of director, with the assistance of Arturo Busnengo as cameraman, and the part of Dante, while Armando Novi takes on the role of Virgil. Closely following the text, Berardi narrates how Dante and Virgil, after meeting Cato Uticensis, reach the shores of Purgatory by boat; in a series of *lever de rideau* several characters appear: the Mantuan poet Sordello, the princes who delayed repenting for their sins up until the moment of their death, a woman from Siena killed by her husband, and others. The highlight of the voyage, according to all the critics, is Dante's dream: to reach each circle he is transported by a golden eagle. The special effects, unprecedented for the times, were painstakingly produced by Busnengo with the help of the cinematographer Ferdinando Politi ... In the *Purgatory*, throughout the 700 metres running length and in rapid succession ... come the proud, the slothful, the wrathful, the greedy, the gluttons, the lovers of luxury ... After the flames of the Seventh Circle, the Poets come into the Terrestrial Paradise and, after the meeting with Matilde, Countess of Tuscany, comes another marvel, the triumphal chariot pulled by a Gryphon, with the seven women who represent as many virtues, and then Beatrice appears. The film ends with Dante bathing in the lustral waters of the Eunoé, which purify him and prepare him, as the last caption tells us, ' to ascend to the stars.']

Martinelli also gives us a taste of what contemporary reviews were like:

Il Bioscope londinese parlò, a proposito della realizzazione de *Il Purgatorio* di 'rugged grandeur,' *Le Courier Cinematographique* di Parigi di 'exécution admirable.' Per lo *Erste Internationale Film-Zeitung* di Berlino: 'Das Fegefeuer übertrifft alles' (*Il Purgatorio* supera tutti), mentre il già citato *The Moving Picture World* si compiace che Dante, 'di cui si aveva sino a quel momento una vaga idea, venga ora fatto conoscere al pubblico americano.' Solo in Italia, tra il generale consenso, qualche aristarco avanza riserve: 'Per quanto non metta in dubbio il nobile scopo che anima coloro che si sono accinti ad un'impresa si ardua, certi colossi dovrebbero essere sacri e non profanati da alcuno' – tuona A.A. Cavallari su *La Vita Cinematografica*. Ma è voce ... nel deserto: critica e pubblico, italiano e straniero, sono concordi nell'assegnare all'impresa della Helios un ampio riconoscimento. (109)

[Speaking of the production of *Purgatory*, the *Bioscope* of London notes its 'rugged grandeur,' while *Le Courier Cinématographique* of Paris praises its 'exécution admirable.' In the opinion of *Erste Internationale Film-Zeitung* of Berlin, 'Das Fegefeuer übertrifft alles' (*Purgatory* beats everything), whereas

The Moving Picture World, earlier quoted, rejoices that Dante, 'who was only vaguely known, is now made available to the American public.' Only in Italy, disregarding the general consensus, do a few doubting Thomases voice their reservations. 'Though I don't doubt the lofty purpose harboured by those who embarked upon such an arduous undertaking, certain giants should be kept sacred and not be desecrated by anybody,' thunders one A.A. Cavallari in *La Vita Cinematografica.* But he is a lone voice in the wilderness, for both Italian and foreign critics and publics agree in showering ample praise on Helios Films' accomplishment.]

Brunetta refers to the Helios *Purgatory* in connection with the Helios *Inferno* and the Psiche *Paradise,* all of which he lumps together:

Una piccola casa cinematografica, la Helios, sfruttando l'attesa pubblicitaria, brucia sul tempo la Milano Film e realizza una pellicola omonima riuscendo a conquistarsi alcuni mercati stranieri. Qualche tempo dopo la stessa Helios realizza il Purgatorio e Paradiso, che senza avere la capacità di invenzione visiva e plastica dell' Inferno della Milano, tenta una serie di effetti visivi abbastanza interessanti. La tecnica di sovrimpressione ha ormai raggiunto ottimi livelli, mentre manca quella cura nella regia che si sentiva nel film della Milano. Qui Dante ogni tanto benedice qualche peccatore e la ricostruzione delle scene o i movimenti dei personaggi sono piuttosto approssimativi. Il flash-back comunque funziona da elemento conduttore e il continuum narrativo è spezzato da un variare dei piani, dei punti di vista e della unità spazio-temporale. Trionfano, più che nell' Inferno, i moduli iconografici e figurativi del simbolismo e della pittura liberty. Le metamorfosi sono continue e gli effetti visivi sono il vero punto di interesse del film che culmina, nel gran finale, con la visione della trinità e l'apparizione di Cristo all'interno della croce. (*Storia del cinema italiano* 159)

[A small film studio, Helios Films, taking advantage of the suspense created by advertising, beats Milano Film to the post, producing a film by the same name and managing to conquer some foreign markets for itself. Some time later, the same Helios Films produced *Purgatory* and *Paradise,* which, without exhibiting the same visual and plastic inventiveness of Milano Films' *Inferno,* attempt a series of rather interesting visual effects. Double exposure techniques had by then reached high levels, though the direction lacks the precision evident in the Milano production. From time to time Dante gives his blessing to some sinner and the reconstruction of

scenes or the movements of characters are rather vague. Flashbacks, nonetheless, act as a unifying element and the narrative continuum is broken
up by variations in perspective, point of view, and space-time relations.
Here, more so than in *Inferno*, the representational and figurative techniques of symbolism and *Art Nouveau* painting predominate. There are
continuous metamorphoses and the visual effects are the real point of
interest of the film, which culminates, in a grand finale, in the vision of the
Trinity and the apparition of Christ within the cross.]

The copy of the *Paradise* which I was able to see presents a different
finale. In agreement with Dante's text in Canto xiv, the apparition of
Christ within the Cross is placed toward the middle of *Paradise* by
Psiche Films, which ends with a smiling Dante, sitting at an escritoire,
who puts down his quill, rolls up a parchment, and presses it to his
heart, under the light of a three-branched brass oil lamp. I was also able
to screen a fragment of *Paradise*, in the possession of the British Film
Institute, at the British National Archives, the sole copy of which is also
listed in the American Film Institute database. Just over four minutes in
length, with ten captions in English, some in prose and some in verse
(sometimes equivalent to those of the longer film), the fragment opens
with Cacciaguida (Scene Ten of the other film) and ends with a flight of
souls in the sky following Dante's prostration to the Madonna. Scenes
and framing of shots are the same as in the longer film, but they are
edited differently.

   It is impossible to form a precise and definite opinion of these three
films, given the lack of complete and unequivocal information about
these productions. But many elements, such as the originality and
ingenuity of the films and the pleasure they still bring to viewers, attest
that these films, so little known, are anything but the low-quality product of an inferior competitor to Milano Films. On the contrary, from
what one can gather, the Dante trilogy by Helios and Psiche Films can
be placed at the top of contemporary Italian and world productions for
the following reasons: (a) the complexity of the project; (b) the running
time and distribution; and (c) the conception of an original film vernacular (all the more so in the case of *Paradise*).

   (a) It is true that *Inferno* and *Purgatory* seem to have been produced by
one film studio (Helios) and *Paradise* by another (Psiche), but we have
already discussed the close relationship between the two. Furthermore,
the entire project clearly seems to have been coordinated, not from the
start perhaps, but certainly not long after. It would also seem reason-

able to suppose that the dynamic Frieda Klug may have influenced this coordination. From her Turin office, at the prestigious address 'Door D, Mezanine, National Gallery,' she appears in those days to have been one of the most formidable rivals of Lombardo, given her exceptional public relations skills and wide web of contacts internationally on the distribution front. In an article dated December 1910 (*La Vita Cinematografica* 11), that is, during the gestation period of *Visioni dantesche dell'Inferno*, Klug figures already as 'world agent for the well-known Helios film studio' (as well as for Unitas, Lux – not to be confused with Lombardo's publication by the same name – and Pharo Film).

(b) Helios's *Inferno* is only 400 metres long, but we know that it was distributed in France as a two-reel print 450 metres long and in the United States, apparently, in two reels (Bernardini, *Archivio* 266). We know that in 1911 in Italy 1,029 films were produced with an average length of 203.05 metres (cf. Bernardini, *Archivio* 266). According to contemporary advertisements, *Purgatory* and *Paradise* are each between 660 and 700 metres long. Compared to the 1,400 metres produced by Milano Films, both the Lazio productions seem diminutive, but screened together (or even just the last two, as is often the case), they are certainly 'competitive' for quantity. An American ad of April 1912 (*The Moving Picture World* of 6 April 1912) shows six frames of the film, without giving the length, and informs theatre managers that '*Paradise and Purgatory*' (*Paradise* is set in larger print and attracts more attention) are now available, produced at a cost of $150,000, accompanied by 'special literature, eight-page booklets,' and produced – as if they were one film – by Helios alone. In Italy, the ads by '*Maison Klug*' tell us that the two films were distributed separately and were attributed to the correct film studio, whereas a whole page is dedicated solely to *Paradise* by Psiche (*La cinematografia italiana ed estera* 1735) with an outlandish graphic display which shouts out: '*True work of art.*'

(c) The distinct language conceived to portray the environment of *Paradise*, which contrasts strongly against the background of historical flashbacks, seems unequalled in other productions of the time. The scenery for the clouds where Dante's meetings take place brings to mind stage decor à la Méliès. The effect, however, is rather different: the scenes are not intended to provoke a grotesque or unconventional or hyper-fantastic effect, a baroque accumulation of elements. They are simpler, even 'naïve,' thus creating a serene and 'realistic' atmosphere for Paradise. The same observations could apply to the heavens and their planets, which act as background and connecting thread to the different scenes. Not at all naïve, however, are the special effects employed in some of the difficult transitions. For example, in the first flashback of the death of Cacciaguida during the Crusades, a sort of *ante litteram* split-screen is employed: on the left, separated by an edge in mid-frame, the meeting between Dante and his ancestor in the clouds goes on while on the right Cacciaguida is being killed by the infidels. In 1911, it must have verged on the miraculous! Other effects, such as points of light and double exposures, actually manage to reproduce faithfully and convincingly Dantean passages which are extremely difficult to translate into images, such as the verses 'ché quella croce lampeggiava Cristo' [Christ / Beam'd on that Cross (14.104)], or 'mostrarsi dunque in cinque volte sette vocali e consonanti' [vocal and consonant, were five-fold seven (18.87–8)], 'poscia ne l'emme del vocabol quinto rimasero ordinate' [in the *M* of the fifth word they held their station (18.94–5)], and 'la testa e 'l collo d'un aguglia vidi rappresentare a quel distinto foco' [the head and neck then saw I of an eagle, lively graved in that streaky fire (18.107–8)]. The American critic was absolutely right when he wrote (*The Moving Picture World* of 6 April 1912): 'It would be impossible to describe in detail the many changing glimpses ...'

These three films, therefore, and most especially *Purgatory* and *Paradise*, constitute a watershed in the history of early Italian cinema. With their abundant and refined visual effects, the 700 metres under consideration cause the scope and nature of cinema to move far away from its original ability to 'refaire la vie,' and so enter a world of 'virtual reality' in order to embody poetical images which would otherwise have been lost. In so doing, they do justice to Dante's failed memory (cf. *Par.* 1.5–9), which, as Sapegno maintains in reference to the paradisiacal experience, must be interpreted 'as imaginative memory, which, in the condition of "*excessus menti*" is no longer capable of managing its task of collecting and handling the data of the senses' (6). They thus capture Dante's trans-humanized condition (cf. *Par.* 1.70–1) as something that cannot be conveyed in words.[4] Above all else, they convey the early magic of cinema which consisted in the creation of a fantastic environment, not existing in nature, but made 'real' by film, by it sets and its 'exteriors,' a world to be visited by the new 'homo cinematographicus' as a sort of fortunate 'icononaut' (Brunetta, *Il viaggio dell'icononauta*). They also, with their light, incessant movement, and extreme rapidity herald the arrival of Futurism, a fact underscored by Brunetta in his remarks above. To be sure, they lack the abiding greatness of such colossal films as *Cabiria* and *Intolerance*, but they far outweigh the everyday cinematic endeavours of the times. Unfortunately, it is with the former and not the latter that they are often compared, and so they are omitted from the standard histories of world cinema, such as the monumental *Storia del cinema mondiale,* edited by Brunetta, of which the first volume, on European cinema, has just been published. In a passing remark, this same scholar sheds light on another reason for their omission:

> Se da una parte nella fase iniziale ne sono l'alimento indispensabile e vanno a formarne il patrimonio e il marchio d'identità non bisogna nascondersi il fatto che la letteratura e il teatro nel tempo medio-lungo costituirano una sorta di peso morto per il cinema europeo, rispetto a quello americano che se ne libererà assai presto, senza provare alcun complesso di inferiorità. (28)

> [If in the initial phase literature and theatre are indispensable fodder and offer a heritage and a means of identification, we should not hide the fact that in the medium-long term they constitute a sort of dead weight for European cinema, in comparison to the American industry, which would free itself from that bondage without feeling any sense of inferiority.]

The gist of this quote, although quite interesting, seems a bit strained. For it is clear that Dante is present at the birth and the coming of age of Italian cinema, as is evident in the Helios-Psiche Dante trilogy as discussed above and, of course, in the colossal 1911 Milano *Inferno,* the first feature film of world cinema. The latter (I would like to add) precedes by two years the American *Richard III* of 1915, recently rediscovered and wrongly designated as the first feature-length film. Moreover, Italian cinema never quite managed to rid itself completely of the 'dead weight' of literature, and certainly never rid itself of the shadow of Dante. The influence of the great Florentine poet would continue to be felt in subsequent Italian cinema through the transition from silent to sound movies, and then in the flourishing of Italian cinema in the post–Second World War period, but never with the same clarity and the same intensity of inspiration as in its foundational moment.

Notes

1 Associazione Nazionale Industrie Cinematografiche e Audiovisive. It represents all of those active in the areas of audio-visual creation, production, and distribution.

2 Passages from unpublished notes edited by Aldo Bernardini, which he graciously allowed me to use for this research.

3 Another unpublished note by Bernardini.

4 The following remarks by Jacqueline Risset (5–12) from the introduction to her French translation of *Paradise* are particularly relevant: 'Le coeur du grand projet, c'est le *Paradis*. L'*Enfer* et le *Purgatoire* n'en sont peut-être que des préliminaires ... Le *Paradis*, poème de la lumière, est doublement abstrait. Il n'y a pas de paysage, sinon celui des astronomes, et des cosmonautes – air et lumière, étoiles (et aussi la vue de la terre lointaine, cette *petite aire*, à partir de la constellation des Gémeaux). Dante, pour décrire l'apparition des élus au ciel de la Lune, emploie une "anti-image": "comme une perle sur un front blanc" – sorte de dissolution du voir habituel. Blanc sur blanc: naissance de la différence; la perception s'affine ... Décrire le Paradis est une entreprise excessive – elle signifie "*trasumanar per verba*" – outrepasser l'humain par les mots. Écrire prend le sens d'un défi, d'un passage à la limite – il faut donc forcer les resources du langage, et risquer, à mesure que le voyage se rapproche de son centre indicible, l'échec pur et simple, le silence, l'aphasie ... La mémoire et l'imagination se révèlent incapables de *suivre* l'expérience "parce qu'en s'approchant de son désir / notre intellect va si profond / que la mémoire ne peut l'y suivre" (I, 7–9). Approche du désir et perte de la mémoire sont actions simultanées: ce qu'on peut écrire sera par conséquent non le royaume lui-même mais l'*ombre du royaume*. Tout le *Paradis* est scandé par la réflexion de Dante sur ce qu'il écrit, et aussi sur l'impossibilité d'écrire le paradis. Et c'est là, précisément, dans ces zones réflexives, mais d'une réflexivité directe, transparente, interrogative, que réside la plus étonnante modernité de sa poésie. Car si la poésie contemporaine – et sans doute la littérature en général – est tournée, dans ses expressions les plus significatives, vers l'expérience des limites, l'exploration des confins du dicible et la tentative d'extension de ces confins, le *Paradis* appartient à la poésie contemporaine. Il vogue déjà sur ces eaux, il les ouvre ...' [The heart of the great enterprise is *Paradise. Hell* and *Purgatory* are but preliminaries. *Paradise*, the poem of light, is doubly abstract. There isn't a landscape apart from that of astronomers and cosmonauts – air and light and stars (and also the view of the distant earth, this little whiff of a planet, from the constellation Gemini). In order to describe the appearance of the elect in the Heaven of the moon, Dante employs an 'anti-image' – 'as a pearl on a white brow' – a sort of dissolution of habitual sight. White on white – birth of difference – and perception is refined. To describe Paradise is an exercise of arduous excess which signifies 'trasumanar per verba' – to go beyond the human in a search for words. Writing therefore takes on the sense of a challenge, a

passage pushed to the limit. It is therefore necessary to force the resources of language and risk (as the journey moves inexorably toward its ineffable centre) failure, pure and simple, silence, *aphasia*. Memory and imagination reveal themselves incapable of following experience 'for nearing its desired end, / our intellect sinks into an abyss / so deep that memory fails to follow it' (*Par.* 1.7–9). Approaching desire and losing memory are simultaneous actions: what one describes will be by consequence not the kingdom itself but the mere shadow of the kingdom. All of *Paradise* is scanned by Dante's reflection on what he has written and on the impossibility of describing Paradise. And it is precisely in these reflexive zones – reflexive in a direct, transparent, and interrogative manner – that there resides the most stunning modernity of its poetry. For if contemporary poetry, and without doubt literature in general, is turned in its most significant expressions toward the experience of the ultimate, the exploration of the limits of the utterable and the tentative extension of these confines, then *Paradise* belongs to contemporary poetry. It sails already on these waters and opens them up.]

Bibliography

Bernardini, Aldo. 'I film dall'*Inferno* dantesco nel cinema muto italiano.' *Dante nel cinema*. Ed. Gianfranco Casadio. Ravenna: Longo Editore, 1996. 29–33.
– 'L'*Inferno* della Milano-Films.' *Bianco e Nero* 46 (1985): 91–111.
– ed. *Archivio del cinema italiano*. Vol. 1. Roma: Edizioni ANICA, 1991.
Bernardini, Aldo, and Vittorio Martinelli. *Il cinema muto italiano. I film degli anni d'oro. 1912*. Part 2. Special number of *B & N* (*Bianco e Nero*). Roma: Centro Sperimentale di Cinematografia, 1995.
Brunetta, Gian Piero. *Storia del cinema italiano*. Vol. 1. *Il cinema muto 1895–1929*. Roma: Editori Riuniti, 1993.
– *Il viaggio dell'icononauta*. Venezia: Marsilio Editore, 1997.
– ed. *Storia del cinema mondiale*. Vol. 1. *L'Europa. I. Miti, Luoghi, Divi*. Torino: Giulio Einaudi Editore, 1999.
Capra-Boscarini, Giulio. *Lux*. [Napoli] 93 (April 1912): 1–3.
Iannucci, Amilcare A. 'From Dante's *Inferno* to *Dante's Peak*: The Influence of Dante on Film.' *Forum Italicum* 32 (1998): 5–35.
La cinematografia italiana ed estera 5.114 (15–20 Sept. 1911).
Lizzani, Carlo. *Il cinema italiano 1895–1979*. Vol. 1. Roma: Editore Riuniti, 1979.
Martinelli, Vittorio. 'Filmografia Ragionata.' *Dante nel cinema*. Ed. Gianfranco Casadio. Ravenna: Longo Editore, 1996. 103–19.
The Moving Picture World Magazine [New York], 6 Jan. and 6 April 1912.

Paolella, Roberto. *Storia del cinema muto.* Napoli: Giannini Editore, 1956.

Risset, Jacqueline, ed. *Dante: La Divina Commedia.* Paris: Flammarion, 1992.

Sapegno, Natalino, ed. *La Divina Commedia.* Vol. 3. Firenze: La Nuova Italia, 1992.

Welle, John. 'Dante in the Cinematic Mode: An Historical Survey of Dante Movies.' *Dante's 'Inferno': The Indiana Critical Edition.* Ed. Mark Musa. Bloomington: Indiana University Press, 1995. 381–95.

Back to the Future: Dante and the Languages of Post-war Italian Film

MARGUERITE R. WALLER

> There is always a tendency to identify historical breaks and to say 'this begins there,' 'this ends here,' while the scene keeps on recurring, as unchangeable as change itself.
>
> – Trinh T. Minh-ha, 'Surname Viet Given Name Nam,' 56

I. Thinking the Relationship

It is becoming well known among Italianists that Dante's inquiry into, map of, and innoculation against most of the signifying possibilities we creatures of discourse have created in the West has offered filmmakers, no less than writers, a remarkably rich discursive universe in terms of which to locate themselves. But, given the disciplinary boundaries in the North American university, it has been more difficult to persuade non-Italianist film theorists that the languages of Italian cinema, however they may participate in the movements, strategies, or periods associated with 'modernism' or 'postmodernism,' also problematize such insulating categories through their consistent engagement with Dante's great fourteenth-century experiment.[1] While a score of other film communities, ranging from the Lucas/Spielberg/Scorsese generation in the United States to the post-Communist generation in Central Europe, have mined post–Second World War Italian cinema for its innovative narrative structures, constructions of character, and cinematography, the profound engagement of Italian filmmakers with questions of signification and subjectivity that have surfaced repeatedly for at least six centuries has not been widely acknowledged.[2]

Offering us a kind of critical *mise-en-abyme*, Dante's *Commedia*, too, looked back in innovative ways. The poem does not so much break with, as reframe and perspectivize, the culture of Latin, the hegemonic, pan-European language of law, knowledge, and being. To accomplish this reconfiguration, Dante looks to vernacular dialect and to contemporary visual culture – to painting, sculpture, architecture, and civic pageantry – for alternative models of textuality and readership. The poem presents itself, notably, not as a text to be submitted to, but to be walked around, lived in, interacted with. With the *Commedia*, hierarchies such as those between author and text, or text and reader/auditor, become at best contingent and heuristic. Characters within the poem, drawn from different ontological and temporal dimensions, also mix freely, comparing perspectives and swapping stories. (Viewers of Maurizio Nichetti's *Ladri di saponette* [*The Icicle Thief*], supposedly the canonical instance of postmodern Italian cinema, may be struck by how well this description of the *Commedia* works for Nichetti's film as well.)

But the poetics of the *Commedia* bring the significance of post-war Italian cinematic strategies into sharper focus through more than coincidental parallelisms. Writing in the context of a highly aural/visual culture, Dante's poem combines extensive ecphrases (descriptions in words of visual images) with dialogue, actually *making* movies, of a kind. (From Dante the pilgrim's point of view, the *mise-en-scène* also resembles a three-dimensional, interactive virtual environment.) As Walter Benjamin argues in 'The Work of Art in an Age of Mechanical Reproduction,' new media seem always to have been prefigured by works made with existing technology. The yearning for certain possibilities, Benjamin implies, precedes and summons the technologies. 'Dadaism,' he offers as an example, 'attempted to create by pictorial – and literary – means the effects which the public today seeks in the film' (237). If we follow Benjamin as he provocatively reframes print as 'merely a special, though particularly important case' (219) in a history of mechanical reproduction whose yearnings are most fully embodied in cinema, then Dante's exploration of vernacular language as a new technology of signification appears to prefigure *both* the transformations of writing in the age of vernacular print culture *and* the metamorphoses of word and image in the new age of visual culture announced by photography and film. It should come as no surprise, then, that filmmakers familiar with Dante (which would include virtually all Italian directors) have been profoundly influenced by the *Commedia* in both ways – as the poem brilliantly explores a new medium (vernacular poetry) and as it rigorously investigates the still-to-be-invented audio-visual moving image.

In reading the languages of post–Second World War Italian cinema and Dante's poetics in relation to one another, then, we discover that there are several, interconnected ways of thinking the relationship. There are the demonstrable thematic references, which commentators such as Barbara Lewalski, P. Adams Sitney, and John Welle have elaborated. With or without explicit reference to Dante, there are also the rich possibilities of analysing the languages of Italian cinema rhetorically in relation to the rhetorical forms of the vernacular in *Inferno*, *Purgatorio*, and *Paradiso*. And, finally, we can watch filmmakers, as they experiment with film as a theoretical and political/ideological medium, testing, so to speak, Dantesque hypotheses about audio-visual representation and signification.

II. Rossellini: Making Cinema Useless for Fascism

At the beginning of 'The Work of Art in an Age of Mechanical Reproduction,' Benjamin announces that his intention in the essay is to introduce certain concepts that will be 'useless for the purposes of Fascism' (218). The cinematic language of Roberto Rossellini's 1945 film *Roma, città aperta (Rome, Open City)* might be described in the same words. Rossellini's 'neo-realism,' is 'neo' because it 'breaks with the coordinates of the old realism,' writes Gilles Deleuze, who makes Rossellini's work pivotal to his discussion of a metamorphosis of cinema from the representation of action to the representation of thought (*Cinema 1* 121, 212; *Cinema 2* 1–3). This break is evident precisely in Rossellini's use of intersecting, but not congruent, coordinates; that is, in his contruction of a heterogeneous visual space that proves ungovernable by the film's would-be authority figures. Challenging the spectator to read the action occurring along each coordinate in relation to the other coordinates, the on-screen images thus deliteralize each other, displacing the theatre of signification from the screen to the mind's eye. What we see on screen, no matter how authentically 'documentary,' will evoke the real, but will not, and cannot possibly, coincide with it.

A brief example from *Roma, città aperta* will illustrate this aspect of Rossellini's 'rhetoric.' In the opening sequence of the film, the figures of German soldiers move along a horizontal axis that coincides with the left/right axis of the picture plane. Then, through the eyes of the resistance hero Manfredi and, moments earlier, of his landlady, the camera looks down on this axis from a vertical axis of which the soldiers seem unaware. The third axis in this montage of spatial orientations runs from the foreground to the background of the screen, articulated first by the terrace outside the apartment where Manfredi has been hiding and then by the interior hallway, the camera maintaining an unusually great depth of field in both shots. Juxtaposing the sound of the German soldiers pounding on the door and a radio broadcast (the famous 'London Calling') from England, the image of the empty terrace itself organizes a montage. The pounding reminds us of the Germans' horizontal trajectory, already being exposed as incommensurate with the more complex spatiality of Rome; the radio broadcast connects the terrace with the non-contiguous space of London, further suggesting that any attempt to fascicize this terrain is doomed from the start. The Germans' delusion that they can control this multidimensional space seems based on a fundamental misconception of both their own position and the reality they are dealing with. Later in the film, various of the Italian characters also move in and out of the reductive horizontal axis, making it clear that fascist thought is not a matter of national identity, but a particular way of trying to organize relations.

Almost any passage of *Inferno* could serve as an analogue to Rossellini's construction here of a reality that is, to quote Deleuze, 'dispersive and lacunary' (*Cinema 1* 212). The sequence of rapid changes in altitude and orientation embodied in Virgil's report to Dante of Beatrice's charge to him offer a concentrated example.

> L'amico mio, e non della ventura,
> nella diserta piaggia è impedito
> si nel cammin, che volt'è per paura;
> e temo che non sia già sì smarrito,
> ch'io mi sia tardi al soccorso levata,
> per quel ch'i'ho di lui nel ciel udito. (*Inf.* 2.61–6)

> [My friend, not fortune's,
> is so obstructed on the desert slope
> that he has turned back for fear;
> and I am afraid, from what I have heard about him in heaven,
> that he may already be so far astray
> that I may have risen too late to help him.]

Dante the pilgrim, like the Germans, had thought to forge straight ahead toward his goal. Within these few lines, though, his movement is contextualized within a strangely convoluted cosmic space that has somehow required Beatrice to 'rise' in order to address Virgil, even though Virgil resides in the first circle of *Inferno* and she in *Paradiso*.[3] Where the desert slope might be in relation to either of these two dimensions there is no way, at this point, of knowing, which is precisely what Dante will need to be convinced of if he is ever to escape its gravitational pull.

The sign under which the Germans have chosen to perpetrate their raid, meanwhile, evokes Dantesque form and content explicitly. Looking down from the terrace axis at the roof of the German soldiers' truck, the camera notes that they have commandeered a Red Cross vehicle, hiding their violence beneath a signifier that, by international convention, signals the cessation of hostilities. Aligning themselves with a number of Dante's sinners who practised their tyrannies under the sign of the cross – Popes Nicholas III and Boniface, for example – the Germans are similarly misled by their reductive understanding and appropriation of signs. The polysemy of Rossellini's Red Cross, a palimpsest of both the Christian cross and the Swiss flag, signifying complex theological and historical frameworks to which the Germans appear oblivious, immediately ironizes the logic of killing people as a way of stabilizing meaning. The means being used to enforce fascist ideology puts the goal out of reach from the start. The crossed bars themselves figure the film's own, very different rhetorical strategy – its repeated crossing of univocal with multivalent readings of signifiers (like the example we have just seen) that constantly erodes ones' faith in the former. The film, that is, insists that no cinematic image, no matter how dramatic, painful, or seemingly definitive, can be simply true.

The test case, the sequence which has engraved itself indelibly in cinema history, is the death of Pina. Pina (Anna Magnani), working-class widow and mother, engaged to be married to the resistance printer Francesco, with whom she is expecting a baby, is killed on her wedding day as she races after the truck taking away Francesco and several other men caught up in a German raid of their apartment building. As she runs, a shot suddenly rings out, and Pina's body crumples to the pavement. The resistance priest, Don Pietro, and Pina's son Marcello reach her almost at the same moment, and Don Pietro, after pulling Marcello off her lifeless body, cradles it for a moment in his arms, forming a tableau clearly alluding to the *Pietà*.

The shot of Pina running, taken as if from the back of the moving truck, and the reverse shot of the truck receding from her desperate reach have achieved classic status in world cinema. But two other shots in this sequence interrupt this particularly dramatic use of the shot / reverse-shot technique. First there is an anomalous shot of Pina that is not a reverse shot from the truck, but is taken from a camera placed perpendicular to the truck/Pina axis, catching Pina for a moment in the deadly horizontal axis I have been associating with the Germans or with fascist reading and signifying practices. Then there is an unexpectedly abrupt edit from the *Pietà* image formed by Don Pietro holding Pina's limp body (also composed along the horizontal axis) to a shot of a *partigiano* emerging vertically from an underground hiding place. The figure of the *partigiano* and the figure of Pina 'rhyme,' which is to say that they are placed in exactly the same position on the screen in successive shots. Syntactically, that is, the sequence reads as a resurrection, as if Pina were rising from the dead.

Thus, even Pina's death (or especially Pina's death) does not signify univocally. We don't see which German shoots her, or even that it is a German. Instead the axis of literalism itself appears to cut her down. Pointedly not reinscribing essentialist 'us/them' binaries, the sequence representing Pina's death, then, implicitly proposes a subtle and highly subversive response to the Italian fascist / German Nazi alliance. Its visual language inaugurates a shift away from interpreting war and politics in terms of easily dichotomized national and personal identities.[4] The brisk editorial rhyming of Pina's lifeless form with that of the anonymous *partigiano* leading the band of men who will liberate Francesco and the other prisoners from their captivity reinforces this suggestion. Pina's death (like Beatrice's) constitutes a terrible loss, but only within the monologic, monocular regime that has transfixed her with a bullet can her death be read as a tragic ending. It remains, in fact, surprisingly unelaborated as the film rushes ahead to model an increasingly decolonized, multidimensional 'open city' that ultimately succeeds in throwing open even the doors of the Germans' strictly compartmentalized headquarters.

My last example from *Roma, città aperta* draws upon an intriguing verbal-to-visual cross-reference to challenge the way in which the character Marina, Manfredi's sometime lover and Pina's younger sister, has sometimes been critically construed. Marina, who betrays her former lover to the Germans, falls in a dead faint when she catches sight through a doorway of Manfredi's horrifically tortured dead face. I read this faint in relation to Dante the pilgrim's swoon at the end of canto 5 of *Inferno*, after he has heard Francesca's account of the double seduction – by the book of Lancelot and Guinevere and by her illicit lover, Paolo – that led to the lovers' double murder at the hands of Francesca's jealous husband, Paolo's brother. Dante the poet writes of Dante the pilgrim the onomatopoeic line: 'E caddi come corpo morte cade' [And I fell as a dead body falls (*Inf.* 5.142)]. The trochees help us hear the fall of that dead body five times over, as if it were being shown repeatedly from different angles, or perhaps in slow motion, such that the thud of each body part became separately audible as it hit the ground. This line could also describe Marina at the moment she registers how her desire to punish Manfredi for his rejection of her has played fatally into the desire of the Germans to destroy the Italian underground. Her faint is registered on the sound track by a highly audible, subtly prolonged, thud.

The similarity of their body language points to a similarity in their metaphysical/moral positions, as well. The Dante of canto 5 seems to faint in acknowledgment of his overwhelming identification, as a vernacular love poet, with both the sexual and textual seductions represented by Francesca. Francesca's seduction – the particular misreading of desire that places her in the circle of the lustful – not coincidentally involved intense identification. She and her lover, Paolo, are figured as doves who appear to navigate the murky textuality of the second circle at will, and yet also to be driven by the elements they appear to have mastered:

> Quali colombe dal disio chiamate
> con l'ali alzate e ferme al dolce nido
> vegnon per l'aere, dal voler portate ... (*Inf.* 5.82–4)

> [As doves, called by desire, with wings open and fixed
> come to their sweet nest,
> borne through the air by their will ...]

Reading the romance of Lancelot and Guinevere, they construed the signifiers constituting the characters in the romance as representative of unified, stable, self-identical subjects, which they, in turn, could imitate. Such a subject may enjoy the illusion of autonomy and self-determination, but only by submitting to a single, univocal – what we might call fascicizing – field of signification that allows signifiers to masquerade as ontologically based representations.[5] In part, what floats some remainder of the character 'Dante' free of Francesca's gravitational pull at the beginning of canto 6 is his having lost the sense of any *via diritta* from sign to referent. As the poet so interestingly puts it at the opening of the new canto, his mind was finally closed or shut down, 'si chiuse' *(Inf.* 6.1), by his encounter with Francesca. Though identification, especially with aristocratic courtly lovers, may still be a potent desire, it no longer computes on a conceptual level for a subject who has painfully experienced the non-coincidence of representation and subjectivity, the contradiction of an autonomy based on iterability.

Similarly, Marina, shocked out of a stupor induced by the drugs to which the Germans have addicted her, seems to encounter in the ruined face of her dead ex-lover a devastating image of her own implicatedness in the violence of the Nazi occupation. This amounts to a radically different position from the one she seemed, to herself and to those around her, to have occupied throughout most of the film. Marina's subjectivity is extensively elaborated in an earlier mirror scene, set in her backstage dressing room, where it is the mirror image of the actress, a univocal projection of glamour, desired and directed by the scripts of others, with which she identifies and on the basis of which she acts. Her performance of selfhood could, that is, be read as a kind of cultural passivity (like that of Paolo, Francesca, and Dante the love poet), which acts to obscure the unstable, indeterminate, and relational nature of subject construction. What Marina encounters in the torture room scene (as Dante does in the second circle) is a shocking deconstruction of the boundaries between active and passive, self and other, conformity and transgression. She comes face to face with an indeterminacy which bears with it the prospect of a moral and political subject very different from the one assumed by either the Germans or the Italians in this film, or by most of the film's commentators (Sitney 36).

If Marina's faint is analogous to Dante's, Rossellini's film is not, then, locating her unequivocally as a 'bad guy.' One of the few potential survivors, along with the gentle Francesco, among the adult characters in the film, she, in a sense, joins the children (otherwise all male, it must be noted) at the end of the film, whose subjectivities are relatively unformed, uncolonized, and whose authority figures have all died. The film leaves us to ponder what kinds of society and what ways of being 'Italian' these orphans may create out of the rubble (evocative in this dimension as well of the *Commedia*) of the various systems – political, cultural, familial, religious – whose seductions (for better or for worse) the cataclysm of the war has ruptured.

III. Fellini: The Ruin of Representation

By 1960, fifteen years after *Roma, città aperta*, Fellini appeared to many commentators to have left the poetics of neo-realist cinema far behind. In *La dolce vita*, his experiments with sound and image, narrative form, character, and something I would term the address to the spectator made privileging any mimetic reading of the film – even one displaced from screen to spectators' imaginations – distinctly problematic. So problematic, in fact, that surprisingly little has been written in English on this watershed film, as if Anglo-American critics sensed how much was at stake in engaging it critically.[6] I would argue, though, that it is precisely because Fellini took so seriously the anti-fascist projects of such films as *Roma, città aperta*, *Paisà* (on which, of course, he also worked), *Ladri di biciclette*, *Sciuscià*, and others that his cinematic language had to change. As the intriguing instance of Marina (as read through *Inferno* 5) suggests, it is the ruin of representation and identification that reveals the subject in potentially transforming ways. The centrality of Dantesque allusions in *La dolce vita*, commented on by John Simon, John Welle, P. Adams Sitney, and others, should probably come, then, as no surprise. But, perhaps more helpfully than the thematic references, it is Dante's exemplary exploration of the properties of his medium that can serve as Virgilian guide to the critic who sets out on the deep waters of Fellini's experimental film language.

Let me sketch an example. In canto 1 of *Inferno*, when Dante is driven back from his attempted ascent of the Mountain of Purgatory by the she-wolf, the verb 'ruvinare' is used to describe what he is doing when Virgil first appears to him :

> Mentre che'i ruvinava in basso loco,
> dinanzi alli occhi me si fu offerto
> chi per lungo silenzio parea fioco. (*Inf.* 1.61–3)

> [While I was crashing down into the low place,
> before my eyes was offered one
> who seemed hoarse from long silence.]

The verb *ruvinare* also carries the connotation 'to ruin,' and indeed what seems crucial to Virgil's suddenly being offered to the pilgrim's eyes is the ruin of Dante's attempt to master the obstacles that have appeared to him. These have taken the shape of three beasts, the leopard, the lion, and the wolf, which later, in retrospect, appear to have been allegories of the three major divisions of *Inferno*, which itself will eventually appear to have been an exfoliation of the dark wood, which, in turn, can be read as a projection of the pilgrim's own distressed subject position. Periodically in *Inferno*, the image of ruins and the notion of ruining its architecture come up again, always as positive signs of the ultimate lack of ontology of Infernal imagery.[7]

As one reads each canto, then, ruining becomes an appropriate strategy of reading. Chiselling apart the self-fashioned, self-fashioning narratives of the damned, one begins to hear multiple meanings in their excuses and rationalizations. Ruining their stories releases the inherent polyvocality of language. Ugolino's sons, for example, inviting their father to eat of them – 'Padre, assai ci fia men doglia / se tu mangi di noi' (*Inf.* 33.61–2) – and, later, the words of one of them asking, 'Padre mio, che non m'aiuti?' (*Inf.* 33.69) evoke the Last Supper and the Crucifixion, implicitly inviting Ugolino to turn away from isolation, imprisonment, and death toward communion and salvation as his life's principle of intelligibility. Ugolino, though, maintaining his stony silence throughout their ordeal, hears in the words only a projection of his own paternal impotence, a reading predicated on his refusal to give up a rigid patriarchalism that, the poem's suggestion of cannibalism strongly implies, devours rather than nourishes its young. Quite literally, instead of talking to his children, which would require him to acknowledge the commonality of their situation, he *watches* them die, arrogating to himself the position of owner of the defining gaze. He finally acknowledges their appeals only after they are dead, when he can safely play the grief-stricken father to their inert bodies without risk of losing his centrality as tragic protagonist. The suggestion that he then ate these bodies shockingly images the perversity of this tragic mode, wherein children's humanity is sacrificed on the altar of an inessential, contingent (but all the more devouring) patriarchal hierarchy.

Ruining, unframing, undoing the story – these are also the gestures that *La dolce vita* calls upon the spectator to perform, the verb *rovinare* itself coming up early in the film's diegesis. Marcello, upon returning home at dawn to his new, still sparsely furnished apartment, discovers that Emma, his mistress, has overdosed on pills in an apparent suicide attempt. 'Ma chi vuoi rovinare?' he asks incongruously. 'A me?' His deafness to Emma's bid for communication, his blindness to the pain his machismo inflicts on her, his indifference, for that matter, to the pain of Maddalena, the woman with whom he has just spent the night, and to the poverty of the prostitute in whose flooded basement apartment he and Maddalena have made love, suggest that his position is in dire *need* of 'ruining.' For the rest of the film, though, Marcello remains hellbent (so to speak) on making a career of appearing to be the master of signifiers, first as a journalist for a semi-fascist newspaper and then as a PR man who constructs the identities of Italian actors in the image of American and English superstars (reprising the pattern of Paolo, Francesca, and Marina). And he continues not to listen to women.

The spectator, though, at whatever point s/he becomes aware that Marcello is blind and deaf (not unlike Ugolino) to most of the signs around him, becomes free to ruin the journalist's status as central character and focalizer, to read his ubiquitous presence on screen as obstructing, rather than guiding, the gaze. When Marcello walks (horizontally) along a corridor in the castle of Bassano di Sutri, for example, the very fact that his body obscures, while the frame truncates, the marble busts and oil canvases past which he moves comments on his way of looking. But unlike *Roma, città aperta*, where a reductively literal axis could be read in relation to what it excluded to suggest a richer, more inclusive, polyvalent reality, not directly representable by the film image, *La dolce vita* offers layer upon layer of signifiers that seem equivalent to one another and do not relationally evoke a richer reality always ready to breach the borders of those in power. The film creates moments and spaces in which the fundamental activity could be described, not as representation or even signification *per se*, but as a catachresis of images and ideas, selves and projections, all of which are presented as *products*, not sources, of systems and logics of authority.[8]

Following the night that has culminated in Sylvia Rank's (Anita Ekberg's) excursion into the Trevi Fountain, the confrontation of Sylvia, Marcello, and Sylvia's 'fiancé' Robert (Lex Barker) is just such a moment. Both diegetically and extra-diegetically, Barker/Robert is an exemplar of Hollywood machismo, the real-life Barker having played Tarzan, and 'Robert,' according to the Fellinian *paparazzi*, having done the same. Marcello, meanwhile, both Mastroianni and Fellini's character, 'Rubini,' epitomizes sophisticated European masculinity. The Tarzan subtext, not too distantly, also evokes a concatenation of colonial situations – at least two in Africa – the British and the Italian – as well as the post-war cultural imperialism of the United States in Italy, one of whose aspects was, of course, the tidal wave of Hollywood movies swamping Italian screens. The presence of three major Hollywood actors, Sylvia (Ekberg), Robert (Barker), and Frankie (Alan Dijon), at a Roman night-club indexes the Hollywood juggernaut. Taken out of their different generic contexts and mixed up together, though, these characters lose the charisma they radiate within their respective genres. Robert/Lex/ Tarzan looks anything but heroic, drunkenly slapping Sylvia and punching the unmuscular Marcello. Marcello's Latin lover persona looks decidedly unromantic being punched. And Sylvia's glamour seems to invite victimization, allegorizing the colonial structure of heterosexist gender roles, even as the conspicuously nordic star herself is being deployed to colonize the Italian unconscious.[9] Barker's real-life homo-sexuality, another reason he and many other Hollywood actors went to Rome, also brings heterosexist homophobia into this complex of West-ern phallocentric avatars. Finally, since even the *mise-en-scène* has been contrived by predatory *paparazzi*, hoping to get marketable photographs, the task of the spectator would seem not to try to synthesize these images into a coherent narrative, but to navigate among the discourses producing and reproducing them. When we do so, these ruined figures, each suggestive of a whole field of images and narratives, are freed to combine and recombine with other similarly suggestive elements to create immense and unexpected new fields of analysis and action.

The film does not simply imply these linkages, furthermore, but later shows them in action. At a *soirée* at the elegant apartment of Steiner, Marcello's excessively rational, intellectual friend, a young woman of colour wearing a sari sits cross-legged on the floor singing and accom-panying herself on the guitar. An old colonial anthropologist, express-ing his admiration, discourses pretentiously on the 'Eastern' woman as the essence of true femininity, hinting that his field work has included intimate investigation in this area. Steiner and Marcello, oblivious to the feelings of Steiner's wife and Marcello's girlfriend, enthusiastically lionize the old man. Several beats later, Steiner and Marcello repair to the terrace to speak about their despair over the state of the world and their own inability to work out a viable relation to it, while the singer, now centred in the frame, begins a new song. As she sings the words 'Look away' (in clearly American-accented English), it becomes obvi-ous that she is not Asian at all, but African-American, not 'Eastern,' but a particularly complicated representative of 'Western' culture, recalling the history of the murderous Middle Passage and the roots of U.S.

economic and military dominance in the institution of slavery. In other words, if the spectator refuses to privilege the white male figures and follows the sound cue to 'look away' from these contingent focalizers of the scene, then new logics become 'visible' to the mind's eye, logics which radically displace and delegitimate Steiner's and Marcello's sense of identity and location.

Subsequent to the *soirée*, Steiner's subject position reveals itself as untrustworthy – indeed, conceptually and literally homicidal. As P. Adams Sitney, John Welle, and others have pointed out, Steiner's murder of his two young children and his own suicide gruesomely reinforce whatever connections spectators might be making between Fellini's male characters and Dante's since the moment Marcello's father describes himself in the words of Dante's notoriously stony father figure, Ugolino: 'Tu vuo' ch'io rinovelli / disperato dolor che 'l cor mi preme' [You want me to renew desperate grief that presses on my heart (*Inf.* 33. 4–5)] (Sitney 112–16; Welle 111–12). Ugolino's line recalls, in turn, the words with which Aeneas, founding patriarch of Rome, begins the story of the fall of Troy, as requested by Dido, the woman he will subsequently abandon in order to pursue the trajectory of the Roman imperium: 'Infandem, regina, jubes renovare dolorem' [You ask me to renew an unspeakable pain, o queen (*Aen.* 2.3)].

At this point, a Baudrillardian postmodernist might interject that this infinite regress of images without origins is the reason for Marcello's degeneracy. Marcello is a victim of the age of simulation, a poor modernist, nostalgic for the old master narratives, elegantly adrift in a world in which everyone sounds like everyone, and distinctions are impossible to maintain. But Fellini's engagement with Dante's forest of simulacra suggests that ontology and its history are not the issues here, or at least not as represented within Baudrillard's patriarchal European framework. The obstacle to Dante the pilgrim's ascent lies not in the universe's ontology, or lack of it, but in the configuration of the subject, specifically and explicitly of the masculine subject as constructed within Western culture. Such a subject seeks, desires, and requires the conditions I associated earlier with identification and mimetic representation. Its mastery, its ability to freeze signifiers in univocal meanings and therefore to universalize its own perceptions, while construing itself as neutral and transparent, depends upon not only political dominance but also a logic of the same, a centrist logic, that constantly writes difference as otherness, falseness, fiction, femininity, and inferiority in relation to which its own position appears to coincide ever more convincingly with the real. Before Dante can enter the Earthly Paradise and begin to take his own desire as his guide, he must finally come to know male subjectivity otherwise than as a pseudo-neutral position that, of necessity, desires to master and objectify all others. That is, he needs to experience himself as sexual and his sexuality as a fundamental sign of the differential, situated nature of his own cognitive position, a sign that, as Beatrice points out, has been staring him in the face since he was first attracted to her.[10]

When Dante catches sight of Matelda, on the opposite shore of the river Lethe, which appears to block his entry into the Earthly Paradise, he finally discovers the difference between these two 'male' positions. The effect that Matelda has on the pilgrim is unambiguously sexual. He compares her to Venus, the goddess of sexual love, and himself to Leander, one of mythology's greatest and, I might add, most tragic lovers. In contrast to his attraction to and identification with Francesca, though, he does not experience any narcissistic self-gratification. On the contrary, he registers a radical sense of separation and loss:

Tu mi fai remembrar dove e qual era
Proserpina nel tempo che perdette
la madre lei, ed ella primavera. (*Purg.* 28.49–51)

[You make me remember where and what
Proserpina was at the time that her mother
lost her and she the spring.]

In other words, sexual attraction to a woman, once a man is beyond what Dante calls sin, seems violently to disrupt his sense of being in control of his world. Dante here shares the feelings of a mother who has lost her child and, simultaneously, the feeling of a child to whom part of the world is lost. (The comparison of his situation with that of two female figures is in itself suggestive, as if to say that there is something metaphorically 'female' about his predicament.) In the comparison of himself to Leander, the situation appears even more desperate. Leander was drowned, lost in the waves of the Hellespont, as he was trying to return home after visiting his beloved Hero. But if Dante, having passed through the barrier of fire that eliminates lust, now experiences sexual attraction as a kind of loss, as a drowning, even a rape, he nevertheless stands to gain everything by it. He becomes at last permeable to the 'other' as he painfully surrenders the last vestiges of mastery. In a sense central to the sexual politics of the entire *Commedia*, this is his first real sexual experience, and, like Proserpina, he loses half the world – the female half, which suddenly appears as a strange, new, uncharted territory. As Matelda points out, though, it is not she or the territory that is new: 'Voi siete nuovi' [You are new (*Purg.* 28.77)], she comments to Dante and his companions. What Dante loses, then, is his sense of being at home in, and central to, half the world, but his is a loss which is tantamount to the saving realization that one is also a stranger, a passer-through, a pilgrim in one's own world.

Marcello, at the end of *La dolce vita*, conspicuously *fails* to come to a similar realization in relation to the Matelda figure presented by the young Umbrian waitress Paola, as she hails him from the far side of a small, tidal estuary.[11] In a sequence I have analysed in greater detail elsewhere, Fellini's cinematic text finally breaks away from Marcello, its central and centric male focalizer, to remain with Paola, who, in turn, in the film's famous final freeze-frame, redirects her gaze from Marcello to the lens of the camera, or, in other words, to the audience ('Whose *Dolce Vita*?' 129–31). What happens as a consequence of this handing off of the gaze from Marcello to Paola to the spectator depends in interesting ways on the spectator. To the extent that we accept her invitation to give up the 'male' gaze, the film undergoes a strange metamorphosis, which, as I have already intimated, actually depends upon its non-ontology, its not being locatable as a determinate text. Determinations of centre and periphery, foreground and background, actions and setting, shift dramatically, characters' needs and anxieties no longer appearing as innate, individual, or unilateral, but readable also, or instead, as products of economic and sexual politics. The situations of the women in the film, every one of whom is beaten or brutalized, speak eloquently to the malaise from which the men are suffering, a connection it is in the nature of the men's malaise not to be able to make. But nothing *except* Marcello's point of view prevents *us* from recognizing the violence of his objectifying and increasingly commodifying readings of the world. It is this kind of seeing, the acceptance of constant invitations to *shift*, compare, and link different focuses and perspectives, that Fellini's film offers. The project is literally to change the subject, for screen and spectator mutually to reconfigure each other.[12] Broached by neo-realism, that is, the project of making cinema useless for fascist purposes and ruining representation becomes linked explicitly to questions of gender and sexuality, and understood to necessitate a radical decentring of patriarchal masculinities.

IV. Cavani, Wertmüller, and Nichetti

This project was soon brilliantly elaborated by Fellini himself, by female filmmakers Lina Wertmüller and Liliana Cavani, and by anarchic comedian Maurizio Nichetti. Unfortunately space and time do not allow me to unfold this continuing history in detail, but I can offer a kind of trailer of subsequent developments, starting with the concluding sequence of Wertmüller's *Mimi metallurgico, ferito nell'onore*, a film that from beginning to end relentlessly exposes the seductions of identificatory masculinity. Having assumed precisely the role against which he defined himself at the beginning – that of *mafioso* flunky distributing threats and election propaganda – Mimi encounters his lover Fiore and their son leaving him for a Communist, once Mimi's friend, who makes his living selling refreshments from the back of a small, red, three-wheeled truck. After a shot of Fiore and her son sitting in the back of the truck as it crosses the desert wastes of a salt mine where Mimi and his gang have come to propagandize the workers, Mimi is shown running toward her in a series of short reverse shots. The iconography of the truck, the action, and the camera work all recall the death of Pina in *Roma, città aperta*. In fact, the truck is a palimpsest of allusions to both that film and *La strada*, conflating Zampanò's makeshift Harley Davidson caravan with the German army vehicle that takes away Francesco. Americans, Germans, Italians, entertainers, Communists, films themselves: their conflation in this image suggests that they are all equivalent ontologically – all performative tropes and potentially all tropes of the performativity of identities, roles, and power relations. Appropriately, Fiore, a thoroughly catachrestic soul, as her knitted harlequin costumes suggest, leaves Mimi when his performance of 'male honour' becomes too literal, finally transforming him into one of the neo-fascist thugs he initially rebelled against. The desert waste of the salt mine, meanwhile, takes us back to the desert shore at the beginning of the *Commedia*, another indication of the scene's rhetorical mode. Like both Dante and Zampanò, Mimi finds himself lost and depleted in the absence of the female figure in relation to which male authority knows itself. Our response to Mimi's screen *figura*, though, is likely to be quite different from our response to Zampanò – or to the pilgrim. Since the film text itself from the beginning has been flamboyantly performative rather than mimetic, while sexual behaviours and gender identities have been thoroughly denaturalized, we do not have to go through the painful process of dis-identification and ruining representation in order to start 'seeing' Mimi's situation. We are, you might say, already in *Purgatorio*.[13]

Much harder to look at, but more explicitly both Purgatorial and performative, Liliana Cavani's Holocaust film *Portiere di notte* is often watched as if it were mimetic, but changes dramatically when the spectator no longer assumes a position of voyeuristic domination. If we assume, for example, that everything is as it looks when we see a close-up of the character Lucia, with her hands chained above and behind her head, being sexually assaulted by a concentration camp officer named Max, we may – and many viewers do – find the images unbearable, as physically and mentally painful as it is for Dante in *Purgatorio* 10 to look at the souls of the Prideful bent double beneath their stones. Especially if Lucia's enigmatic passivity is read as acceptance, even pleasure, then viewers may find themselves wishing they were not watching, wishing the filmmaker were not showing them this, wishing Lucia would let us off the hook by appearing to suffer more. The image is presented as Lucia's own flashback or fantasy, though, and we have no objective rendering to compare it to. Instead, as Max and Lucia work their way to an embodied understanding of the performativity of identities, even the identities of concentration camp officers and prisoners, the spectator, too, is discouraged from mistaking him- or herself for the kind of global, knowing subject the Nazis took to its extreme. The imperializing view and substantializing effects of such a subject are frustrated throughout the film by a camera that continually reframes the characters from moment to moment, never purporting to be objective. It pans, tracks, zooms, pulls focus – a conspicuous textual effect in its own right, which seems to want us never to mistake for mimetic representations its signifying plays on the images it offers us. Representation, in the sense that one position or effect could stand for another (whereby, for example, Lucia could stand for women, who could stand for victims, who could stand for Jews), would require an inert, monocular vision that produces a 'truth' in which people and events appear to stay put.[14]

And what of the poetics of *Paradiso*, the canticle of the *Commedia* apparently least referenced in cinema history? While I would not try to establish a relationship of influence between the poetics of *Paradiso* and

Maurizio Nichetti's *Volere volare*, it does happen that they hit upon comparable images for a happy ending to the story of the metamorphosis of the male subject. In *Purgatorio* 10, reacting to his own horrific rendering of the Prideful bent double under their loads, Dante the poet apostrophizes:

> O superbi cristian, miseri lassi,
> che, della vista della mente infermi,
> fidanza avete ne' retrosi passi,
> non v'accorgete voi che noi siam vermi
> nati a formar l'angelica farfalla
> che vola all giustizia sanza schermi? (*Purg.* 10.121–6)

> [O proud Christians, weary wretches,
> who with the sight of infirm minds,
> have faith in backward steps.
> Can you not see that we are worms,
> born to form the angelic butterfly
> who flies to justice without defensive screens?]

In *Volere volare*, the main character, Maurizio, under the influence of his attraction to Martina, herself a rather unconventional woman, undergoes just such a metamorphosis. At first horrified and ashamed, Maurizio wraps himself in bandages like the Invisible Man, a get-up in which he strongly resembles a butterfly in its chrysalis stage, but, gaining confidence in the warmth of Martina's affection, he decides, for better or for worse, to emerge. What he emerges as is a brightly coloured, anatomically correct, animated version of himself, gifted with all the properties of motion, including flight, of a cartoon character. Curiously, the film almost received an X rating in the United States for frontal male nudity, even though the male genitalia under scrutiny consisted only of a small, very abstract pen and ink doodle. What was being censored, I strongly suspect, was not the exposure of a penis, but the exposure of the possibility that a penis could be represented by such an innocuous abstraction. The substitution of a doodle for the 'real thing' suggests that the meaning of male sexuality is just as constructed and metaphorical as other significations, that the penis need not, to borrow from Lacanian terminology, function as the phallus. The implications of this shedding by the male body of its phallic integument are powerful. As Martina's reaction when she tries on Maurizio's glasses suggests, they amount to a whole new optic. The metamorphosis of desire *(volere)* from the longing for presence, essence, and mastery to the weightless, but definitely not sexless, *jouissance* of flying *(volare)*, comparable to the metamorphosis of Dante's phallic earth-bound worm into angelic butterfly, may require a metamorphosis of filmmaking. The techniques and possibilities of such a transformation, of a profound change in cinema's ways of associating identities with bodies, have already been richly elaborated, I would predict, in the third movement of Dante's metamorphic journey.

Notes

1 For a discussion of the centrality of Dante to the history of Italian cinema from its very beginnings, see Amilcare Iannucci's essay 'From Dante's *Inferno* to *Dante's Peak*: The Influence of Dante on Film.'

2 Gilles Deleuze and Frank Burke in their highly fruitful rhetorical analyses of Fellini's film language, for example, emphasize its newness and, in the case of Burke, 'postmodernity' in relation to chronologically earlier stages in cinema history (Burke, 'Fellini: Changing the Subject'; Deleuze, *Cinema 1* 205–15, *Cinema 2* 1–13, 68–9, 88–94). Deleuze, though, also ironizes his narrative of cinema history, linking Italian neo-realism with the French *nouvelle vague* and New German Cinema and suggesting that these rhetorical shifts have as much to do with ideology as with chronology. He also asks provocatively whether the 'crisis' he sees occurring 'first' in Italian neo-realism might not be implicit in the medium itself: 'But can a crisis of the action-image be presented as something new? Was this not the constant state of the cinema?' (*Cinema 1* 205).

3 For a detailed reading of the geometry of the *Commedia*, the analysis of which has deeply influenced my focus on constructions of space in Italian cinema, see my book *Petrarch's Poetics and Literary History* (70–5). I cannot help but suppose that Italian filmmakers have been even more profoundly influenced than I by Dante's understanding and production of different kinds of space. For the clear references in Peter Greenaway's *A TV Dante* to Dante's correlation of geometries with epistemologies and their corresponding subjectivities, see Vickers.

4 It is interesting in this regard to reflect upon Rossellini's reversal of genders in the *Pietà* tableau. Western gender construction is among the most fundamental binary oppositions underwriting the us/them, self/other, inside/outside construction of modern national identities. For a collection

of strong essays extensively investigating the inter-implications of nation, gender construction, and sexualities, see the remarkable volume *Nationalisms and Sexualities*, edited by Andrew Parker, Doris Sommer, and Patricia Yeager.

5 Carla Lonzi in her feminist manifesto 'Let's Spit on Hegel' comments upon the binary gendering of identificatory relations: 'Identification has a compulsive male quality. It strips the bloom from an existence and subjects it to the demand of a rationality which would control, day by day, the sense of success or failure' (57). Film theorist Anne Friedberg, working from a Freudian framework, comes to a similar conclusion: '[I]dentification ... replicates the very structure of patriarchy. Identification demands sameness, necessitates similarity, disallows difference' (36).

6 Notable exceptions to Anglo-American avoidance of *La dolce vita*, interestingly, are mostly scholars with a strong background in Dante studies, including Barbara Lewalski, P. Adams Sitney, and John Welle. Otherwise, Peter Bondanella and Frank Burke, both of whom have written extensively and brilliantly on all of Fellini's films, are almost alone in having critically engaged this film.

7 Examples of references to infernal ruins include the opening of *Inferno* 11, where Virgil explains the plan of Hell as he and the pilgrim pause on the threshold of the descent into the circles of the Violent and the Fraudulent. In the next canto, Dante compares the scree-like slope to damage caused by an earthquake or some other form of geological instability, and Virgil indicates indirectly that 'quella ruina' dates from Christ's harrowing of Hell.

8 Theorists use the term *catachresis* in a variety of ways, but I am using it here in its etymological sense of 'the abuse or perversion of a trope or metaphor' (*OED*). Fellini, I am arguing, mixes levels, modes, icons, and styles as a way of denaturalizing or 'decolonizing' them, restoring what may pass for the real to a contingent, metaphorical, constructed status.

9 For a more extensive reading of the similarly colonizing/colonized image of Rita Hayworth in Vittorio de Sica's *Ladri di biciclette*, to which I think Fellini's Ekberg/Sylvia clearly refers, see my essay 'Decolonizing the Screen: From *Ladri di biciclette* to *Ladri di saponette.*' In Wim Wenders's film *Kings of the Road*, one of the protagonists makes the now well-known observation 'The Yanks have colonized our subconscious' (Elsaesser 231).

10 For a fuller version of the following argument about the sexual politics of the *Commedia*, see my essay 'Seduction and Salvation: Sexual Difference in Dante's *Commedia* and the Difference It Makes.'

11 I concur with P. Adams Sitney's and Anne Paolucci's association of the

waitress Paola with Dante's Matelda in contradistinction to John Welle's
and Barbara Lewalski's association of her with Beatrice (Sitney 113). Since
Matelda prefigures Beatrice, though, I do not see these readings as mutually exclusive.

12 Frank Burke reads Fellini's cinematic rhetoric similarly in his 'Fellini:
Changing the Subject,' but he locates the shift I am describing in the film
language of *8 1/2*, three years later (280).

13 For a more extensive treatment of this film, see my '"You Cannot Make the
Revolution on Film": Wertmüller's Performative Feminism in *Mimi
metallurgico, ferito nell'onore.*'

14 I have discussed this film and its theoretical ramifications more fully in
'Signifying the Holocaust: Liliana Cavani's *Portiere di notte.*'

Bibliography

Baudrillard, Jean. *Simulations.* Trans. Paul Foss, Paul Patton, and Philip
Beitchman. New York: Semiotext(e), Inc., 1983.

Benjamin, Walter. 'The Work of Art in an Age of Mechanical Reproduction.'
Illuminations. Trans. Hannah Arendt. New York: Schocken Books, 1978.
217–51.

Bondanella, Peter. *The Cinema of Federico Fellini.* Princeton: Princeton University Press, 1992.

Burke, Frank. 'Fellini: Changing the Subject.' *Film Quarterly* 43.1 (1989): 36–48.
Rpt. in *Perspectives on Federico Fellini.* Ed. Peter Bondanella and Cristina
Degli-Esposti. New York: G.K. Hall, 1993.

– *Fellini's Films: From Postwar to Postmodern.* New York: Twayne Publishers,
1996.

Dante Alighieri. *La Divina Commedia.* Ed. and annotated by C.H. Grandgent.
Boston: D.C. Heath and Company, 1933.

Deleuze, Gilles. *Cinema 1: The Movement Image.* Minneapolis: University of
Minnesota Press, 1986.

– *Cinema 2: The Time Image.* Minneapolis: University of Minnesota Press, 1989.

– 'Fellini and the Crystals of Time.' *Perspectives on Federico Fellini.* Ed. Peter
Bondanella and Cristina Degli-Esposti. New York: G.K. Hall, 1993. 260–74.

Elsaesser, Thomas. *New German Cinema: A History.* New Brunswick, NJ:
Rutgers University Press, 1989.

Fellini, Federico, dir. *La dolce vita.* With Marcello Mastroianni, Anita Ekberg,
Lex Barker, and Yvonne Fourneaux. Prod. Giuseppe Amato and Angelo
Rizzoli. Riama Film and Consortium Cinema, 1960.

Friedberg, Anne. 'A Denial of Difference: Theories of Cinematic Identification.' *Psychoanalysis and Cinema*. Ed. E. Ann Kaplan. New York and London: Routledge, 1990.

Iannucci, Amilcare, A. 'From Dante's *Inferno* to *Dante's Peak*: The Influence of Dante on Film.' *Forum Italicum* 32 (1998): 5–35.

Lewalski, Barbara K. 'Federico Fellini's *Purgatorio*.' *Massachusetts Review* 5.3 (1964). Rpt. in *Federico Fellini: Essays in Criticism*. Ed. Peter Bondanella. New York: Oxford University Press, 1978.

Lonzi, Carla. 'Let's Spit on Hegel.' *Italian Feminist Thought: A Reader*. Ed. Paolo Bono and Sandra Kemp. Cambridge, MA: Basil Blackwell, 1991. 40–59.

Marcus, Millicent. 'Rossellini's *Open City*: The Founding.' *Italian Film in the Light of Neorealism*. Princeton: Princeton University Press, 1986.

Paolucci, Anne. 'Italian Film: Antonioni, Fellini, Bolognini.' *Massachusetts Review* 7.3 (1966): 556–67.

Parker, Andrew, et al. *Nationalisms and Sexualities*. New York and London: Routledge, 1992.

Rossellini, Roberto, dir. *Roma, città aperta*. With Aldo Fabrizi, Anna Magnani, Marcello Pagliero, and Maria Michi. Excelsa, A Minerva Film, 1945.

Simon, John. *Acid Test*. New York: Stein and Day, 1963.

Sitney, P. Adams. *Vital Crises in Italian Cinema: Iconography, Stylistics, Politics*. Austin: University of Texas Press, 1995.

Trinh T. Minh-ha. 'Surname Viet Given Name Nam.' *Framer Framed*. New York and London: Routledge, 1992.

Vergilius Maro, Publius. *Vergil's Aeneid Books I–VI*. Boston: D.C. Heath and Company, 1930.

Vickers, Nancy. 'Dante in the Video Decade.' *Dante Now: Current Trends in Dante Studies*. Ed. Theodore J. Cachey, Jr. Notre Dame: University of Notre Dame Press, 1995. 263–76.

Waller, Marguerite. 'Decolonizing the Screen: From *Ladri di biciclette* to *Ladri di saponette*.' *Revisioning Italy: National Identity and Global Culture*. Ed. Beverly Allen and Mary Russo. Minneapolis: University of Minnesota Press, 1997. 253–74.

– *Petrarch's Poetics and Literary History*. Amherst, MA: University of Massachusetts Press, 1980.

– 'Seduction and Salvation: Sexual Difference in Dante's *Commedia* and the Difference It Makes.' *Donna: Women in Italian Culture*. Ed. Ada Testaferri. Ottawa: Dovehouse Editions Inc., 1989. 225–43.

– 'Signifying the Holocaust: Liliana Cavani's *Portiere di notte*.' *Feminisms in the Cinema*. Ed. Laura Pietropaolo and Ada Testaferri. Bloomington and Indianapolis: Indiana University Press, 1995.

- 'Whose *Dolce Vita* Is This Anyhow? The Language of Fellini's Cinema.' *Quaderni d'Italianistica* 9.1 (1990): 127–35.
- '"You Cannot Make the Revolution on Film": Wertmüller's Performative Feminism in *Mimi metallurgico, ferito nell'onore.' Women and Performance: A Journal of Feminist Theory* 6.2 (1993): 11–25.

Welle, John. 'Fellini's Use of Dante in *La Dolce Vita.' Studies in Medievalism* 2.3 (1983): 53–65. Rpt. in *Perspectives on Federico Fellini.* Ed. Peter Bondanella and Cristini Degli-Esposti. New York: G.K. Hall, 1993.

Beginning to Think about *Salò*[1]

GABRIELLE LESPERANCE

> Four manner of things appear: good and evil, life and death: but the
> tongue ruleth over them continually.
>
> – Sirach 37:18:1[2]

When analysing films based on written narratives (other than screenplays, naturally), one always runs the risk of oversimplifying the cinematic critique, basing it on points of intersection and divergence
between the original and filmic texts (Marcus 1–25). Delineating
Dantesque allusions in Pier Paolo Pasolini's films is a relatively easy
exercise, as Pasolini borrows repeatedly from the *Divine Comedy*, in
spirit and in kind, from his first film, *Accattone* (1961), to his last, *Salò o le
120 giornate di Sodoma* (1975). This paper is less an attempt to enumerate
these *accenni* to Dante than a means of returning to an analysis of
Pasolini's cinematic texts, in this case through the filter of the *Divine
Comedy*, with the goal of offering a new perspective on a film which all
too frequently in the past has been maligned as some psychotic, homo-
sexual, sadomasochistic fantasy. While a thorough analysis of Pasolini's
final film would require more space than is available in this volume,
this essay will focus on *Salò's* more subtle connections with Dante's
influential poem.

The main issue to be considered in this inquiry is Pasolini's treatment
of justice, crime, and punishment, much of which depends, as it does in
the *Commedia*, on spatial structure, symmetry, and how identity is developed in *Salò*. In Dante's world, punishment is perfectly suited to the
sins committed and is, in fact, the mirror image of sins. Because retribution is divine, punishment is viewed as both fixed and logical: fixed
(and preordained) because Hell is created simultaneously with the rest

of the world, and therefore created together with original sin; logical because it is made in the image of God. In this sense, justice can exist only because a perfect system of punishment is in place.

In Pasolini's world, punishment is enforced because of the existence of dysfunction and bureaucracy. Here, the rules are stated and even scripted in the form of a code of conduct, but then are subject to change at the will of the libertines. For example, in the *Antinferno* the Eccellenza establishes the villa's laws in a speech from the balcony. One of these rules is that no heterosexual intercourse among the prisoners will be allowed. The punishment for any male prisoner in violation of this law is said to be the loss of a limb. Yet when Enzo, one of the recruited soldiers, is caught *in flagrante* with his servant girlfriend, both are fatally wounded. Not only does this action gravely exceed the penalty set forth by the 'law,' but it also arbitrarily punishes another party where no discipline had been prescribed. Also, while the libertines try to project the image of a preordained system of punishment to the extent that the laws are written in book form, much is legislated on a case-by-case basis. When one of the female victims reveals Enzo's secret affair in order to save herself, she asks, 'What will become of me?' The Monsignore responds, 'I don't know ... it will be decided tomorrow ... many things will be decided tomorrow.' Because of the fluid nature of punishment (and the imaginary status of 'sin') in *Salò*, there is no justice here.

According to David Schwartz, Pasolini 'had wanted for some time to do a work built on the principle of Dante's "theological verticalism": levels of blessing, layers of Hell' (Schwartz 640–1). Naomi Greene appears to agree that this is what Pasolini actually accomplishes in his film when she states that '*Salò* echoes the "theological verticalism" of *The Inferno* as, like a descending spiral, it takes us from one circle of horrors to the next' (Greene 197). I would contend that *Salò* does not follow Dante's principle of 'theological verticalism' because the punishment is not just, and there are no blessings. However, the film's moral relativism, a result of such an 'imperfect' Inferno, serves only to underscore the perfection and ideological symmetry in the *Divine Comedy*. Any viewer of *Salò* who recognizes Pasolini's Dantesque references will almost certainly also have expectations of theological verticalism in the film in recalling Dante's system of grace and retribution. Instead, when the viewer is confronted with the contrary system in *Salò*, the effect is much more powerful than had Pasolini utilized 'theological verticalism' in its purest form.

At the same time that there exists an uneven bureaucracy in *Salò*, the film's physical symmetry could be considered overwhelming. This degree of glacial perfection has both political and semiotic implications. While *Salò*'s symmetry gives the impression of complete dominance by man over his surroundings, it, in fact, reveals the limits of human control. 'The obsession with precise formulas and bureaucratic regulations that characterizes his libertines represented, [Pasolini] declared, the strategies embraced by *all* power in its pure arbitrariness, that is, its own anarchy' (Greene 204). Though power is arbitrary in *Salò*, it is manifested in an extremely organized fashion.

Concerning the physical symmetry found in *Salò*, Naomi Greene notes: '[T]he world of *Salò* is one where everything is mathematically composed, geometrically balanced, endowed with a precise function and meaning' (Greene 198). Greene does not go on, however, to explain precisely how this world is composed, balanced, and endowed. I would like to offer the following explications as they resonate with the structure of the *Divine Comedy*.

While Dante's threes are a constant reminder of the divine structure of the afterlife, where there is perfection through forgiveness, Pasolini's fours (4 libertines, 4 narrators, 16 [4 x 4] victims, 4 guards, 4 conspirators, 4 companions, 4 wives/daughters) suggest symmetry. However, this symmetry is not divine, but apocalyptic, if we consider the biblical significance of the number four.[3] Furthermore, the repetition of the number four suggests, in spatial terms, a cubic construction or box. A closer look at the artwork decorating the villa reveals Cubist paintings, which serve to emphasize this pattern of thought. The majority of the film consists of interior shots, which repeatedly present viewers with almost identical boxes.[4]

I would go so far as to suggest that Pasolini is, in fact, consciously toying with the interplay of Dante's divine threes and *Salò*'s apocalyptic fours, with the theme of fours appearing in the narrative structure of the film. For example, while it might seem that there are three acts or circles (the *gironi delle manie, della merda, e del sangue*), there are really four when we include the *Antinferno*. Additionally, the male and female victims begin as nine each (3 x 3), but they number sixteen in total (four squared) after one male and one female victim are killed. It should be noted that Pasolini underlines the numeric aspect of the killings, when after the murder of each of the first two victims the President offers a joke based on the change in numbers. Even the narrators appear to be three, but are actually four since the accompanist is classified as a narrator.[5] In the *girone del sangue*, Pasolini seems to attempt a reversal, insinuating a divine finale with a destruction of the symmetry he had so carefully constructed earlier in the film. Enzo's death signals a reduction from four to three soldiers, which is soon followed by a similar reduction in the number of narrators when the accompanist commits suicide. Both deaths seem sacrificial and somewhat Christ-like. In the sequence directly following the suicide, the four libertines separate for the torture with the three torturers and the one spectator, rotating roles so that each man is both spectator and participant. In other words, even though there is a physical division between the spectator and the three participants, the manner in which the libertines exchange these roles so effortlessly suggests that there is very little practical difference between the functions of the two roles. Therefore, the 'trinity' of torturers is actually a foursome.

Besides the numerological aspect of the symmetry found in *Salò*, there is also the important question of symmetry as it relates to physical perfection and to identity. Unlike *Inferno*, where shades are grotesque, here physical imperfection (i.e., a missing tooth) results in the rejection and/or immediate death of the victims. As opposed to the disfigurements of the libertines in Sade, Pasolini's libertines are perfectly typical, making their behaviour seem simultaneously more heinous and thoroughly conceivable (Schwartz 644). In other words, the grotesque appearance of Sade's characters renders them fantastical in semblance to the reader, thereby making their actions sublime but innocuous, as the characters are unabashedly fictitious. Instead, the lack of hyperbole in Pasolini's depiction of the libertines is odious in that monstrous behaviour is perpetrated, not by aberrant, unbelievable characters, but by those of 'normal' superficies.

The film's symmetry skews identity and, through the use of mirrors and the employment of certain lighting techniques, camera shots, and angles, makes all things equal. The first identity crisis occurs with the introduction of the libertines in a darkened room where it is nearly impossible to distinguish one from another. Not only are their identities obscured by the low lighting of the shot, but the libertines prolong the confusion by addressing each other by titles which are similar (Monsignore, Presidente, Eccellenza, Duca) and which reveal little about their personalities or backgrounds other than the bureaucratic nature of their roles.[6] In all, there is little effort made to differentiate them. As a consequence, the act of the libertines marrying each other's daughters becomes incestuous and further obfuscates their relationships and identities.

Contrary to Dante's *Inferno*, where the names of the shades take on a great deal of importance, here, after the initial listing of victims' names, they nearly cease to denominate the characters. The one exception to this tendency is the crimes list, where the President writes down names and offences. In his capacity as record keeper, the President becomes a modern Minos but does not allow the 'sinners' to distinguish themselves by listing their own sins; instead, this becomes another mundane, bureaucratic duty. In the *Comedy*, the punished find solace and remembrance in their speech acts; in *Salò*, utterances by the victims usually result in obliteration. Besides the lack of identity attributable to the victims' 'namelessness' and relative speechlessness, the children also are deemed interchangeable because of their nudity (Greene 203) or, in the case of the guardsmen, because of their sumptuary uniformity.

In the transition from the *Antinferno* to each of the *gironi*, Pasolini adds complexity to the identities of the narrators more so than he does with any other group of characters within the film. The title shot of the first circle, the *girone delle manie*, dissolves into a shot of the image of the first narrator, Sra. Vaccari, in a mirror as she prepares for her 'performance.' The problem? The shot presents an image with no referent. Sra. Vaccari then visits another mirror on a closet door, where we see two images of her and the image of another vanity with a mirror. Furthermore, the act of opening and closing the closet door catapults her reflected image across the room and across the screen. When she exits the room, we see yet another mirror. Clearly, this is a hall of mirrors. Cinematically, such a multiplicity of disparately positioned reflections already signals an identity crisis. The reproduction of images confuses the audience; which is the image we should watch? As Sra. Vaccari walks down the marble steps to the storytelling room, her image is reflected in the table, making her appear to rise as she descends. Her descent into the first 'circle,' unlike Dante's descent, is easy. The children, guards, wives, other narrators, and libertines are placed in groups around the room, against the wall, not in a circular formation, as would be the expected arrangement of an audience about to hear a story or an oral history, but in the shape of a square. At this point, Sra. Vaccari initiates her narrative by recounting her childhood.

The second circle, the *girone della merda*, is nearly identical to the first, involving a different but remarkably familiar room with a storyteller in front of a mirror. This narrator is seen on both the left and right sides of the frame as both referent and mirror image. In her grooming, screen position, and reflections, Sra. Maggi is identical to Sra. Vaccari, reducing the viewer's ability to demarcate the two women. Given the Dantesque reference to the *gironi,* one would expect to find the characters in a distinct location, as this is a new circle. Instead, Sra. Maggi descends the same stairs in the same way to the same room where the audience is in the same configuration as in the previous *girone.* Sra. Maggi says she will not tell the audience of her childhood as Sra. Vaccari has done. Of course, given the continuum of the characters, there is no need for her to do so, as the two narrators experienced what must be considered, for all intents and purposes, the same childhood. Rather, she begins her narration where the first storyteller left off. In other words, Sra. Maggi is being 'plugged' into the role formerly inhabited by Sra. Vaccari, with no discernible differences between the two. In this way, the film suggests that what passes for identity is very slippery, indeed, and here degenerates into what could be better deemed prefabricated standardizations than true identity.

Because, cinematically speaking, Sra. Vaccari, Sra. Maggi, and Sra. Castelli are being constructed as one character divided or fractured, we expect to see the image of Sra. Castelli in a bedroom mirror in a transition from the *girone della merda* to the *girone del sangue.* Instead we are met with three cross-dressed libertines, each looking in a different mirror as he finishes his preparations, and each reflected in the others' mirrors. This transvestism presents the crisis of a third sex, which 'puts in question identities previously conceived as stable, unchallengeable, grounded, and "known"' (Garber 12–13). Instead of being introduced to one woman (or rather, our three women in one), in this episode Pasolini positions the three men where they are neither expected nor, in some ways, welcome. In Western cinema, women are generally assigned to the centre of the frame to emphasize their 'to-be-looked-at-ness' or to the left side of the screen because this is the weaker, less active position. Here, instead, the three libertines inhabit a traditionally female, spectacular space. Additionally, the topos of the dressing room could be considered almost exclusively feminine or feminized, and certainly has been a feminine locus within the film until this moment.

It should be noted that this act of transvestism should not be seen merely as a case of sexual or gender role *jouissance,* but as a serious challenge to power and gender construction. These men are not trying to 'pass,' as neither the Eccellenza nor the Duca depilates for his performance, but the three are co-opting female functions while maintaining their masculinity. The libertines' interruption of the narration implies their incontrovertible mastery over categories. They are allowed to slide in and out of roles, but with deadly results. In other words, the libertines may seem to be only burlesquing in this sequence, but because of the real effects of the torture and because the others are not permitted the same kind of spatial and gender freedom, it really must be viewed as something graver. Aside from the identity crisis resulting from the cross-dressing episode, the highly fragmented and multiple images arising from the numerous mirrors utilized here serve to emphasize the libertines' physical dominance of the room and the screen, while suggesting something akin to a reproduction or cloning of their power. Pasolini is making us question the nature of power, gender, and position through his constant interplay of the same. It should be noted that the narrative tension created by the sequence of transvestment is eventually relieved when the temporarily displaced Sra. Castelli later makes the descent to the storytelling room in the same manner as the first two storytellers had, thus resuming the female ritual.

The presentation of the third circle purposely interjects the libertines into the 'space' of the narrators in order to show that the females are every bit as culpable in the torture as the libertines, because they are responsible for producing the stimuli which result in torture. In other words, the libertine bureaucrats are barren of ideas and must rely on the narrators for 'original' ideas. Without the narrators, the libertines would be impotent. Ironically, because the libertines have managed to infiltrate and colonize the narrators' space, the women are ultimately and literally eliminated from the screen. After attempts to surfeit the men's appetites have been made, the galvanizing presence of female creativity is no longer deemed necessary as a stimulus for the libertines.

Finally, ascension in Dante signals the transition from Inferno to Purgatory. Since the pilgrim's climb toward Purgatory begins in Inferno, the two regions are described as being physically connected as well as created concurrently, so that the one could not exist without the other. Ascension here is classified as hopeful since sinners can be redeemed. Pasolini instead creates ascensions which are every bit as diabolical as the descents. The rituals that occur on the top floor of the villa seem promising at first glance, with wedding ceremonies associated with both societal approbation and eventual procreation, but they prove fruitless when the libertines once again subvert these events. Instead, these rituals serve to reinforce another kind of sterility demonstrated by the libertines' dependence on the narrators for stimulation. In the film's final ascension following the three wedding ceremonies, the accompanist, who has tried to intervene on behalf of the victims, manifests her inability to influence the destiny of the children when she plunges to her death. She is no Beatrice, Mary, or Lucia. Perhaps the key to Pasolini's rendering of 'theological verticalism' is to be found in the convoluted role of the four narrators, who, rather than mediating divine intervention leading toward salvation, inspire only torturous death.

Notes

1 This title is a play on words on the title of a painting by artist-translator Tom Phillips. That work, entitled *Beginning to Think about Dante* (1978), served as an important springboard to Phillips' illustrated translation of Dante's *Inferno* (1983), which led to his collaborative television series on the *Inferno*, *A TV Dante* (1988). Both *Beginning to Think about Dante* and *A TV Dante* are examined in this collection.

2 This biblical (KJV) reference to the number four seems particularly apt in light of the importance of the speech act in Salò. The role of the number four and symmetry in the film is discussed later in this paper.

3 Frequently, the number four appears in the Bible in describing winds (Job 1:19 and Dan. 7:3); punishment or destruction arising from God's anger (Ezek. 7:2 and Amos 1:3–2:7); beasts (Dan. 7:3–8); and the number of enemy troops, companies, or deceased (Gen. 32:6, 33:1, Judg. 9:34, and 1 Sam. 4:2). The apocalyptic usage of the number four is most sensational, of course, in the Book of Revelation.

4 A viewer familiar with the Italian retro films of the 1970s cannot avoid associating the cubism of *Salò* with a striking flashback in Liliana Cavani's *Night Porter* (1973). In this flashback, the Nazi protagonist presents his victim-lover with a box containing the decapitated head of a man believed to be a threat to their relationship.

5 This is done cinematically in the balcony sequence. While the Eccellenza discusses the daily orgies, the camera holds on each of the storytellers, with the accompanist presented as the second of the four narrators in the series of shots.

6 As Greene suggests, Sade's aristocrats are replaced by bureaucrats (203).

Bibliography

Adair, Gilbert. 'Salò o le 120 giornate di Sodoma.' *Monthly Film Bulletin* 46.548 (Sept. 1979): 200–1.

Bachmann, Gideon. 'Pasolini and the Marquis de Sade.' *Sight and Sound* 45.1 (Winter 1975–6): 50–4.

– 'Pasolini on de Sade.' *Film Quarterly* 29.2 (Winter 1975–6): 39–45.

Barthes, Roland. *Sade, Fourier, Loyola*. Trans. Richard Miller. New York: Hill and Wand, 1976.

Boarini, Vittorio, Pietro Bonfiglioli, and Giorgio Cremonini, presentati da. *Da Accattone a Salò: 120 scritti sul cinema di Pier Paolo Pasolini*. Bologna: Tip. Compositori, 1982.

Cavani, Liliana, dir. *Portiere di notte*. 1973.

Dumont, P. 'Salò ou l'impossible représentation du fantasme.' *Cinéma* 302 (Feb. 1984): 8–10.

Finetti, U. 'Nella struttura di Salò: La dialettica erotismo-potere' and 'La condanna di Salò nella sentenza del tribunale.' *Cinema Nuovo* 25.244 (Nov.-Dec. 1976): 428–43.

Garber, Marjorie. *Vested Interests: Cross-Dressing and Cultural Anxiety*. New York: Routledge, 1992.

Greene, Naomi. *Pier Paolo Pasolini: Cinema As Heresy*. Princeton: Princeton University Press, 1990.

Klossowski, Pierre. *Sade My Neighbor*. Trans. Alphonso Lingis. Evanston, IL: Northwestern University Press, 1991.

Marcus, Millicent. *Filmmaking by the Book*. Baltimore: Johns Hopkins University Press, 1993.

Pasolini, Pier Paolo, dir. *Salò o le 120 giornate di Sodoma*. 1975.

Rumble, Patrick. *Allegories of Contamination: Pier Paolo Pasolini's Trilogy of Life*. Toronto: University of Toronto Press, 1996.

Rumble, Patrick, and Bart Testa, eds. *Pier Paolo Pasolini: Contemporary Perspectives*. Toronto: University of Toronto Press, 1994.

Sade, Marquis de. *The Marquis de Sade: The 120 Days of Sodom and Other Writings*. Ed. and trans. Austin Wainhouse and Richard Seaver. New York: Grove Press, 1966.

Schwartz, Barth David. *Pasolini Requiem*. New York: Pantheon Books, 1992.

Waller, Marguerite. 'Signifying the Holocaust: Liliana Cavani's *Portiere di Notte*.' *Italian Women Writers from the Renaissance to the Present: Revising the Canon*. Ed. and introd. Maria Ornella Marotti. University Park, PA: Pennsylvania State University Press, 1996. 259–72.

The Off-Screen Landscape: Dante's Ravenna and Antonioni's *Red Desert*

VICTORIA KIRKHAM

Modern Italian cinema, mirroring national culture, often centres on geographic regions with their physical features and on cities with their defining monuments. It was the neo-realists, departing from stagy boudoirs and drawing rooms typical of 'white telephone' movies in the 1930s, who came out of the studios into real towns and countrysides to establish the importance of place in film. In this they took their cue from local colour integral to *verismo*, the late nineteenth-century literary school that defined those directors after the Second World War as the 'new realists.' As early as Visconti's proto–neo-realist *Ossessione* (1942), setting was to become an essential element of verisimilitude. Millicent Marcus has reminded us how Rossellini's *Rome, Open City* (1945), the founding film of neo-realism, programmatically cites Christian structures to make an anti-fascist statement.[1] Landmarks of the Roman past like the Colosseum and Forum are replaced by Trinità dei Monti, whose twin towers rise against the background of a shadowy establishing shot as the film opens with German troops tromping ominously to the clipped, jarring sounds of a song in their language through the very heart of the city, Piazza di Spagna. The cupola of St Peter's, against which in the original Italian version of the film the titles unfold,[2] returns powerfully as a symbol on the skyline for the closing sequence after the execution of Don Pietro, as the boys two by two, in symmetrical opposition to the German troops at the beginning dawn scene, silently re-enter the city. Fascist Rome, by contrast, would trumpet itself in the grandiose documentary footage that launched Scola's *Una giornata particolare* (1977), the mass spectacle of Hitler's and Mussolini's historic meeting in May 1938 captured by newsreel that covers their motorcade down the Via dei Fori Imperiali, pauses at the seat of government, and then leads to the Vittorio Emanuele Monument ('Altare della Patria'), concluding at the Duce's balcony over Piazza Venezia.

Sightings of such monuments in Italian movies can remind us of snapshots in an album. They are the most familiar sights, what all tourists go to see. The neo-realists in their own evolution, as well as later generations of Italian directors, have continued to invoke land-marks like these, forming a corpus that I call the Italian album-film. With Rossellini's *Viaggio in Italia* of 1953, the film actually became a travelogue in its structure, one that could well be subtitled 'Napoli e dintorni,' as Katherine Joyce's cultural outings lead us from a guided tour of the National Museum in Naples, with its busts of Roman emper-ors and statuary excavated from Herculaneum, to the Temple of Apollo, a steamy Vesuvius, and catacombs stacked with piles of human bones, while her husband visits Capri, ironically without being smiled on by Venus. Their split paths cross again dramatically as together they visit Pompeii, still re-emerging from its blanket of ash.

Other directors have given us more personal albums. Fellini's recol-lections of Rome come to mind, usually warm, humorous, wry. Early snatches anchor *The White Sheik* (1952), his first solo film. Newlywed Ivan's planned day, complete with a visit to the Tomb of the Unknown Soldier at the 'Altare della Patria' and an audience at the Vatican, parodies the predictable itinerary, but his arrangements go awry when his wife runs off starry-eyed to join a seaside shoot with the *fotoromanzo* troop. Back in the city that night, disillusioned and bedraggled, she makes a bathetic suicide attempt by hopping into the Tiber's muddy shallows near the Castel Sant'Angelo bridge. At the close of their 'comic odyssey through Rome,'[3] echoing Rossellini's final assertion of St Peter's, the director reassembles his characters before the cathedral façade for a final procession, at Bernini's ellipse, its colonnade surmounted by an angel who smiles down on Ivan and Wanda with a wink as they trot dutifully into the waiting arms of the Church and the tedium of bour-geois life. Fellini's colourful *Roma* of 1972 is a cinematic scrapbook fully dedicated to Italy's urban hub, culminating with the wonderful motor-cycle ballet through the city at night, a graceful sweep of its landmarks: Castel Sant'Angelo, St Peter's, Piazza Navona, the Spanish Steps and Trinità dei Monti, Piazza del Popolo, the Quirinale, Campidoglio, Aracoeli, the Forum, the Colosseum. Nanni Moretti in *Caro diario*, re-leased in 1993, rides his own motorcycle (perhaps in a nod to Fellini) through his favourite neighbourhoods, to the empty summer movie houses, and then to dismal coastal fields on the outskirts, where a small marker commemorates Pasolini's murder. Pasolini himself attached his films to Rome, not the tourist centre but that desolate periphery where he died, breeding ground for violence and tragedy. *Mamma Roma* (1962) alludes to a better social order and finer past by showing just the segment of a Roman aqueduct, now standing solitary on the barren, rough ground occupied otherwise only by sterile towers of low-rent apartments. Pasolini had already recalled the metropolitan overlay of papal history in scenes from *Accattone* (1961) set under the Ponte Sant'Angelo, whose presiding angels are physically close but poetically distant from the young men of the *borgata*. The time Accattone and his friends spend eating, drinking, card playing, and horsing about on the underside of the bridge is a visual metaphor for their existence in the underbelly of society.

In both Rossellini's *Open City* and *Voyage in Italy*, setting defines character, but whereas in the former it lends sociological realism, in the latter it serves psychological symbolism. Rossellini makes Rome speak for an entire post-war generation; Fellini makes it speak for himself, and Moretti makes Rome the stage for meditations on the recent history of Italian cinema.[4] Pasolini's Rome aggressively reverses the stereotype, bespeaking a terrible political failure, yet what is absent – the beautiful, historic, and supposedly functional city off-screen – is present implicitly, by virtue of its absence. Rossellini's Naples, registered in scenes that give the impression of unmediated documentary, rises as a pan-Italian symbol, synecdoche for all Italian history and culture, an emblem of the collective psyche.

Pasolini's anti-Rome of the *borgate* and the cerebral Rossellini of *Viaggio in Italia*, where setting assumes existential resonance, bring us closest to Antonioni and his choices for *Red Desert* (1964). Antonioni had already explored a variety of locations, both in northern and southern Italy: the Po Valley for his early documentary *Gente del Po* (*People of the River Po* [1943–7] and for *Il grido* (1957), choices that connect with Visconti's *Ossessione* and with the final episode in Rossellini's *Paisà*; Turin for *Le amiche* (1955); Sicily and the Aeolian Isles for *L'avventura* (1960); Milan for *La notte* (1961); Rome for *L'eclisse* (1962). Later he would rove in his cinematic ventures to London, Los Angeles, Death Valley, North Africa, Spain, and even as far as China. Unique in his corpus for its setting, *Red Desert* takes us to Ravenna.

Situated south of the Po on the Adriatic shore and stratified with a Roman, Byzantine, and medieval past, Ravenna is rarely seen even in the larger history of Italian cinema, except for that celluloid family that revolves around Dante. Late in life, the outcast Florentine accepted an invitation from Guido Novello da Polenta to live there, and under Guido's patronage Dante was able to finish writing the *Divine Comedy* before his death in 1321. Just a generation later, in 1346, Boccaccio briefly sojourned at the court of Ostasio da Polenta, cousin and successor to Dante's host, and he visited again as an ambassador from Florence to deliver money to Alighieri's cloistered daughter in 1350, the period that saw him draft his life of Italy's founding poet, *Trattatello in laude di Dante* (*The Little Treatise in Praise of Dante*). From then on, that 'most ancient city of Romagna,' as Boccaccio calls it, hallowed site of Dante's death and grave, entered the circuit of the master's cult. In the fifteenth century, a *tempietto* was raised to enshrine his remains, decorated over the altar with a bas-relief bust by Pietro Lombardo showing the poet bent over his books (illus. 1 and 2).[5] Recognizing an ideal subject, especially for the Italian public, cinema's early promoters capitalized on Dante's life story as well as indelible episodes he had painted with words in his *Divine Comedy*. An extravaganza of 1921, *La mirabile visione* (*The Amazing Vision*), used on-location shooting to depict his early days in Florence, his exile in Verona as a guest of Can Grande della Scala, and his ultimate haven in Ravenna, where he is seen composing his masterpiece. Francesca da Rimini, one of the most famous residents of Dante's *Inferno* and an enduring dramatic subject, could also provide occasion for invoking Ravenna since she had been a native of that city and the niece of Guido Novello. So when Raffaello Matarazzo directed *Paolo e Francesca* for Lux Film in 1949, his version of her ill-fated romance was partially shot in Ravenna, under siege by the Lord of Rimini as the film begins.[6]

Antonioni's vision of Ravenna departs radically from such album-film treatments, inspired by a literary classic. It is a chilly, ugly, and dehumanized port synonymous with the desert of the film's title. Against Ravenna, he and his co-writer, Tonino Guerra, insert other secondary settings, both by way of echo and contrast – Ferrara, Patagonia, and an imaginary Edenic isle. Nearby Ferrara is the first. Early in the film, the protagonist, Giuliana (Monica Vitti), the psychologically troubled wife of Ugo, managing engineer in a large factory, accompanies her husband's friend Corrado (Richard Harris) to recruit workers there for his industrial project in Patagonia. Set on the banks of the Po, that mythic river with such appeal for the neo-realists, Ferrara obviously had added significance for Antonioni, himself Ferrarese, as he returns with this sequence to the region featured in his earlier *People of the River Po* and *Il*

Illustration 1. Camillo Morigia, *Dante's Tomb* (1780), Ravenna.

Illustration 2. Pietro Lombardo, *Portrait of Dante* (marble bas-relief, 1483). Interior of Dante's tomb. Courtesy of Istituto Centrale per il Catalogo e la Documentazione, Rome.

grido.[7] Through his lens for *Red Desert*, there is no hint of Ferrara's flowering in the fifteenth and sixteenth centuries as one of Europe's great courts under the ruling Este dukes, patrons to Ariosto and Tasso, or of its important Jewish community. Rather, Ferrara presents itself as a satellite of Antonioni's Ravenna, an inland city seen only at the periphery with sterile white blocks of impersonal worker housing, near which rise new high-tech towers for a radar installation that stalk weirdly in a line like monstrous robots. Nothing at all is revealed of the Renaissance jewel at its historic centre, landmarks Vittorio de Sica would later cite for climactic scenes in his *Garden of the Finzi-Contini* (1972). After her arrest, from the back of a police car whose driver's fascist fez with a fat tassel partially obscures her view, de Sica's Micol glimpses the Este Castle and Palazzo dei Diamanti. Then at the schoolhouse where Ferrara's Jews have been herded together for deportation, she clings to the father of her friend Giorgio, and as he speaks the last words of dialogue in the film, 'Let's hope they let us stay together, those of us from Ferrara,' both look out on the skyline, across which the camera slowly, wrenchingly pans. What de Sica asserts for emotional effect disappears from camera view in Antonioni's Ferrarese scenes, which are voided of the past and distinctive markers of place. These latter have been pushed to the off-screen landscape, where we as viewers picture them mentally, inevitable connections arising from what we know about the city's heritage. On-screen, after Antonioni has deliberately filtered away those traditional images, regional depth has been levelled into a barren present of pan-global modernity.[8]

Most of the film, reflecting Giuliana's depressive state of mind, is set in the foggy, colour-drained, and polluted environment of Ravenna's industrial periphery. High-tech factories have foreign or artificial names that fit perfectly the alienating surroundings they at once cause and occupy, labels like Phillips, ANIC, and Sarom. Maritime traffic comes and goes in the background, passing behind damp flats in sandy lowlands where the characters walk (illus. 3), or glimpsed through long high horizontal windows in Giuliana's ultra-modern house, or docked on the quay outside Max's hut, where Giuliana, her husband, Ugo, and Corrado join several friends for a pseudo-orgy in a room painted bright red. Except for the fairy-tale island sequence, the brightest most saturated colours are not outdoors, in the landscape, but inside in such bits and pieces as the swatches painted on the walls of Giuliana's empty shop, the red boards inside the hut, or on metallic structural elements in the bowels of the factory where Ugo works. Not content with the

Illustration 3. Michelangelo Antonioni, *Red Desert* (1964). Ugo, Corrado, and Giuliana on the dunes with the *pineta* in background. Courtesy Film Stills Archive, Museum of Modern Art, New York.

dreariness of the dismal landscape as it actually was, Antonioni used filters to drain objects of what colour they had. He painted grey the sooty industrial waste littering the ground around Ugo's factory, the fruit on a street vendor's cart, and the pine trees growing on Ravenna's sandy coastal land, its well known *pineta*.[9] If anything, this urban wasteland is just the opposite of picturesque settings associated with the home-town spirit of Italian *campanilismo* or cultural icons like the great basilica of *Open City*, the vacated but still defiant Uffizi in the Florentine episode of *Paisà*, and Venice's Teatro la Fenice, resonant with rustling silks and the strains of Verdi in the brilliant opening sequence of Visconti's *Senso*.

Yet Ravenna too has its high artistic traditions. All Italians know her ties, proud and jealously guarded, with Italy's founding poet, whose remains the city has for six centuries steadfastly refused to yield back to Florence. Each year the Florentines send olive oil from the Tuscan hills to refuel the eternal flame that burns at the base of Pietro Lombardo's marble relief, housed in its early Renaissance *tempietto* outside the church of San Francesco (illus. 6 and 7). Ravenna's most famous magnets by far, unique in the world, are her splendidly preserved Byzantine religious monuments animated within by stunning mosaics. Dating from the fifth and sixth centuries, these treasures are the churches of Sant'Apollinare in Classe, Sant'Apollinare Nuovo, and San Vitale, the Mausoleum of Galla Placidia, the Arian Baptistry, and the Neonian Baptistry. We see none of them in the movie, neither tessellated icons nor the shrine of Dante, at least not from a sightseer's perspective. They are present, however, in other more oblique ways.

Most obvious is the allusion to Dante, whose family name occurs explicitly and early in Antonioni and Guerra's screenplay. Emerging from the factory where he works in dim, windowless chambers filled with space-age control panels and labyrinths of metal pipes, Giuliana's husband, Ugo, casually tells Corrado of his wife's 'accident' and month-long hospitalization. Mostly, he says, it was shock, and she still doesn't seem able to reconnect with reality. 'Now,' Ugo continues, 'she wants to set up a shop, but I don't have any idea what she wants to do. In Via Alighieri. For that matter, I don't even think it's proper.'[10] As if to underline his indifference, Ugo lights a cigarette. The subject is then quickly dropped, as metallic hammering sounds interrupt the conversation, and attention shifts to their source in a gigantic rusted empty silo at the factory exit. The Alighieri name slips by quickly, wedged into a brief exchange of words whose main point is Ugo's impatience with

Giuliana for her failure to recover emotionally from what we later learn was actually a suicide attempt triggered by her isolation, her lovelessness, her desperation.

Later that morning, Corrado goes to find Giuliana in her shop. The deserted medieval street that we are to take as 'Via Alighieri,' although finely preserved, appears not quaintly picturesque but spooky and surreal, even threatening.[11] Like the street outside, the space Giuliana has rented is empty. All it holds are some cans of paint, a bare hanging light bulb, a telephone on the floor, and test swatches of colour splashed on the white walls. Giuliana and Corrado talk about what she might sell. Lurching and pacing restlessly, she speaks and moves disconnectedly; and in a spasmodic impulse, she tries unsuccessfully to make a phone call. Her failure to reach anyone at the other end of the line confirms what Ugo had said in the previous sequence: 'Non riesece a riingranare' [She isn't able to reconnect]. Unlike Giuliana, who is tied down to her husband and son in Ravenna, Corrado reveals that he is a wanderer who has lived peripatetically, in Trieste, Milano, Bologna, and now South America. Later that day, the two will drive to Ferrara, and eventually she will go to his hotel room, where they have a sexual encounter, more physical writhing than passionate transport or affectionate intimacy. Afterwards, she and Corrado return to her shop for a scene much shorter than the first one there. Near tears, Giuliana blurts out, 'There is something terrible in reality, and I don't know what it is. No one will tell me.' Through Corrado, she had hoped to find relief from her unhappiness – love in an affair, or escape, at least, in contemplated travel, as when they talk of Patagonia over the map she spreads on the floor in his hotel room. But at the door to her shop, she looks at him with final words of disillusionment: 'And you didn't help me either, Corrado.' Her exit marks the end of the affair. In Antonioni's tightly edited film, these two scenes are the only ones at Giuliana's Via Alighieri shop. Structured in symmetry, they are markers in the narrative that bracket the abortive affair between Giuliana and Corrado, whose first and last conversations take place there.

The interior of Giuliana's house provides the setting for other allusions to the medieval past. As she packs for Ugo, who is leaving on another of his frequent business trips, he urges her to invite a friend to keep her company at night. Over their bed hangs a small painting, a wooden panel of *St George and the Dragon* (illus. 4). Its identity is at first withheld from us since the *mise-en-scène* keeps most of it just beyond the right edge of the picture frame. Each time the camera cuts back to

Illustration 4. Michelangelo Antonioni, *Red Desert*. Truncated image of *St George and the Dragon* over Giuliana's bed. Courtesy Film Stills Archive, Museum of Modern Art, New York.

Giuliana, we are allowed to see a bit more of it, until finally, before quickly moving down to the suitcase on the bed, the camera pans over to reveal the whole object. Even then, the picture comes and goes so quickly that it is just a minimal presence, a tantalizing trace. The point seems to be more to deny than to assert this saint from the legends of the Middle Ages, represented on the panel in *Red Desert* in the same style as the mosaics of the city's celebrated Byzantine churches.

They, too, are conspicuous by their absence from Antonioni's Ravenna. In the hotel room with Corrado, Giuliana at one point walks over to the window and looks out on another deserted street, now at night-time. As in her shop, just one light bulb hangs over the scene. Following her gaze, the camera pans down over what the screenplay describes as 'un sagrato,'[12] the space outside a church, to focus fleetingly on black-framed death notices plastered around it and a solitary passerby. This dark funereal view is the only sign of a church building in the entire film. It is significant that we are excluded from it, viewing it from the outside, momentarily, and in a nocturnal shot that makes the brick exterior look dark, especially if we make the mental connection with the glowing gold mosaics that probably brighten its interior.

To deny the past, Antonioni must paradoxically recall it, but only minimally, in reminders invoked with a maximum of economy. *St George and the Dragon* over Giuliana and Ugo's bed is not quite alone among the selected few antiques that decorate their ultra-modern house. The most striking, and surely the most incongruous, is an antique wooden chair on the landing in an otherwise aseptic stairwell. Like the shop in Via Alighieri, this piece makes a coordinated pair of appearances in the film. When we first see Giuliana at home, she awakens thrashing in the night, anxiously thrusts a thermometer under her arm, and then wanders into her son's room, where she turns off a toy robot that has been whirring back and forth eerily beside his bed. Finally, her anxious pacing leads her to the landing, where the chair receives her restless, twisting body. Solitary, anachronistic, and oddly placed, this piece of furniture focuses our attention, as we watch Giuliana slowly heading toward it in her insomnia, then sitting. The shot has been framed in such a way as to create tension by pushing it off-centre, over into the right half of the composition, leaving nothing to fill the left. Before we glimpse the seat the second time, Giuliana's little boy, Valerio, terrifies her with his supposed paralysis, and she tells him the fairy tale about an island inhabited only by a young girl, whose companions are a cormorant, sea gull, and rabbit. The fantasy sequence ends with a full screen of sapphire blue sky, which dissolves directly to Giuliana, stand-ing numb with worry outside her son's room, this time in broad day-light. Here the frame is more sharply bisected vertically, revealing in the mid-distance behind her the same antique chair, now empty (illus. 5). This time, in symmetrical opposition to its first appearance, the chair occupies the left half of the screen, and Giuliana does not sit in it. The camera cuts from Giuliana and the distinctive chair, backless with two juxtaposed semicircular arches forming the cradle-like seat and curving legs, to the view from her window, where a large bright merchant vessel pulls away from the dock. Like the magical island, the ship represents her own yearning to escape the dreary reality of her sur-roundings. Twice framed in corresponding reversed 'visual cells,'[13] the wooden seat, so out of key with its setting, is nonetheless an apt prop for this drama that takes place in Ravenna. In both English and Italian, it is known as a 'Dante chair.' From a similar chair, Dante presides in Giorgio Vasari's often copied *Portrait of Six Tuscan Poets* of 1544, perhaps the origin of the term (illus. 6).[14]

Via Alighieri is a verbal allusion; the *St George* over Giuliana and Ugo's bed and their Dante chair are visual allusions to the past, a past nearly obliterated by the all-encompassing present. Antonioni's present exists, not as an age that has gracefully evolved out of what came before, but in hungry opposition to the past. Around the dichotomy between present and past, as Angela Dalle Vacche has suggested, *Red Desert* develops related polarities: technology versus humanistic tradition, scientific progress versus nature, reality versus fantasy, masculine versus femi-nine, reason versus intuition. Ugo, who first appears in the factory talk-ing on the telephone and later demonstrates to Valerio the principle of a gyroscope, embodies all the former terms. Practical in his reasoning, he is perfectly comfortable surrounded by machines that are the result of technological advancement through science. Giuliana, in contrast, em-bodies the feminine of classical Western epistemology, an opposite set of values associated positively with nature, tradition, the arts, sentiment, and imagination. She wears a green coat in a film where green otherwise is scarcely present, for it is winter, trees are barren, flowers do not bloom, and industrial waste and mud cover the ground, not grass. Incapable of making a single call from the useless phone on her shop floor, Giuliana stands near the Byzantine saint, looks down wistfully from the hotel window on the church apse, sits in the Dante chair, invents for Valerio a fairy tale island, and in the end actually climbs the gangplank of a ship in a futile attempt to escape her predictable, confining life.

Illustration 5. Michelangelo Antonioni, *Red Desert*. Giuliana outside her son's room with a 'Dante chair' in background. Courtesy Film Stills Archive, Museum of Modern Art, New York.

Illustration 6. Giorgio Vasari, *Portrait of Six Tuscan Poets* (oil on panel, 1544). Minneapolis Institute of Art. The John R. Van Derlip and William Hood Dunwoody Funds.

In the iconography of the film, ships are synthetic vessels of meaning. There is an ambivalence about them. Some are sleek inviting things; others, grim tramps, rusted or poisoned with contagion. Emblems of instability, they can remind us of the characters, who also keep moving about but without really connecting, reified beings in perpetual motion like ships plying the seas and passing in the night. These boats also remind us of Ravenna's long history as a maritime community, reaching back to Roman times and preserved in the proper name Sant'Apollinare in Classe, which comes from the Latin *classis* for 'navy.' Classe, which gives the Italian variant 'Chiassi,' refers to the fleet that anchored in orderly ranks in the port of Classe, not far from Sant'Apollinare in Classe and Sant'Apollinare Nuovo. Mosaics in both churches recall the ancient city of Classe and the fleets that sailed in and out of Ravenna's harbour. Antonioni's ocean-going ships, a real part of Ravenna's history and industry, can be antidotes to the 'desert' of his film's title, for they are signs of exotic, distant places like Patagonia, where Corrado is headed with a new crew of labourers, or the nameless island of Giuliana's fable.

Although Patagonia will never appear directly in *Red Desert*, it hovers over the horizon, invoked later on a huge map of Latin America as Corrado answers workers' questions about what it will be like to work there, and in Corrado's hotel room as Giuliana runs her finger over the paper charting that far, unreachable country. A land at the antipodes, both spatially and spiritually, it implies unspoken possibilities of escape from her deadening Ravennate environment, in much the same way as the merchant vessels that endlessly come and go near her house, mysterious voyagers free to criss-cross the world's high seas. The film's symbolic topography assigns Patagonia a part similar to that of the Sardinian island in the fairy tale that Giuliana tells her son, Valerio, when he pretends that his legs are paralyzed. By far the most vivid sequence in *Red Desert*, this pink beach answers her fantasy of breaking away as she struggles to recover from her depressive neurosis. The nameless island is a place of brilliant colours and stunning natural beauty, inhabited only by a pre-pubescent girl, flourishing plants, and small tame wild creatures. The sail boat that approaches her fantasy island, unmanned and mysteriously self-powered like a bark of Arthurian or Breton legend, cannot land there because the island only remains perfect in isolation.

This is obviously an Eden, its features like those of the Earthly Paradise in medieval imagination. Separated from the rest of the world, it is a place where animals peaceably dwell, blossoms scent the air, song wafts on the breezes, and spring reigns perpetual in primeval, unspoiled nature. But why is there a little girl there? It is Giuliana who tells the fairy tale, and hence as a woman she imagines a female counterpart. For purposes of the film's pairings, the girl complements Valerio, its male child. In contrast to the adults who wander aimlessly through landscapes of alienation, she symbolizes a lost world of childhood innocence, uncontaminated by civilization. Poetically, the girl alone on Giuliana's pink beach has an ancestress in another solitary maiden, just as mysteriously alone in an older Earthly Paradise. Her name was Matelda. She was guardian spirit of the 'ancient forest' benevolently shading Dante's Garden, a salvific corrective for the terrifying 'selva oscura' where he had nearly perished in sin before beginning his pilgrimage to God.[15]

In the film's dialectic economy, Giuliana's Edenic island is the counterpart of Antonioni's infernal Ravenna, and both are informed by the director's memories of the *Divine Comedy*. As the camera jumps from Ravenna to Sardinia, dazzling colours explode over the screen in sharp contrast to all the greyness up to then dominant in the film, and simple natural harmonies bring sudden relief from the irritating cacophony of industry. Such an abrupt shift can remind us of the moment Dante emerges on Purgatory, like Giuliana's utopia a warm, sunny island skirted by beaches, after his descent through the dark, clangorous depths of Hell.[16] Giuliana, too, had visited the 'depths' earlier in *Red Desert*, descending a stairway into the cavernous gut of Ugo's factory to pick her way among machines howling deafeningly, to sidestep hissing steam, and to fend off the assault of mechanically generated wind. Tellingly, on the threshold of that infernal place, Ugo had dropped the name 'Alighieri' as he belittled Giuliana's shop. Dante's Earthly Paradise, at the peak of the island, differs from the dry, desert-like landscape of Giuliana's tale. His Eden is a forest, suffused with caressing breezes and birdsong. In one of the most famous canto openings and similes of the *Divine Comedy*, Dante compares this privileged spot to the pine grove on Classe's shore:

> ... [li augelletti] con piena letizia l'ore prime,
> cantando, recevieno intra le foglie,
> che tenevan bordone a le sue rime,
> tal qual di ramo in ramo si raccoglie
> per la pineta in su 'l lito di Chiassi,
> quand'Eolo scilocco fuor discioglie. (*Purg.* 28.16–21)

[... singing (the little birds) greeted the morning hours with full joy among the leaves, which kept such burden to their rhymes as gathers from branch to branch through the pine forest on Chiassi's shore when Aeolus lets forth Sirocco.][17]

Breezes hum with a pleasant constant low note, making a bass accompaniment (or 'burden') to the birds who chirrup in the upper registers. It is as if Antonioni had transposed this musical image into a grotesque anti-natural imitation when he stages the hellish factories early in the film to produce a deep humming against which we hear intermittently higher pitched shrieks and whistles of industrial production. Never once in *The Red Desert* is there any sound so gentle as a singing bird; instead, only technological noise – motors whirring, machines clanking, vapours sibilant – punctuated at intervals by ghostly fog horns of the ever-present sailing vessels. The 'little birds' are not absent, though. They figure in Antonioni's landscape, too, in the final scene, as Valerio asks his mother why smoke puffing from the factory chimney is yellow, and she explains that it is poisonous:

CHILD: Then if a little bird flies through it, it will die.
GIULIANA: Yes, but by now the little birds know that, and they don't fly through it any more.

In Valerio's childish language, it is not surprising that the birds are 'little' ('uccellini'). The diminutive noun, of course, also emphasizes the absurd contrast between those tiny, fragile creatures of nature and the monstrous man-made instruments of pollution that threaten not only Ravenna's birds and fish, but also sensitive human beings like Giuliana who can only try to survive by adapting to the poisons in the modern industrial environment. Perhaps with the form 'uccellini,' which the screenplay prefers to the standard 'uccelli,' Antonioni and Guerra echo the Dante they would have learned by memory and his 'augelletti,' precisely the same word in a diminutive poetic form borrowed from the Provençal of the troubadours.[18]

In Dante's verses, the pine grove is the defining natural feature of Chiassi, Ravenna's ancient port, and by metonymy cultural tradition soon made the *pineta* an attribute of Ravenna itself. A generation after Dante, the region's characteristic umbrella pines return in a famous novella by Boccaccio (*Decameron* V.8) attached to Ravenna, the story of Nastagio degli Onesti, whose astonishing vision of a ghostly couple one day in the forest guides him to a happy resolution in marriage of his own amorous suit. Sandro Botticelli and his assistants retold the popular novella around 1483 with four influential panels, commissioned for a marriage. Florentines like Dante, both Boccaccio and Botticelli construct their stories with the *Commedia* as a point of reference. Botticelli's first two paintings are dominated by the dense *pineta*, which metaphorically resembles Dante's 'dark forest' in *Inferno* 1 as labyrinthine symbol of man's uncontrolled passions. The pines' heavy, vertical trunks give the pictorial space three-dimensionality and articulate the action into successive narrative episodes beneath the overarching branches; against a brighter background, beyond the forest, we glimpse sailing vessels in the harbour. An almost identical shot occurs in *Red Desert*, interjected in a scene where Giuliana, Ugo, and Corrado are out walking in the swampy land around Ugo's abandoned shack.[19] She looks up as a large ship glides by, just on the other side of the thick pine forest with its deep stand of heavy, vertical trunks. This frame, unique in the film, is as close as Antonioni ever brings his camera to the *pineta*. The shot resembles so uncannily Botticelli's compositions that it must be a citation. Yet since they reveal Ravenna's past and a still surviving slice of natural beauty, the trees on the dunes cannot be an occasion for lingering. The *pineta* in close-up comes and goes as quickly as the vessel passing through Giuliana's narrow field of vision, in the blink of an eye.

Thanks to the art of Dante, Boccaccio, and Botticelli, Italians associate the *pineta* with Ravenna as much as they do its Byzantine monuments and history of Dantism. Although *Red Desert* only once brings us into visual proximity with it, in the scene I have just described, the *pineta* makes significant appearances in earlier sequences of the film. From his subterranean factory command chamber, Ugo telephones administrators in two other offices to help find workers for Corrado to send to Patagonia. In deliberate contrast to Ugo's dim windowless setting, the offices of the men to whom he speaks are both flooded with bright natural light from large windows. As the film cross-cuts between Ugo and his colleagues on the phone, we realize that their windows function as frames, drawing our eye to what lies without. From one office, in the first of two parallel compositions, we see bulbous silver storage tanks of the new, progressive, industrial Ravenna; from the second, rounded dark green umbrella pines, reminders of Ravenna's once unspoiled natural beauty and its cultural heritage, both of which are fast disappearing. The same point is made again as Corrado and Giuliana stroll under a grey sky, and he speaks of his credo:

> We don't really know what we believe in. We believe in humanity, in a
> certain sense. A bit less in justice. A bit more in progress. We believe in
> socialism maybe ... The important thing is to do what is right, right for
> oneself and for others, that is, to be at peace with your conscience.[20]

Just as he says the word 'progress,' he and the camera look up to a
structure that appears to be an electrical pole or antenna. In the background, far in the background of this deserted swamp, a few characteristic umbrella pines can still be discerned, dwarfed by the man-made
metal tower in the foreground.

The film's final sequence, with chimneys belching yellow smoke that
the birds have learned to avoid, brings it full circle to the beginning
scene and, even before that, to the credits, which flash over a yellow
sky. In an ironic way, this sky that is yellow, not from the sun but from
chemical smog, can recall the golden heavens of Ravenna's Byzantine
mosaics, where birds also fly, especially the dove who hovers in scenes
of Christ's baptism. At the start of the credits, the very first frame of the
film shows us, against that yellow, polluted air, the pines of Ravenna.
We see only their tops, not the trunks. Visually, they have been up-
rooted, just as in history they are dying. Sickly remnants of Dante's
Edenic *pineta*, they give the film its master establishing shot, but the
camera does not stay with them any more than it will pause to let us
make out the *St George* over Giuliana's bed or allow us to stroll inside
the *pineta* with its sheltering umbrella of boughs. As the credits continue, the camera immediately pans through a choking haze to the
petrochemical setting that has replaced the trees, those smoke stacks
and fire-puffing pipes that announce Antonioni's cinematic anti-album.
His industrial scene is like Pasolini's Roman peripheries, barren lands
of new shanties and 'sub-urban' sprawl that speak in contrast to the
great classical and Christian city they encircle, a Rome within Rome
present by virtue of its absence. It can recall, too, Rossellini's *Viaggio in
Italia*, where landscape becomes mentality, and exterior setting mirrors
interior states of mind. So it is in Antonioni's film, as we see what
Giuliana sees, filtered through her mood. In *Red Desert*, with its forest of
factory towers, we can also now intuit Dante's infernal counterpart to
the Terrestrial Paradise, that 'dark forest' on a 'piaggia diserta,' a 'desert
shore' (*Inf.* 1.29). Here rises a modern-day Ravenna that we cannot visit
without remembering what it replaces – the other, older Byzantine city,
Dante's Ravenna, and the *pineta* that has lasted as long as the monuments, all surviving only in the merest verbal and visual traces, fragments of the implied setting and off-screen landscape.

Notes

1 Marcus, 'Rossellini's *Open City*: The Founding,' 33–53. Sorlin (137) has argued that place becomes even more important in Italian film after the neo-realists, in films made after the 1950s, which 'instead of being grouped into themes or chronological clusters, could be divided into locations.'

2 The Roman skyscape behind the titles has disappeared in the version of the film released in the United States, replaced by a blank background. With this unfortunate cut, the circularity of structure linking beginning and end to the cupola of St Peter's is lost.

3 The term is Bondanella's (88). He also calls attention to the irony in the final shot of the smiling 'guardian' angel.

4 Marcus, '*Caro diario* and the Cinematic Body of Nanni Moretti,' 233–47.

5 When he lived in Ravenna in the 1340s, Boccaccio met men who still remembered Dante. He returned to deliver ten gold florins on behalf of the Confraternity of Or San Michele in Florence to Dante's daughter, 'Suora Beatrice,' a nun in the convent of San Stefano dell'Uliva (Branca 75, 83). Boccaccio's *Trattatello in laude di Dante* is a fictionalized construct, which I discuss in 'The Parallel Lives of Dante and Virgil.' The classic description of Dante's tomb sculpture, commissioned by Pietro Bembo's father, Bernardo, remains that of Holbrook 53–6.

6 *La mirabile visione* was a major production of 4,026 metres. Synopses of this, Matarazzo's *Paolo e Francesca* (85 min.), and other known films on Dante and his *Commedia* appear in Casadio 128–9 and 150–1.

7 Rhodie 7.

8 Arrowsmith (92) speaks in an elegant essay on *Red Desert* of how Antonioni gives 'the *sense* and *degree*, the universality, of modern mobility. Mobility is here such that it makes all ages and cultures simultaneously contemporary – for instance, American blacks in Italy (*Eclipse*), Italian smugglers in Australia (*L'avventura*), Italian workers in Argentina (*Il grido*).' For Antonioni's views on his industrial landscape, see Brunette 96–7.

9 Actually, he painted the *pineta* white, to achieve the effect of grey (Liehm 228–30). Antonioni himself wrote about how he had altered colour in the objects he was filming in an introduction to the published screenplay: 'I want to paint the film as one paints a canvas; I want to invent the colour relationships, and not limit myself by photographing only natural colours' (cited in Chatman 131–2; cf. Cameron and Wood 121). Critics concur that the reds and pinks in the film reflect Giuliana's repressed sexuality. On the choice of periphery generally in Italian film, see Ferzetti.

10 'Adesso ha voluto mettere su un negozio, ma non so mica cosa ne voglia

fare. In via Alighieri. Tra l'altro non mi sembra neanche decoroso' (Antonioni 440).

11 This 'Via Alighieri' has, in fact, been compared to the surrealist style of the Italian painter Giorgio de Chirico, whom Antonioni admired (Dalle Vacche 43–80).

12 'D'improvviso balza dal letto per andare a chiudere lo sportello dell'armadio. Poi va alla finestra e guarda giú, il sagrato di una chiesa. Infine si rannicchia sulla poltrona del salottino, seminuda' (Antonioni 493).

13 The term is from Marcus, 'Antonioni's *Red Desert*,' 188–207.

14 Discussions of the painting can be found in Bowron; in Kirkham, 'L'immagine del Boccaccio'; and in Kirkham, 'Dante's Phantom, Petrarch's Spectre.'

15 For a discussion of this episode, see Kirkham, '*Purgatorio* xxviii,' 411–32.

16 I thank Peter Armour for suggesting the parallel in colour contrasts between *Purgatory* 1 and the fantasy island sequence.

17 The translation is that of Singleton. After first presenting this paper at 'Cinema across the Disciplines: A Colloquium on Italian Film,' University of Pennsylvania, March 1998, I discovered that Sitney (213–18) had already suggested this literary parallel, but to somewhat different ends. Sitney develops his analysis to suggest that Corrado in *Deserto rosso* is a modern counterpart of Dante's Ulysses.

18 BAMBINO: Perché quel fumo è giallo? / GIULIANA: Perché c'è veleno. BAMBINO: Allora se un uccellino passa lí in mezzo, muore. / GIULIANA: Sí, ma gli uccellini ormai lo sanno e non ci passano piú' (497). Sitney (217) also sees the parallel between Antonioni's 'uccellini' and Dante's 'augelletti.'

19 In Botticelli's last two panels, the trees have been cut down to make a clearing in the woods for a nuptial banquet, the civilized resolution to a threatening passion. For a recent discussion, with reproductions, see Tinagli 36–41. Chatman (124) reproduces a frame from this brief shot in *Red Desert*, where the ship looks so close that it almost seems to sail among the trees.

20 'In fondo non si sa bene in che cosa si crede. Si crede nell'umanità, in un certo senso. Un po' meno nella giustizia. Un po' di più nel progresso. Si crede nel socialismo, forse ... Quello che importa è di agire nel modo che si ritiene giusto, giusto per sé e per gli altri, cioè di avere la coscienza in pace' (457).

Bibliography

Alighieri, Dante. *The Divine Comedy. Purgatorio*. Trans. Charles S. Singleton. Princeton: Princeton University Press, 1973.

Antonioni, Michelangelo. *Deserto rosso: Sei film*. Torino: Einaudi, 1964.

Arrowsmith, William. *Antonioni: The Poet of Images*. Ed. Ted Perry. New York: Oxford University Press, 1995.

Bondanella, Peter. *The Cinema of Federico Fellini*. Princeton: Princeton University Press, 1993.

Bowron, Edgar Peters. 'Giorgio Vasari's "Portrait of Six Tuscan Poets."' *Minneapolis Institute of Arts Bulletin* 60 (1971–3): 43–54.

Branca, Vittore. *Giovanni Boccaccio: Profilo biografico*. Firenze: Sansoni, 1977.

Brunette, Peter. *The Films of Michelangelo Antonioni*. Cambridge: Cambridge University Press, 1998.

Cameron, Ian, and Robin Wood. *Antonioni*. New York: Praeger, 1968.

Casadio, Gianfranco, ed. *Dante nel cinema*. Ravenna: Longo, 1996.

Chatman, Seymour. *Antonioni, or the Surface of the World*. Berkeley: University of California Press, 1985.

Dalle Vacche, Angela. 'Michelangelo Antonioni's *Red Desert*: Painting As Ventriloquism and Color As Movement.' *Cinema and Painting: How Art Is Used in Film*. Austin: University of Texas Press, 1996. 43–80.

Ferzetti, Fabio. 'Città e cinema: La periferia urbana nella filmografia italiana.' *Città come...* Ed. Fausto Fiorentini. Roma: Argos, 1988.

Holbrook, Richard Thayer. *Portraits of Dante from Giotto to Raffael: A Critical Study with Concise Iconography*. London: Philip Lees Warner, 1921.

Kirkham, Victoria. 'Dante's Phantom, Petrarch's Spectre: Bronzino's Portrait of Laura Battiferra.' *'Visibile Parlare': Images of Dante in the Renaissance*. Ed. Deborah Parker. *Lectura Dantis* (1998): 63–139.

– 'L'immagine del Boccaccio nella memoria tardo-gotica e rinascimentale.' *Boccaccio visualizzato*. Ed. Vittore Branca. Vol. 1. Torino: Einaudi, 1999. 85–144.

– 'The Parallel Lives of Dante and Virgil.' *Dante Studies* 110 (1992): 233–53.

– 'Purgatorio xxviii.' *Dante's Divine Comedy. Introductory Readings ii: Purgatorio*. *Lectura Dantis* 12 [Supplement] (Spring 1993): 411–32.

Liehm, Mira. *Passion and Defiance: Film in Italy from 1942 to the Present*. Berkeley: University of California Press, 1984.

Marcus, Millicent. 'Antonioni's *Red Desert*: Abstraction As the Guiding Idea.' *Italian Film in the Light of Neorealism*. Princeton: Princeton University Press, 1986. 188–207.

– 'Caro Diario and the Cinematic Body of Nanni Moretti.' *Italica* 73.2 (1996): 233–47.

– 'Rossellini's *Open City*: The Founding.' *Italian Film in the Light of Neorealism*. Princeton: Princeton University Press, 1986. 33–53.

Rhodie, Sam. *Antonioni*. London: British Film Institute, 1990.

Sitney, P. Adams. *Vital Crises in Italian Cinema*. Austin: University of Texas Press, 1995.

Sorlin, Pierre. *Italian National Cinema 1896–1996*. London: Routledge, 1996.

Tinagli, Paola. *Women in Italian Renaissance Art: Gender Representation Identity*. Manchester: Manchester University Press, 1997.

Spencer Williams and Dante: An African-American Filmmaker at the Gates of Hell

DENNIS LOONEY

Introduction

This essay looks at a unique moment in the reception of Dante: the imitation of the *Inferno* in the film *Go Down, Death!* (1944), by the independent African-American filmmaker Spencer Williams. Williams, by one account 'the most unsung hero of [the] entire era' of early black filmmaking (Jones 173), estranged much of the black intelligentsia for his part in the controversial television comedy *Amos 'n' Andy*, in which he played the leading role of Andy Brown.[1] Consequently, his substantial body of work is not as well known today as it might be.[2] Spike Lee, in a recent piece on 'Black Films' in which he praises 'our pioneers,' fails even to mention Williams. While I intend my discussion of Spencer Williams to draw attention to the filmmaker's career and art in the hope that it may counter the general disregard of this fine artist, I have a larger purpose in mind. My discussion here is part of a project, *Dante in Black and White*, in which I examine the surprising multitude of ways in which Dante has assumed a position of importance in African-American culture. From Frederick Douglass, the abolitionist, to Daunte Culpepper, the quarterback of University of Central Florida chosen by the Minnesota Vikings with the eleventh pick in the 1999 NFL draft,[3] the medieval Italian poet seems to have found a niche in African-American culture. Or rather four niches, to be exact. I note four different moments in this cultural appropriation of the Italian poet, which I designate:

1) the Coloured Dante;
2) the Negro Dante;

3) the Black Dante;
4) the African-American Dante.

This sequence of responses to the Italian bard takes us from slavery, abolitionism, and reconstruction in the nineteenth century, to segregation in the South during the first half of the twentieth century, to the Black Revolution of the 1960s, and finally to the tensions between the urban ghetto and suburbia of our own day. It is a chronology of reception that has been, as far as I can tell, ignored by Dantisti.[4] It is as if this tradition of reception, complex and worthy of study, had suffered the fate of Ralph Ellison's narrator in *Invisible Man*; it is as if this tradition were itself invisible.

But first, before I focus on Williams's striking example of a Negro Dante, a bit more about the project as a whole. I go back approximately 150 years to a moment when the slave took control of writing to tell his or her story, which could touch on Dante. After all, the pilgrim's passage from Hell to Heaven, like the narrative of the children of Israel fleeing Egypt in search of the Promised Land, would be of heightened interest to a people with a memory of slavery.[5] Moreover, Dante, the historical man in addition to the character in the *Divine Comedy*, had become an important symbol of freedom for some of the abolitionists who maintained ties to the new Italy, 'la giovine Italia,' during the period of the Risorgimento, from the 1840s to the foundation of the unified Italian state by 1870.[6] Cordelia Ray (my example of an author who writes a Coloured Dante), whose father was an associate of Frederick Douglass in the abolitionist movement, subtly alludes to the medieval poet in this politicized way in her fifty-two-line poem 'Dante.'

Spencer Williams, an independent filmmaker who worked from the 1920s into the 1950s, uses Dante's allegory of good and evil to shed light on the daily existence of the Negro's segregated world in the first half of the twentieth century. Williams splices cuts from a silent film, *L'inferno*, into his own *Go Down, Death!* and in so doing, he uses Dante-the-character to integrate his 'All-Negro Production.' We'll consider this charged example of creative imitation in more detail below.

During the Black Revolution, Dante retains his potential as a powerful model of emancipation, exemplified by LeRoi Jones, who uses the medieval poet to articulate an unexpected crossing over into a new kind of literary campground: Jones creates a Black Dante. If Lévi-Strauss is correct that the function of writing is to enslave, or, as Barbara Johnson restates that claim, that the control of access to writing en-

Poster for Spencer Williams's *Go Down, Death!* (1944).

slaves, then the function of writing about Dante, and the control over access to the part of the tradition that Dante inhabits, can liberate the Black writer.[7] At least it liberates LeRoi Jones, turning him into a new man with a new name, Amiri Baraka, who becomes, then, a model for the hip-hop poets of the urban ghetto in Gloria Naylor's novel *Linden Hills*. The African-American artists she creates follow in Dante's footsteps, although they actually eschew writing, as if they, too, were wary of its potential to enslave, opting instead for a new oral tradition, which takes its inspiration in part from Dante's poem.

It is in this context that I would like to examine Spencer Williams's cinematic art in his film *Go Down, Death!* which will lead us to the gates of Dante's Hell. And beyond.

The Negro Dante

Born in Louisiana in 1893, Spencer Williams, who worked in the film industry in the 1920s, 1930s, and 1940s, went on to achieve fame, if not notoriety, as Andy Brown in the television version of the slapstick comedy *Amos 'n' Andy*, which was in production from 1951 to 1953.[8] While the TV show gave white America a safe glimpse into a world it mainly knew through racial stereotypes, Williams's films were another thing altogether, though it's unlikely that many whites ever saw them. Folk dramas like *The Blood of Jesus* (1941) and *Go Down, Death!* (1944), deceptively simple tales of good and evil, are set against the backdrop of the religious experience of Southern blacks on the eve of the great migration that took many men and women out of the South in search of decent jobs and a better life in the urban North.

Williams's films have the feel of documentaries with their gritty depiction of daily life in stark black and white images: a preacher intones rhythmically from the pulpit; a big man (played by Williams himself) tears into some fried chicken at the dining-room table of his boarding house; young couples do the jitterbug across the dance floor of a local juke joint. The films Williams made during the 1940s were financed by a Jewish entrepreneur, Alfred N. Sack, 'a hands-off backer who enabled him to do what few other black artists ... had been able to do – to direct a large number of his own screenplays as he saw fit' (Jones 34). It turned out to be a good business decision, for Williams's films played very well throughout the small-town theatres of the South, *The Blood of Jesus*, for example, quickly recovering the $15,000 it had taken to make it. Southern blacks in the 1940s were aware that the way of life portrayed in many of Williams's films had all but vanished; Williams as narrator says as much in a voice-over accompanying the opening frames of *The Blood of Jesus*, in which a farmer tills his field behind a mule: 'Almost gone are the days when Peace ruled the earth with a firm and gentle hand ...' These films were not as popular in the North, where the newly urbanized emigrant blacks were hardly nostalgic for views of what they had left behind.[9] Williams's films, then, document the end of an era: the rural existence of the Negro in the South.

In one of his quasi-documentary pieces, *Go Down, Death!*, Williams made use of Dante in an unprecedented way.[10] *Go Down, Death!* takes its title from a funeral eulogy composed by James Weldon Johnson and collected in his volume of 1927, *God's Trombones: Seven Negro Sermons in Verse*. The film's opening credits conclude with a dedicatory frame that contains an inscription in praise of 'the Pen of the Celebrated Negro Author, JAMES WELDON JOHNSON, *Now of Sainted Memory*,' who had died in 1938, six years before the film came out. The text of Johnson's sermon is the focus of the penultimate sequence of the film. The film tells the story of Jim, played by Spencer Williams, whose bar has been losing money ever since a charismatic Baptist preacher arrived in town. The filmscore emphasizes the two worlds at odds in the story as it shifts from church hymns to jazz and back again. This is a film about good and evil, symbolized by the church and the juke joint, the pastor and the bar owner. Jim and his cronies scheme to frame the preacher, by photographing him with three floozies who are posing as potential converts to his congregation. His henchmen snap the shot just as one of the women, brandishing a whiskey bottle and revealing a glimpse of her thigh, plants an unexpected kiss on the preacher. Jim's landlady, Carrie, an older woman who raised him after his parents died when he was a baby, sees through his dastardly plan to blackmail the preacher. With the help of divine intervention, she finds the incriminating photographs, but Jim catches her with them and, wrestling her to the ground, he inadvertently knocks her head against the metal safe in which he had hidden the photographs. Sister Carrie, as her fellow congregation members call her, never recovers, dying peacefully with the pastor and her friends from church at her bedside. The last words to issue from her lips are coordinated with the text of Johnson's sermon: 'I'm going home.'

The narrative cuts to her funeral with the preacher delivering the eulogy, lifted from Johnson's text with slight alterations. The conceit underlying the sermon is that God tells Death to 'go down' and relieve Carrie of the burden of life:

Day before yesterday morning,
God was looking down from his great, high Heaven,
Looking down on all his children,
And his eye fell on Sister Caroline,
Tossing on her bed of pain.

God commands his right-hand angel to call Death.

And Death heard the summons,
And he leaped on his fastest horse,
Pale as a sheet in the moonlight.
Up the golden street Death galloped,
And the hoofs of his horse struck fire from the gold,
But they didn't make no sound.
Up Death rode to the Great White Throne,
And waited for God's command.

And God said: Go down, Death, go down,
Go down to Savannah, Georgia, ...
And find Sister Caroline.

Here we have our first glimpse of the genius of Williams as a cinematic imitator. At those points in the sermon where the text refers to Death on the horse, Williams splices in frames from an unidentified earlier film of a figure cloaked in black riding on a white horse over the horizon. Necessity is the mother of invention. Constrained by a tight budget, Williams used what he could find in the archives to illustrate details in Johnson's sermon rather than shoot new frames or keep the camera fixed on the preacher for the entire eulogy. When the sermon refers to 'Heaven's pearly gates,' the camera cuts to another borrowed sequence: two figures, an angel welcoming a soul, stand outside large metal gates cushioned comfortably among the clouds, which then swing open to the soul's delight. Repeated four times, this image is recycled from Williams's earlier film *The Blood of Jesus*, along with a recurrent image of angels moving in a slow geometric dance.[11]

Sister Carrie is resting in the bosom of Jesus, but things are taking a turn for the worse for Jim, whose conscience begins to speak out about the murder. While we see him chain-smoking and frantically downing shots of whiskey, the voice of his conscience cackles away, harping on what he has done. Sitting at a table in his bar, Jim leaps up, pulls out a pistol, and begins to shoot at the disembodied voice. Harassed to distraction, he leaves the building and wanders aimlessly until he enters a desert-like terrain where he eventually collapses. Before him looms an image of the Gates of Hell decked out with a skull and crossbones and crowned with an inscription in English, 'Abandon all hope, ye who enter here,' an obvious imitation of the entrance to Hell at the beginning of *Inferno* 3. The line in English and the simple design suggest that it was a prop created by Williams for the shot. While the vision of these gates provides an effective structural counterpoint to the pearly gates seen earlier during the preacher's sermon, their construction is markedly inferior, even shabby by comparison with the wrought-iron gates that swing open to welcome Sister Carrie's soul to Heaven. Williams is hard-pressed to match the production quality of the films he incorporates into his work.

If Williams improvises a cardboard or plywood prop for his Gates of Hell, what follows is of another order altogether. To illustrate Jim's experience of Hell, Williams turns once again to the archives, to the 1911 silent film *L'inferno*, by Adolfo Padovan and Francesco Bertolini of Milano Films, from which he literally clips frames that he splices into his movie.[12] We suddenly see Hell through the eyes of Jim's soul as Dante and Virgil step gingerly around the traitors frozen in the River Cocytus, with Lucifer in the distant background champing on the body of Judas. The camera cuts back to Jim lying on the ground looking at the scene before him as his conscience reprimands him for killing the woman who brought him up. There are, then, short clips from the filmed version of the *Inferno*: from cantos 5, 6, and 18; a quick cut to Jim again; then cantos 19, 21–2, and 34, once more, before the gates of Hell shut. The entire sequence of frames in Hell takes less than one minute. We return to the boarding house of Mama Carrie (Jim's name for her), where the pastor tells Betty Jean, his fiancée and Carrie's niece, that Jim has been found dead at the mouth of Buck's Canyon.[13] The film ends with Jasper, the pastor, consoling Betty Jean, which parallels another scene earlier in the film where he reports her aunt's death.

The poor production value of *Go Down, Death!* might lead one to assume that a financially strapped Williams made do with whatever pieces of the Dante original he could get his hands on. But the quality of the final product does not detract from the deliberate, intelligent reading of Dante behind Williams's allusive adaptation of the cinematic *Inferno*, from whose fifty or so scenes he chooses six that suit the allegorical purposes of the narrative of *Go Down, Death!* That we first race down to the bottom of Hell among the traitors suggests that this is the ultimate destination for Jim, who murdered his surrogate mother. The narrative then pulls back and focuses briefly on other circles where Jim might have gone had the sin of his undoing not been so heinous.[14] The image of windswept lovers illustrating canto 5 alludes to Jim's jealous lust for Betty Jean, about which his conscience pricks him as he begins to hallucinate at the movie's end: 'You love her, don't you, Jim. But she's not your kind, Jim.' There is a brief image of gluttons from canto 6, recalling how Jim, a big man, shoved food in his face as he taunted Mama Carrie about the photographs. The snipped sequence from canto 18 of the flatterers immersed in their own excrement recalls several moments in the film when Jim tries to use flattery to get his way. The image from canto 19 of simonists, of those who use church power and office inappropriately, may reflect what Jim tried to get the church members to do or it may simply allude to his disrespect for the holiness of the pastor's position. This is followed by a scene from cantos 21–2 in which devils punish grafters. Mama Carrie acknowledges Jim's entanglement in graft and other ill-conceived uses of money when she says: 'I'm going to one that you can't bribe, one that you can't pay off with money and lie to. I'm going to the Lord.' And finally we return to Lucifer, whose massive face gnaws incessantly on the sinner in his mouth. When the Gates of Hell shut, Jim is dead.

I cannot say with certainty how Williams came upon his copy of the 1911 *L'inferno*, though examination of various copies makes it clear that he did not work from the version of the film distributed in the United States.[15] The Italian financier of the original project, Gustavo Lombardo, marketed the film cleverly and distributed it widely after it was released in 1911. In keeping with his description on the film's publicity poster as 'concessionario per tutto il mondo' [distributor for the whole world], Lombardo saw to it that the film was released in England and the United States, with the title *Dante's Inferno*, in France as *L'Enfer*, and in Germany as *Die Holle*.[16] By one estimate, the film grossed $2,000,000 in the United States alone.[17] Williams's active life in the film industry put him in a position to acquire a copy of the Italian original, which, with intertitles in Italian, would have been less valuable to an American distributor.[18] It's likely that Williams got his copy from his distributor, Alfred N. Sack of Sack Amusement Enterprises, who put up the money for the production of *Go Down, Death!* and saw to its distribution. In addition to producing many all-Negro feature films and shorts, Sack distributed foreign art films in the South. And 'in Dallas – where his various companies had their headquarters – [he opened] the Coronet Theatre, in 1948, which he claimed to be the first art- and foreign-film theatre in the Southwest' (Slide).

Although no one has yet found any contemporary reviews of *Go Down, Death!*, the Production Code Administration (PCA) files in the Library of the Academy of Motion Picture Arts and Sciences provide an interesting glimpse into the way in which the film was received upon distribution. The presence of a file on it in the PCA Collection indicates that the film was submitted for certification, which suggests that it may have been intended for larger venues beyond the boundaries of the chitlin' circuit in the South. In fact, the PCA files include reports from regional censorship boards in Maryland, Ohio, and New York, all of which recommend specific deletions from the film. The Maryland board censors the scene where Mabel, one of the prostitutes, reveals her leg while flirting with the preacher, and requests that the line of dialogue 'Gee, but I could really go to town with that guy!' be cut. Maryland censors make these recommendations twice, first in October 1944, then later in July 1946, suggesting that the film might not have been ready for release until the later date. The New York board recommends the following deletion: 'In Hades episode, eliminate all views of women where naked breasts are visible.' The Ohio board proposed the most radical cuts, at least for my project: 'Eliminate entire sequence depicting "hell" including scenes of "devil" chewing man and all scenes of people in "hell."' In the version as it now stands, none of these cuts was made, which would have reduced the film to a very mundane status. One would like to know more about the composition of the Ohio board and the specific reasoning behind its radical proposal. Was it an all-white board that passed judgment on this all-black film? Did the board members have any inkling of what Spencer Williams was doing with his elaborate allusions to Dante through his use of the Milano Films *L'inferno*? Was there, perhaps, the sense that this black man had no right to lay claim to a white man's hell? Did the noticeably white devil of Padovan and Bertolini make them uncomfortable? We don't have any information to allow us to answer these questions, as far as I know, beyond the brief reports in the PCA files I've cited above.[19]

Dante Meets Amos 'n' Andy

Go Down, Death! is a race movie, made by a black director with an all-black cast, meant for black audiences primarily in the segregated theatres of the South. But one white presence in the film stands out: Dante. To be sure, Dante's guide through Hell, Virgil, whom we see throughout the frames Williams uses, is also white, but he is a special case, a spirit from Limbo, the refuge in the *Inferno* for saintly pagans. The sinners we glimpse in the frames from the cinematic Hell are also white, but it is the pilgrim who stands out. Why does Spencer Williams privilege Dante, the ultimate 'dead white European male' in this way, making him the only living white person in his film? What value does Dante have for Spencer Williams?

Dante's authoritative appeal as a source for Williams is enhanced by the gothic horror of his particular vision of Hell, rendered all the more striking when it is cast in moving pictures. Many of the sets in the Milano Films version of the *Inferno* owe their iconographic design to Gustave Doré's illustrations, which in their own way seem to anticipate cinema.[20] The citation from the Milano Films *L'inferno* is a source you don't have to understand completely to appreciate. It has the advantage over a literary allusion of using an actual piece of the cinematic source to provide the viewer a glimpse of Hell, as seen through Jim's eyes. Imagine the experience of someone who doesn't know Italian reading a translation of the *Inferno*, who then comes upon an untranslated passage still in Italian *and is able to understand it as if it were English!* That is the effect of coming upon the frames from the Milano Films *L'inferno* spliced into *Go Down, Death!* Suddenly we are there in Hell with Dante as our guide to good and evil; suddenly Dante is called upon to gloss the injustices of the Negro's segregated world in the South, to pass judgment on an example of what we might call nowadays 'black on black crime.' Suddenly Dante is the Negro director's moral compass.

In the reception of the *Inferno*, it is common for Dante to serve as this sort of authoritative gloss on evil, though one may wonder how many in Williams's intended audience appreciated the magnitude of the medieval authority. In fact, Dante had acquired moral currency in African-American culture in the nineteenth and early twentieth centuries. He was an important symbol of freedom among the abolitionists, including Frederick Douglass (who kept a bust of the Italian poet alongside those of Lincoln and John Brown in his private library at Cedar Hill outside Washington, DC). Douglass followed with great interest the political fortunes of the new Italy, 'la giovine Italia,' during the Risorgimento, through which Dante was interpreted as a symbol of political and moral liberty, a voice that spoke out against hypocritical bureaucracy. If not exactly sanctioned as canonical, Dante was a figure to be reckoned with in the newly articulated African-American tradition.

African-American culture was becoming more bourgeois, more middle-class, less rural with each passing year as more and more Southern blacks moved north and became urbanized. Readers were coming into their own. W.E.B. DuBois had to argue that he had the right to read European authors in 1903: 'I sit with Shakespeare and he winces not' (67). But in the next generation, as the Harlem Renaissance artist Aaron Douglas recalls almost nonchalantly, a boy growing up in a middle-class family outside the South could be expected to read Dante as easily as any other author (1). Adrienne Seward has speculated that Williams minimizes the folk elements of the religious drama in *Go Down, Death!* in order to appeal to this new middle class. Seward also comments that the hymns in the film's soundtrack are associated more with the rather staid Methodist Church than with the rural Spiritual tradition (2). In fact, 'Ave Maria' plays at a crucial point in the soundtrack, not exactly what comes to mind when you think of that old-time religion in a black church down South. There is no question that the film is much less of a religious folk drama than Williams's first success, *The Blood of Jesus*. Sack and Williams probably hoped the new film would circulate in areas of the country like Maryland, New York, and Ohio, where they submitted it to the censorship boards of those states. Perhaps the inclusion of a series of elaborate allusions to Dante is a gesture to the rising intellectual and financial status of the Negro at this time.

The Dantesque source also appeals to Williams for the structure it lends his film. The narrative of the *Inferno* becomes a device to catapult his character, Jim, into Hell, anticipating the way that later African-American writers such as LeRoi Jones and Gloria Naylor use Dante's poem to shed light on the moral inadequacies of their respective characters. These authors, like Williams, are drawn to the structural rigour of Dante's system of moral classification. LeRoi Jones, for his part, calls his imitation of Dante's *Inferno*, *The System of Dante's Hell*, while Naylor structures the narrative of her novel *Linden Hills* around the descending crescent circles of an infernal suburb in which her middle-class African-American characters lose their souls. In each of these examples, the medieval source functions as a narrative model to which the artist refers in organizing the modern work. But Williams (and these other African-American artists) could have found and borrowed a sense of structure from other sources, for a rigorous moral order is not unique to Dante. The Bible and religious rituals, for example, function as organizing principles of this sort in *The Blood of Jesus*. Why else, then, might the artist turn to Dante?

By splicing cuts from *L'inferno* into his film, Williams uses Dante-the-character to integrate his 'All-Negro Production' (to borrow from the film's publicity flyer), engaging in a charged act of creative imitation that we might call 'artistic integration.' Ten years before the Supreme Court ruling that began the dismantling of official segregation in the United States, Williams is pushing the envelope in his art. As the white character integrates the world of the Negro film, so the filmmaker mixes or integrates his sources: the literary sources, James Weldon Johnson and Dante, on the one hand; the cinematic sources, cuts from *The Blood of Jesus* and other silent films, including *L'inferno*, on the other. It may seem contrary to propose that this 'All-Negro Production' refers to the other race, the white race, which seems to be present only in its absence until Dante appears at the film's end. But the absence is a conspicuous one, for the characters in Williams's film repeatedly make comments that suggest the extent to which the other race (ostensibly nowhere near) is in fact just around the corner (or just over the other side of the tracks). Jim tells his cronies to go down to 'Coloured Street, and round up two or three of them little fly chicks,' prostitutes to use as bait for the preacher. These are women whose sex appeal is measured by their whiteness and by their modified, affected accents that sound like caricatures of Caucasian speech: they talk white. Carrie criticizes Jim for even hoping for reciprocal love from Betty Jean with the claim: 'You love her, don't you, Jim. But she's not your kind, Jim. Oh, she's coloured all right, but she's not common!' As if to say, Jim could only love and be loved by a coloured woman in the hierarchy of interpersonal relations in the segregated South, and in that hierarchy, Jim must find his match at the bottom. Carrie contrasts the only kind of love Jim knows with the honest love between Betty Jean and the pastor, 'not the kind of love you find down on Coloured Street.' And there is the odd momentary hallucination of a rope from a lynching on the tree Jim runs into just before he dies.[21] His conscience goads him: 'See that tree over yonder? I'm going to tell you something about that tree. Now listen. They once hung a man on this tree for killing a woman. And let me tell you this. It was this very limb right here. Got enough to hang you too, Jim. Better go on from here, go on. This ain't no place for you. Run! Run! Run, run, run away, boy.' The rope represents a potential flashback that the director doesn't have to give us, for we know how that scene from race relations would look. And if we didn't know, the reaction shot of Jim's terror amply fleshes out the picture for the viewer's imagination.

The revelation of Dante's moral cosmology, however, ultimately transcends issues of race. Jim's vision of his destination through the edited montage made of the frames from the silent film, with the incessant voice-over of his conscience directing his viewing, shows him what happens to those who traffic in evil, white or black. Alas, he is a sinner who learns about Hell too late for it to do him any good. The timing is ironically emphasized in his glimpses of Dante-the-pilgrim, whose own preview of Hell will enable him to confront evil more effectively once he has returned to life on earth. The integration of sources, while it raises legitimate questions about race relations at the time the movie was made, prompts another way of construing the role of Dante in this otherwise predictable race movie. Spencer Williams's unexpected integration of his black film *Go Down, Death!* with the white protagonist from Dante's *Inferno*, forces us to realize that the work of the medieval Italian poet is far more canonical than keepers of the tradition may have ever imagined.

Notes

1 See the articles by Clayton and Cripps ('*Amos 'n' Andy* ...') for discussions of the controversy surrounding the TV show.

2 Thomas Cripps has devoted much attention to Williams, though he has relatively little to say about the film I look at in this essay, *Go Down, Death!*

3 'Daunte Culpepper of Central Florida, who becomes the heir apparent to Randall Cuningham in Minnesota' (*New York Times*, 18 April 99, *Sports Sunday*, p. 34) is one of several prominent African-American athletes with a version of the Italian poet's name.

4 Carole Slade refers teachers to the imitations of Dante by Ralph Ellison and LeRoi Jones in *Approaches to Teaching Dante's Divine Comedy* (21). In fact, very little work has been done; but see the studies of Butler, Cooke, Havely, and Ward.

5 In fact, Dante's journey recalls in many ways the exodus of the children of Israel. See the definitive essay on this parallel by Charles S. Singleton, '"In Exitu Israel de Aegypto."'

6 I explored the use of Dante in abolitionist discourse in a talk at the annual conference of the American Italian Historical Association (CUNY-Hunter College, 14 November 1998), 'Political and Politicized Dante(s) from the

1850s to the 1920s.' That work has now been incorporated into my larger project, *Dante in Black and White* (in progress).

7 See the comments by Barbara Johnson in her essay 'Writing,' which touch on the appropriate passage in Lévi-Strauss (47–9).

8 For a biographical sketch of Williams, see Jones 31-5, and Cripps, *Black Film As Genre*, 90–9. Clayton's article discusses Williams's role in the controversial television show.

9 Cripps discusses the dynamics of the different audiences, urban versus rural, in *Black Film As Genre* (98–9).

10 I am grateful to Wayne Shirley, Library of Congress, for directing me to the films of Spencer Williams. I have yet to find any discussion of Williams's use of Dante in the critical literature.

11 I believe that G. William Jones (*Black Cinema Treasures* 50) is mistaken when he says of this image in *The Blood of Jesus*: '... some unusual scenes which literally interpret the story of Jacob's ladder (which Director Williams borrowed from French director Georges Méliès' 1916 film entitled *Going to Heaven*).' I find no reference to a film of Méliès by that name, nor does the cut look at all like a Méliès film.

12 On this film, see Iannucci. In addition, John Welle's essay ably discusses the Italian film in its national cultural context.

13 Texas, where Williams did much of his work, leaves its mark in this topo-graphical detail: Georgia is not known for its canyons! In a similar move, Williams uses Ferde Grofe's *Grand Canyon Suite* at a climactic moment in the film's soundtrack.

14 Dante the poet also must often choose where to assign a sinner who is guilty of multiple sins; he assigns Dido, for example, to the circle of the lustful rather than the wood of the suicides. Sometimes, as in the case of Dido, the poet's choice is more in line with aesthetic than moral criteria.

15 Comparative examination of the cuts used by Williams and the version distributed in the United States reveals several incongruent passages. The version for U.S.A. distribution does not have the scene of the devils from cantos 21-2 poking their pitchforks at the surface of the boiling pitch in the fifth pouch of the eighth circle, which Williams uses; I assume he found the scene in the Italian version of the film.

16 For a reproduction of the film's publicity broadside in Italy, see the cover of Casadio, ed., *Dante nel cinema*. For a poster used to publicize the film in England, see Havely, ed., *Dante's Modern Afterlife*, plate 6.

17 Havely, 'A Note on Film and Video,' *Dante's Modern Afterlife*, 12.

18 I haven't examined the French and German distributed versions of the original; I assume it's possible that Williams could have worked from one

of those, though it's less likely that he would have found them in circulation in the United States.

19 I would like to thank Barbara Hall, librarian in the Special Collections Department at the AMPAS Library in Beverly Hills, for her assistance in locating these censorship reports.

20 Matilde Serao, Italian critic and novelist, acknowledged the filmmakers' debt to the illustrator shortly after the film came out in 1911: 'A great show ... and if Doré used his pencil to design the best graphic commentary on the divine poem, this cinematographic piece has brought Doré's work back to life' (Brunetta 144). See Welle's discussion of the same passage (386–7).

21 Robert Penn Warren has a similar flashback at the beginning of *Who Speaks for the Negro?* (11–12). The imaginary glimpse of the lynching rope becomes a topos in Southern literature and journalism in the twentieth century.

Bibliography

Alighieri, Dante. *Inferno: Text and Commentary*. Trans. Robert M. Durling and Ronald L. Martinez. New York: Oxford University Press, 1996.

Brunetta, Gian Piero. *Storia del cinema italiano, 1895–1945*. Roma: Riuniti, 1979.

Butler, Robert J. 'Dante's *Inferno* and Ellison's *Invisible Man*: A Study in Literary Continuity.' *CLA Journal* 28 (1984) : 57–77.

Casadio, Gianfranco, ed. *Dante nel cinema*. Ravenna: Longo, 1996.

Clayton, Edward T. 'The Tragedy of Amos 'n' Andy.' *Ebony* 16 (Oct. 1961): 66–73.

Cooke, Michael J. 'The Descent into the Underworld and Modern Black Fiction.' *Iowa Review* 5.4 (1974): 72–90.

Cripps, Thomas. '*Amos 'n' Andy* and the Debate over American Racial Integration.' In *American History, American Television: Interpreting the Video Past*. Ed. John E. O'Connor. New York: Ungar, 1983. 33–54.

– *Black Film As Genre*. Bloomington: Indiana University Press, 1978.

– 'The Films of Spencer Williams.' *Black American Literature Forum* 12 (Winter 1978): 128–34.

– *Making Movies Black: The Hollywood Message Movie from World War II to the Civil Rights Era*. New York: Oxford University Press, 1993.

– *Slow Fade to Black: The Negro in American Film, 1900–1942*. New York: Oxford University Press, 1977.

Douglas, Aaron. 'An Autobiography.' Unpublished manuscript, Aaron

Douglas Collection, box 1, folder 1, Fisk University Archives, Nashville, Tennessee.

DuBois, W.E.B. *The Souls of Black Folk*. 1903. New York: Dover Books, 1994.

Havely, Nick. 'Introduction: Dante's Afterlife, 1321–1997.' '"Prosperous People" and "The Real Hell" in Gloria Naylor's *Linden Hills*.' *Dante's Modern Afterlife: Reception and Response from Blake to Heaney*. Ed. Nick Havely. New York: St Martin's Press, 1998. 1–14 and 211–22.

Iannucci, Amilcare A. 'From Dante's *Inferno* to *Dante's Peak*: The Influence of Dante on Film.' *Forum Italicum* 32 (1998): 5–35.

Johnson, Barbara. 'Writing.' *Critical Terms for Literary Study*. Ed. Frank Lentricchia and Thomas McLaughlin. Chicago: University of Chicago Press, 1990. 39–49.

Johnson, James Weldon. *God's Trombones: Seven Negro Sermons in Verse*. 1927. New York: Viking Press, 1973.

Jones, G. William. *Black Cinema Treasures: Lost and Found*. Denton: University of North Texas Press, 1991.

Kisch, John, and Edward Mapp. *A Separate Cinema: Fifty Years of Black-Cast Posters*. Introduction by Spike Lee. New York: Farrar, Straus and Giroux, 1992.

Lee, Spike. 'Black Films: The Studios Have It All Wrong.' *New York Times*, 2 May 1999, Section 2A, p. 23.

Seward, Adrienne. *Spencer Williams*. The New American Film and Video Series 46. New York: Whitney Museum of American Art, 1988.

Singleton, Charles S. '"In Exitu Israel de Aegypto."' *Dante: A Collection of Critical Essays*. Ed. John Freccero. Englewood Cliffs, NJ: Prentice Hall, 1965. 102–21.

Slade, Carole, ed. *Approaches to Teaching Dante's 'Divine Comedy.'* New York: Modern Language Association, 1982.

Slide, Anthony. *The New Historical Dictionary of the American Film Industry*. Lantham, MD: Scarecrow Press, 1998.

Ward, Catherine. 'Gloria Naylor's *Linden Hills*: A Modern *Inferno*.' *Contemporary Literature* 28 (Spring 1987): 67–81.

Warren, Robert Penn. *Who Speaks for the Negro?* New York: Random House, 1965.

Welle, John P. 'Dante in the Cinematic Mode: An Historical Survey of Dante Movies.' *Dante's 'Inferno': The Indiana Critical Edition*. Ed. Mark Musa. Bloomington: Indiana University Press, 1995. 381–95.

Williams, Spencer, dir. *The Blood of Jesus*. Sack Amusement Enterprises, 1941.

– *Go Down, Death!* Sack Amusement Enterprises, 1944.

Television, Translation, and Vulgarization: Reflections on Phillips' and Greenaway's *A TV Dante*

ANDREW TAYLOR

In July 1990, Channel 4 Television in the United Kingdom broadcast *A TV Dante*, co-directed by Peter Greenaway and Tom Phillips. When term recommenced at Oxford the following October, I remember that the four episodes were the subject of some comment in tutorials and not much of it was favourable! Of course, this negative reaction was the result of expectations of 'textual fidelity' engendered by the long tradition of BBC literary adaptations, such as the recent productions of *Sense and Sensibility* and *Middlemarch* seen in the United States on PBS (Marcus 15–17). In other words, viewers expected a dramatization of the *Inferno* complete with medieval costumes and macabre stage sets that would accurately reflect the images they first conceived when they read Dante in high school. These expectations were severely disappointed by Greenaway and Phillips, and my colleagues' criticisms were thus not the only ones. Sheridan Morley, TV critic of the *Times*, was damning in his faint praise: 'Veering from a schools-television lecture through the high gimmickry of split screens to moments of splendid drama and insight, the television Dante is a hotchpotch of poetry and pedantry, at worst the basis for a Ken Russell musical, at best the first real attempt to get Dante in front of the TV cameras' (19). The humorist Miles Kington reviewed the series for the *Spectator* and was similarly equivocal: 'A reviewer should say what he thinks, but I don't know what to think; watching this film was like seeing a country from a helicopter – the landscape was wonderful but the noise was awful. I think I'll lie down and have another look at it, then come back to it next week' (12). Significantly, he didn't and neither did Channel 4, which has consistently declined to provide funds to finish the rest of the project.

Such puzzled reactions to the series arise almost certainly from the directors' decision to dramatize their own personal reactions to Dante's text, rather than the text itself. A reason for this decision can be found in Phillips' admission that he found the *Divine Comedy* 'disappointingly parochial' (227), preoccupied as it is with dead Florentine literati and extinct political controversies. In one of his many paintings themed around the *Comedy*, Phillips tests out a strategy of eliminating nearly all references to the historical fourteenth-century context and stressing instead the resonances which Dante's poem finds in modern experience. In this work, entitled *Beginning to Think about Dante*, the leopard, lion, and wolf of canto 1 do not spring from the medieval menagerie; rather, they are images appropriated from Phillips' British upbringing (the royal coat-of-arms and Landseer's statues in Trafalgar Square are prominent examples).[1] Similarly, Beatrice is no medieval noblewoman but a glamorized, back-lit portrait of the film star Lee Remick. But at least these fragments of the painting originate with the text; many others are purely Phillips' own gloss on Dante, the artist's attempt to inscribe his own beliefs into the poet's moral system. Within the same painting, Phillips therefore equates the ascent to spiritual truth with the life of the Mahatma Gandhi, the corruption and extortion of Florentine mercantilism with bowler-hatted London businessmen, and religious heresy with the masked terrorists of the late twentieth century. These comparisons demonstrate that Phillips' aesthetic approach to Dante has been consistent throughout his oeuvre:[2] as an artist, he is not content simply to illustrate the *Comedy* in the traditional sense but prefers to represent the train of thought which it touched off in his own mind.

The result of this strategy is unfortunately to make Phillips' visualizations of the *Comedy* just as local and self-reflexive as the original text. For example, it is obvious that the painting *Beginning to Think about Dante* depends heavily on a British audience in order to be intelligible: Landseer's emblems of national pride and ambition are not more recognizable out of their context than Dante's original beasts. At other times, Phillips' imagery is simply too obscure to be understood – even by a British audience – without the aid of lengthy exegesis. Two examples of this from the painting are the stars in the top left-hand corner and the small white flowers in the bottom left-hand corner. In a catalogue entry, Phillips explains that the stars are the constellation of Aries, an auspicious sign for a pilgrimage, as witnessed by the *Canterbury Tales*, which began 'when the young sun is half way through the ram'; likewise, Phillips informs us that the flowers are primroses, recalling Shakespeare's description of the road to hell in *Macbeth* as 'the primrose path to the everlasting bonfire' (220). Given such dependence on arcane references, it seems that Phillips has not so much eliminated Dante's 'campanilismo' as simply replaced it with his own provincialism, rendering his new text just as inaccessible as the old one.

While a fine art painting can perhaps get away with this level of erudition, the same cannot be said for a TV program. The problem is that the very choice of television as a medium implies an address to a mass audience, and, indeed, the intention to make a popular version of the *Comedy* seems confirmed by *A TV Dante*'s use of media knights such as Sir John Gielgud and Sir David Attenborough, whose high name recognition in the United Kingdom certainly boosted its initial ratings. Yet at the same time, the directors continue to speak over the heads of their public, declaring that their work is 'polysemous' and captures Dante's 'literal, allegorical and anagogical' meanings via the use of 'simple actions,' 'imagery,' and something mysterious they call 'texture' (Phillips 246). Thus, when Dante encounters Francesca in canto 5, they expect the ordinary viewer to recognize an electrocardiogram as 'a gauge for Dante's changing emotional state' and interpret its broken graph as an indication of his swoon; similarly, a radar scanner from an air-traffic control tower is supposed to suggest to that same viewer 'aethereal blips of movement, the ideal image of medieval cosmology, complete with angels in flight' (Phillips 243). Once again, these parallelisms are so recondite that even an educated viewer could not pick up on them without the explanatory notes provided in the directors' publicity material. In short, the directors presume too much from a mass audience, which as I mentioned at the outset of this paper, is accustomed to a quite different emphasis on character and plot in BBC literary adaptations.[3]

Of course, by privileging exegesis over diegesis, Phillips' work on Dante had always been designed to appeal to a different, rather more elite audience. He writes:

> I avoided dealing with the anecdotal and atmospheric incidents which abound in [Dante's] text in favour of more analytic and exegetic images [serving] rather as a visual commentary than a blow-by-blow illustrative description of the action. This decision was prompted by the study of previous illustrated versions which so often seem to depict exactly those things that Dante himself describes most pictorially; they render a suggested infinite in finite terms and substitute certainties for the resonant ambiguities of the poem. (237)

Unfortunately, the 'visual commentary' provided by *A TV Dante* is unlikely to satisfy the fastidious tastes of the academic audience whom it addresses since, as Amilcare Iannucci notes, the televised *Lectura Dantis* produced by RAI in 1988 had not even been able to do that with its use of eminent Dantisti such as Nino Borsellino and Giorgio Petrocchi (9). Compared to the exegesis these scholars could offer, one wonders what qualified Sir David Attenborough, a post-Darwinian zoologist, to comment on how medieval theologians viewed the sins of lust, pride, and avarice? How is our understanding of Ciacco's gluttony enriched by a high-street butcher appearing in canto 6 to tell us, 'Pigs will eat anything'? The arbitrary selection of these 'talking heads' cannot fail to disappoint the academic viewer of *A TV Dante* since their expertise is less than that of the specialist audience they address.

However, this may be one of those cases where it is fruitless to consider the receiver of the work of art. For it may be that there was no intended receiver – neither the general public nor specialized Dantisti – except Phillips and Greenaway themselves, who used the opportunity provided by Channel 4 to meditate on the nature of video as an independent medium. Phillips has written that the programs tried to answer the question whether there was 'such a thing as television' (246), while Greenaway has expressed a desire to explore the special 'rules and characteristics' of television that make it independent of cinema (quoted in Vickers 267). To judge the work in its own terms, therefore, we must shift our attention away from the audience who watched the programs to Phillips and Greenaway themselves and the style of TV that they developed.

A useful analysis of their creative process is offered by Nancy Vickers, who notes that the directors use a 'linguistic model' to conceptualize TV (267).[4] Vickers argues that the directors compile a 'vocabulary' that is partly borrowed from archive footage (of Mussolini, Pope John XXIII, and Eadweard Muybridge animals) and is partly indigenous to television (the 'commentary boxes' are a typical graphical device used by TV correspondents reporting back to the studio from outside broadcast units). But the directors also elaborate a 'grammar' of television, for in subsequent phases of production, Phillips and Greenaway placed all these disparate items in a syntactical arrangement that tells the story of each canto and then morphologically altered the chosen images during the on-line editing process by adding colour, etc., with the Quantel Paintbox device. In sum, Vickers's argument demonstrates that *A TV Dante* is only secondarily concerned to adapt Dante for television;

instead, its primary object is to develop television as a 'new vernacular.' This is a fascinating conclusion given Dante's own lifelong concern for developing a 'volgare illustre':[5] television is formally conceptualized as the twentieth-century equivalent of his 'cardinal' language, which was a pivotal force in the development of a national identity.

In saying this, I do not mean to imply that *A TV Dante* is simply a dull theoretical essay. Perhaps it would be more accurate to draw an analogy between these programs and the many 'volgarizzamenti' that were produced during the Middle Ages, for, like Greenaway and Phillips, medieval writers preferred to give practical demonstrations of the versatility and worth of a new medium by translating venerable old texts. The term 'volgarizzamento' can therefore help us to position *A TV Dante* among the literary, artistic, and scholarly spin-offs that the *Divine Comedy* has generated, especially since the directors themselves have referred to their work as a 'translation.' But the meaning of this medieval term is problematic: it includes accurate Italian versions such as Bono Giamboni's rendering of Horace, but also stretches to include paraphrases such as Brunetto Latini's *Rettorica* and even free reworkings of popular stories such as the Arthurian legends (Migliorini 144–5). What kind of 'volgarizzamento' have Phillips and Greenaway made? Are these programs a 'vulgarization' of Dante's meaning, a dumbing-down to suit the reduced intellectual abilities of a TV audience, or have the directors ennobled television and made a 'thinking person's pop-video,' as one reviewer put it?

At first sight, it would seem that Phillips and Greenaway do indeed raise the status of video as an art form. Walter Benjamin provides confirmation that translation or 'volgarizzamento' can celebrate the independence of a new medium: in his words, 'it is charged with the special mission of watching over ... the birth pangs of its own language' (73). However, Benjamin also believes that a good translation will do more than 'reassemble the meaning of the original; rather, it will 'lovingly and in detail incorporate the original's mode of signification' (78). *A TV Dante* does exactly this because it attempts to reproduce the *Divine Comedy*'s 'polysemia,' its plural meanings outlined in the epistle to Can Grande della Scala:

> The work may be described as 'polysemous,' that is, having several meanings; for the first meaning is that which is conveyed by the letter, and the next is conveyed by what the letter signifies. The former is called the literal sense while the latter is called the allegorical or the moral or the anagogical sense. (Took 180–1)

In the video series, the literal story of Dante losing his way in the dark wood is preserved at the beginning of canto 1 as the bronze bust of Dante is brought to life and the actor Bob Peck tells the audience of his disorientation. Allegorically, the dark wood stands for any place of bewilderment and confusion, and the screen fittingly shows the chaos of traffic and neon insignia from an urban landscape. Meanwhile, the soundtrack features mocking female laughter and the noise of police sirens and helicopters, suggesting that disorientation may also have a moral dimension to it. Finally, the anagogical or spiritual type of confusion pervades the whole series in the repeated appearance of triangles on the screen, reminding the viewer that Hell is precisely a dislocation of the soul from the Trinity which created it. This complexity is truly unprecedented in television adaptations, which, as I have stated above, normally concentrate on the bare narrative from a literary text.

Unfortunately, this level of thoughtfulness is not sustained throughout the series, and *A TV Dante* exhibits a great urge toward simplification. Much of the rest of the imagery from canto 1 is not allegorical at all but merely doubles the literal understanding of Dante's journey provided in the actors' narration. For example, as Dante proceeds across the desert toward the hill of Purgatory at dawn on the first day, the screen displays facile images of a desert and a sunrise. Similarly, canto 2 concludes with a clichéd, slow-motion sequence of opening flower buds, exactly mirroring Dante's metaphorical description of his reawakening: 'Quali i fioretti, dal notturno gelo / chinati e chiusi, poi che 'l sol li 'mbianca / si drizzan tutti aperti in loro stelo, / tal mi fec'io di mia virtute stanca ...' [As little flowers, which the chill of night / has bent and huddled, when the white sun strikes, / grow straight and open fully on their stems, / so did I, too, with my exhausted force ... (*Inf.* 2.127–32)]. No matter how these shots are digitized or chromatically enhanced, the sequence represents a departure from Phillips' declared aversion to illustrating the *Divine Comedy* and instead gives in to the viewer's basic preference for images that are easy, accessible, and purely mimetic. In such instances, the TV series is a 'volgarizzamento' in the sense of a vulgarization, encouraging passivity in its viewers rather than engaging them in an active interpretive role.

This process of vulgarization is even more obvious in the commentary, whose simplicity I have already called attention to above. In fact, these 'video footnotes' often say far less about the *Divine Comedy* than they do about the TV audience watching them. The most egregious case are the remarks of a psychologist in canto 8. Originally, the verse 'Benedetta colei che in te s'incinse!' [Blessed is the womb that bore thee!] congratulates Dante for his attitude toward Filippo Argenti and sets up a rather daring parallel between Dante's mother and the Virgin Mary ('Blessed art thou among women and blessed is the fruit of thy womb, Jesus'). However, the psychologist is concerned, not about the blasphemous overtones of the verse, but about how mentioning one's mother in such an angry context indicates a dysfunctional family relationship, and seems inclined to put Dante in therapy! In permitting such anachronism, the directors seem more attentive to television and its need for easily understood sound-bites than to the text and its need for thoughtful scholarship.[6] Repeated instances of such vulgarization suggest that *A TV Dante* proves the truth of the old Italian adage about translation: 'Il traduttore è un traditore' [The translator is a traitor].

As I conclude these few reflections on *A TV Dante*, I am aware that even after several years of graduate study, I have still not escaped the preference for BBC-style literary adaptations that are faithful to the spirit of the original. In my defence, I should explain that those painstakingly accurate BBC costume dramas are viewed in a very particular cultural context: usually, at five o'clock on Sundays, to coincide with teatime, and just before the six o'clock religious service broadcasts, typically from a picturesque Anglican church in the countryside. Literary adaptations are thus intimately bound up in the British imagination with two great rituals affirming national identity, and it is no great wonder that it is difficult to transcend such a barrier. The final judgment of *A TV Dante* should not therefore be a British one; it is more appropriate to finish with the reaction of an Italian audience in Urbino in 1991, who awarded the series the Prix Italia for best arts program of the year.

Notes

1 For a colour illustration of Phillips' *Beginning to Think about Dante*, see Phillips' *Works and Texts* 219.

2 Phillips acknowledges the direct link between this picture and his later TV work: 'Looking at a reproduction of it now I see that it ... nearly predicts the aesthetic of *A TV Dante*' (219).

3 Nancy J. Vickers reports an interesting American proposal to make a version of the *Comedy* that 'reduces Dante's text to pure, albeit somewhat misconstrued, plot: guy dies, guy goes to Hell, guy tries to get out.' Although such a project obviously risks oversimplification, it is at least clear whom it addresses, and Vickers is accurate in noting that its strong

focus on narrative would be 'diametrically opposed to the stated goals of Greenaway and Phillips' (272).

4 Other critics have seemed to use an architectural model in their analyses, most often postmodernism. The 'citationist' techniques and the latent irony of *A TV Dante* suggest that such a paradigm might be fruitful; unfortunately, I do not have space here to explore it fully.

5 I am thinking of the *De vulgari eloquentia*, though, of course, the *Comedy* itself acted as a normative force in the development of the Italian language, despite Bembo's attacks on it.

6 Ominously, the commentators are listed in the program credits under the rubric 'The Authorities.' This is one of the most pernicious imports from television journalism, where *soi-disant* 'experts' routinely give their own personal 'take' on current events. This device satisfies the need for instant opinion but rarely results in insight; moreover, it forestalls the democratic process whereby the viewer may form his/her own opinion of events.

Bibliography

Benjamin, Walter. *Illuminations*. New York: Schocken Books, 1985.

Iannucci, Amilcare. 'Dante, Television and Education.' *Quaderni d'Italianistica* 10 (1989): 1–33.

Kington, Miles. 'Television Review.' *Spectator* [London], 4 Aug. 1990, p. 27.

Marcus, Millicent. *Filmmaking by the Book: Italian Cinema and Literary Adaptation*. Baltimore: Johns Hopkins University Press, 1993.

Migliorini, Bruno. *Storia della lingua italiana*. Vol 1. Firenze: Sansoni Editore, 1988.

Morley, Sheridan. 'Hell to Heaven, via Purgatory.' *Times* [London], 28 July 1990, p. 19.

Phillips, Tom. *Works and Texts*. London: Thames and Hudson, 1992.

Took, J.F. *Dante: Lyric Poet and Philosopher*. Oxford: Clarendon Press, 1990.

Vickers, Nancy J. 'Dante in the Video Decade.' *Dante Now: Current Trends in Dante Studies*. Ed. Theodore J. Cachey, Jr. Notre Dame: University of Notre Dame Press, 1995. 263–76.

Dopo Tanto Veder: Pasolini's Dante after the Disappearance of the Fireflies

PATRICK RUMBLE

Ancor ti priego, regina, che puoi
ciò che tu vuoli, che conservi sani
dopo tanto veder, li affetti suoi.

[This, too, O Queen, who can do what you would,
I ask of you: that after such a vision,
his sentiments preserve their perseverance.]

– Paradiso 33.34–6

In this essay, I propose to offer a general description of the significance of Dante's work for a single Italian filmmaker and writer, Pier
Paolo Pasolini. Pasolini was a profoundly important poet, novelist,
and filmmaker, who produced his work within a span of years from
the end of the Second World War until his mysterious assassination in
1975. It seems to me that, in the Italian culture of the last century, there
is no other figure who so often returned to Dante – especially the
Dante of the *Inferno*. And certainly, among Italian filmmakers, no one
has greater debts to Dante than Pasolini. What I would like to offer is
simply a description of those debts. As we will see, Dante's influence
will not be limited to the usual erudite citations or thematic borrowings. Rather, Dante's *Divine Comedy* is a structuring, informing model
for a great deal of Pasolini's work. Indeed, besides offering Pasolini
the image, with which he could identify, of an offended and outraged
poet, exiled by malign political forces, Dante's *Divine Comedy* provides Pasolini with a form, an architecture, a sort of ready-made
container, in which to place his own narration of a corrupt Italy,

whose citizens are seduced into the sinfulness of contemporary consumerist society.

The title of my essay makes a perhaps strange reference to fireflies, and I should explain why. Early in 1975, the year in which Pasolini was assassinated (and the year he made the film *Salò*), Pasolini wrote a famous essay, generally referred to as 'The Article on the Fireflies,'[1] concerning what he called the 'anthropological degradation' of Italy: traditional Italian culture was, he said, being destroyed and replaced by a new totalitarian culture of commodities and mass consumerism and hedonism:

> Ho visto dunque 'coi miei sensi' il comportamento coatto del potere dei consumi ricreare e deformare la coscienza del popolo italiano, fino a un irreversibile degradazione. Cosa che non era accaduto durante il fascismo fascista, periodo in cui il comportamento era completamente dissociato dalla coscienza. (Pasolini, 'L'articolo delle lucciole,' *Scritti corsari* 164)

> [I have therefore seen with my own senses the compulsory behaviour of the power of consumerism to recreate and fashion the conscience of the Italian people, ending in an irreversible degradation. This is something that did not happen during the height of fascism, a period in which behaviour was completely disassociated from conscience.]

This degradation was experienced in the minds and bodies of Italians, suddenly overwhelmed by the irrational need for superfluous things – but it was also a degradation of the Italian landscape and climate as a result of uncontrolled development and pollution. In this article, Pasolini chose to symbolize the 'trauma storico' [historical trauma] of the massification of Italian culture through the metaphor of the disappearance of the fireflies, which, he argued, could no longer survive in the poisoned environment of contemporary Italy, an Italy that will take on the guise of Hell in many of Pasolini's works. However, fireflies are also present in Dante's Hell, seen at the outset of canto 26, whose lessons involve the powers of rhetoric and dangerous languages of seduction. That is, for both Pasolini and Dante, the fireflies are the poetic signals warning their readers of the spiritual and moral hazards of a vicious world. And importantly, in both Pasolini and Dante, the fireflies have associations with the peasant culture of the countryside – a 'culture of the earth,' which, for Pasolini, was in the process of being eliminated in modern Italy. After a general description of the presence of Dante in Pasolini's work, I will concentrate my essay on Pasolini's film *Salò*, in which Sadean excess and the historical experience of fascism and the Holocaust become metaphors for a totalitarian consumerist culture that would remain the object of Pasolini's outrage and hatred in all the work he produced in the 1950s, '60s, and '70s.

Dante in Pasolini's Poetry and Fiction

I believe that, in order to fully understand the place of Dante in Pasolini's filmography, it is useful to first mention the strong modelling influence of the *Divine Comedy* on his writing. Pasolini is mainly known – especially in Italy – as a poet and author of novels and short stories. The Dantesque influence on his poetry is an enormous and rich subject, and would take a great deal of time to fully explore. Let me simply say that Dante is present in the poetry as a model of civic poetry (or *poesia civile*) – as the author of one of the most 'engaged' works of literature ever written. In stylistic terms, Dante's presence is felt in the metrical structuring of his verses – for example, the use of Dantesque *terzine* in many poems in the volumes *Le ceneri di Gramsci*, *La religione del mio tempo*, and elsewhere. Moreover, Dante's influence is also discernible in the plurilinguism of much of Pasolini's poetry, especially in the the mixing of high and low registers – precisely the sort of *contaminatio* that Pasolini described in his essays on Dante in *Empirismo eretico*. In stylistic terms, Pasolini's Dante has great similarities with Contini's Dante (whose plurilinguism is set in opposition to the monolinguism of the Petrarchan lyric counter-tradition).[2] I would also mention that one of Pasolini's very last volumes of poetry bears the title *Trasumanar e organizzar* – a title that revises verse 70 of the first canto of *Paradise* ('Trasumanar significar *per verba* / non si poria' [Passing beyond the human cannot be / worded]) and contaminates Dante's mysticism with Pasolini's Marxism, while sharing with Dante the writer's concern with finding the most effective mode of articulating a transformational experience for readers. As he writes in the poem 'Manifestar (appunti),' 'manifestar significar per verba non si poria / ma per urli sì' [to signify political struggle through words is not possible, but by yelling, yes].

Leaving aside the poetry and turning now to Pasolini's vast production of fiction – and again being very superficial in my account here – Dante is a strong presence in several of Pasolini's novels and short stories. I will mention the three most obvious examples: in a short story

Pasolini wrote in 1959 entitled 'La mortaccia,' the opening cantos of Dante's *Inferno* are rewritten, with the Pilgrim replaced by Teresa, a prostitute in the Roman slums, and Virgil replaced by Dante, a dark and bitter version of Virgil. Dante guides Teresa past the allegorical beasts (stray dogs in this version), not toward knowledge and salvation, but toward Rebibbia, Rome's Penitentiary, where he abandons her without hope. Only a couple of years later, Pasolini began his other, more well known rewriting of the *Inferno*, entitled *La Divina Mimesis*, an apparently unfinished version of the *Inferno*, in which Pasolini doubles himself as Pilgrim and Guide, and illustrates the novel with photographs of Partisans, Communist rallies, neo-fascists of the Movimento sociale italiano (MSI), student revolts, Italian writers, and impoverished African children. Besides these moral snapshots of the Italian and postcolonial European inferno, the novel's very title, 'divine mimesis,' shows how beholden Pasolini was to Erich Auerbach's explanation of Dantean allegorical figuration in his influential work *Mimesis*. The *Divina Mimesis* is often quite rightly viewed by critics as an early version of Pasolini's last great unfinished novel, published with the title *Petrolio* only in 1992, though Pasolini most often referred to the novel by an alternate title, *Vas* – a reference to *Inferno* 2, verse 28, in which Dante refers to Saint Paul as the *vas d'elezione*, the chosen vessel. The title, and the organization of the novel into Dantesque infernal circles, confirms the guiding significance of Dante in Pasolini's fiction. Furthermore, the protagonist in the novel wanders through a devastated industrial Hell of modern Italy.

Dante in Pasolini's Films

Having established his reputation in Italy during the 1950s as a poet and novelist, in the early 1960s Pasolini turned the better part of his creative energy toward filmmaking. Pasolini would make roughly one feature film per year between 1961 and 1975, as well as very many short features, documentaries, and occasional films. Dante is present throughout Pasolini's film production. *Accattone*, Pasolini's first film (released in 1961), begins with an epigraph from *Purgatory* 5, verses 106–7, in which Satan says to the Angel of God, who has taken Buonconte da Montefeltro's soul from him: 'Tu te ne porti di costui l'etterno / per una lagrimetta che 'l mi toglie' [Do you deny me him? For just one tear / you carry off his deathless part]. This Dantesque citation offers one key to understanding the film, insofar as its tragic story of Accattone, a petty thief and pimp who dies in a banal motor-cycle accident while running from the police, is a story of his salvation or redemption. For at his death, Accattone's last words are 'mo sto meglio' [now I feel better], an utterance that corresponds to Buonconte's *lagrimetta*, signalling his salvation – though it is a salvation that seems so richly undeserved.[3] The only other key citation of Dante in *Accattone* is when one of the other characters in the film intones, 'Abandon all hope ye who enter here,' as he watches Accattone introduce the inno-cent Stella into the life of prostitution. In fact, at one point in the film, Accattone will say to Stella, as she is washing out recycled bottles: 'Stella, indicami er cammino' [Stella, show me the way]. Here the reference to the first verse of the *Inferno* and the symbolic value of Stella's name combine to make of her a degraded stilnovistic angelic lady, a sort of Beatrice of the Borgate. And thus, as in Pasolini's fictional rewritings of Dante that I mentioned above, Rome becomes a consumerist Inferno.

After *Accattone*, Dante remains a strong and guiding influence in his films – and since the references are so numerous, I will limit myself to a brief survey of the clearest examples. In Pasolini's 1962 *Mamma Roma*, a film about the impact of petit-bourgeois, consumerist culture on tradi-tional agrarian life in Italy, the protagonist ends his days in prison for petty theft, surrounded by prisoners who recite from the fourth canto of the *Inferno* during the final scenes of the film. Reacting violently to the Dantesque verses he hears, the protagonist, Ettore, is restrained and confined by guards, and he perishes a sort of humiliated martyr – like the character Accattone, he is another of Pasolini's underworld saints. In the 1966 film *Uccellacci e uccellini* (*Hawks and Sparrows*), we get a glimpse of the opinion Pasolini has of Dante scholars, alas, when he has his characters Totò and Ninetto visit the home of a powerful and exploitative landlord who is also hosting a conference of 'Dentisti Dantisti' – the loathsome Dantean Dentists. Besides this barbed attack on academic Dantisti, which I am quite sure my readers would all agree is so entirely unmerited, I think it is safe to say that Dante's metaphor of the pilgrimage, and the pedagogical relationship between Dante the Pilgrim and his guides – all set into motion by divine intervention – is the same metaphor used in *Hawks and Sparrows*, with its characters – a trinity of father, son, and wise crow – seen following a newly con-structed super-highway along the wasteland of modern-day Italy. While Pasolini's 1971 *Decameron* is an adaptation of Boccaccio's work by the same title (itself an adaptation of sorts of the *Divine Comedy*), it also contains clear homages to Dante and to the tradition of manuscript illustrations of the *Divine Comedy*, as seen especially in the sequence of Giotto's vision of Hell.[4] Pasolini's *I racconti di Canterbury* (*Canterbury Tales*, 1972) also demonstrates Dante's influence, as seen at the conclusion of the film in the Friar's vision of Hell. These dark and bitterly ironic sequences, as in Giotto's vision in the *Decameron*, display Pasolini's debts to past illustrators of Dante's infernal vision as well as to those painters, such as Bosch, who drew upon Dante's allegory in their own representations of Hell.

While only superficial, this survey of Dantean quotations and debts in Pasolini's films might serve to give the reader a sense of the lasting impact of Dante on his work, and also the great faith that Pasolini had that Dante's poem remained as potent a condemnation of corruption and evil in post-war Italy as it was at the time of its writing – thanks, in large part, to the allegorical nature of the poem that continues to guarantee its charge. And Dante's heat is felt nowhere in Pasolini's films more strongly than in *Salò*.

Salò as Dantesque Allegory

It might be unfortunate but also true that Pasolini is known best for his last film, *Salò*, made in 1975 and completed in the days immediately preceding his murder sometime during the night between the first and second days of November. A brief description of the film is in order before I try to account for the Dantesque allegory at work throughout *Salò*. The film is organized into four parts: the *Antinferno* or vestibule of Hell that introduces the film (functioning much like the first introductory canto of the *Inferno*), and three Circles or *Gironi*: the Circle of Perversions, the Circle of Excrement, and the Circle of Blood. As can plainly be seen, Pasolini borrows from the architecture of Dante's *Divine Comedy* in organizing the action of the film. In the *Antinferno*, we witness a fascist round-up presented in the manner of Resistance films ever since Rossellini's *Rome, Open City*: fascist military men chasing down and arresting suspects, while mothers and children cry out in desperation. One young man is gunned down in the river valley as he tries to escape. Eventually, two large groups of adolescent boys and girls are gathered together, organized and coached by three women who will later take up their roles as storytellers or narrators (it will remain for another essay to discuss the strong presence of Boccaccio in the film alongside Dante). The adolescent victims are brought by armed

Nazi guards on military transports to an eighteenth-century villa occupied by four powerful libertines, who are first seen working together on a Book of Regulations. As will be seen throughout the movie, these *regolamenti* will govern every aspect of life and of death for their adolescent victims. Once installed in the villa, the victims are subjected to horrible tortures and humiliations, all for the pleasure of the libertines. Pasolini's camera records in clinical and sadistic detail the scenes of horrifying perversions, coprophaghia, the burning and mutilation of genitalia, the gouging of eyes, scalpings. These actions are often accompanied by the narrations of the three storytellers, dressed in high camp and accompanied by a pianist. (The pianist is noteworthy, given the fact that she will ultimately commit suicide rather than participate any further – the pessimism of the film, in terms of what it says about artists and art, is very dark indeed.)

With this visually horrific film, Pasolini came close to succeeding in his desire to make a totally un-consumable work, an anti-commodity: it is a film that is nearly unwatchable (and given the fact that the film was banned in much of the world for so long, it was legally unwatchable as well). I say nearly unwatchable, and, in fact, the issue of the film's 'watchability' is significant for Pasolini: 'I want to go beyond the limits of the endurable' (Pasolini, *A Future Life* 183). Indeed, it is remarkable how during the scenes of torture and humiliation, the act of watching is itself inscribed into the film: in the form of the libertines' voyeurism – their pleasure in watching the annihilation of the victims or their pleasure in being watched themselves as they annihilate the victims. This is the most meta-cinematic moment of film, and its self-reflexivity has a precedent in Dante. That is, throughout *Salò* the spectator's voyeurism is engaged, but only to be destroyed. For the spectator there is, in *Salò*, the experience of the death of desire, which is, at the same time, the death of the cinema as a medium and industry founded upon the desire and visual pleasure of the spectator, the libertines of the multiplexes.[5] Here Pasolini repeats Dante's sharp criticism of immoral or sinful poetry and secular literature, found most obviously in *Inferno* 5 – the story of the adulterous Paolo and Francesca – and in the parallel cantos *Inferno* 26 (Ulysses as a forked tongue of flame, punished for the sins of rhetoric or seductive language) and *Purgatory* 26, where Dante places the poets Guinizzelli and Arnaut Daniel among the lustful shouting out, 'Sodom and Gomorrah,' as they pass one another in the purifying fires of the seventh ledge of Purgatory. However, while it is possible to associate Pasolini's critique of the cinema industry with Dante's attacks on the work of sinful poets, we will not find anywhere in Pasolini's *Salò* any moral coordinates, and any possibility of redemption. *Salò* concludes with the victims firmly under the control of the libertines. Indeed, the last image of the film is of two of the victims who have agreed to act as guards overlooking the other victims: they are the allegorical equivalents of the Kapós of the Lager camps, or the conformists and *qualunquisti* of Pasolini's contemporary Italian landscape, as seen in the snapshots of *La Divina Mimesis*.

Like most of Pasolini's films, *Salò* is an adaptation of literary texts. In this case, the film is most obviously a remake of the Marquis de Sade's *120 Days of Sodom*. That is, it will be a film that screens the sadomasochistic rituals found in de Sade's work. Pasolini was clearly attracted to the scandalous nature of de Sade's writing, and probably identified with the Marquis – whom he referred to as 'the great poet of the anarchy of power' (Pasolini, *A Future Life* 182) – to the extent that he succeeded in producing a work that was intolerable from any established perspective (that is, de Sade's immorality is absolute). But Pasolini was not satisfied with this. Rather, in order to multiply the scandalous effect of a filmic remake of de Sade, Pasolini decided to make his film an allegory, an allegory of the degradation of life in the consumerist culture of Italy and Europe in the 1970s – after the disappearance of the fireflies. Thus, Pasolini decided to model his adaptation of de Sade on Dante's *Divine Comedy*, in such a manner that the sexual exploitation of the victims in *Salò* would have multiple meanings: thanks to repeated allusions to a Dantean structure of the film, the scenes of brutal subjugation and sexual torture of the adolescent victims of the powerful men found at the literal level in the film are scenes that invite an allegorical interpretation. That is, below the surface horror of sexual domination and the murderous desire of the powerful Bureaucrats who control the Sadean villa, there lies the subterranean message regarding the way the citizens of contemporary Italy are being forced to submit to the will of those controlling the commodity economy in Europe: making 'real' human beings into 'statistical' consumers, a transformation and petrification of life that is symbolized in Pasolini's journalistic writings as the disappearance of the fireflies. Moreover, and very importantly, the use of the highly theatrical storytellers in cahoots with the libertines implicates the labours of writers and filmmakers in the exercise of power. However, the allegorical interpretation of the film is further encouraged, and also complicated, by the director's decision to set the action of the film in the northern Italian republic of Salò in 1944, that is, during the last years of the Second World War, Mussolini's last months in power, and the last months of genocide in the Lager camps. By restructuring de Sade's *120 Days of Sodom* according to the Dantesque model and then immersing it all in the context of the last period of anti-semitic Nazi fascism, the necessity of allegorical interpretation is made clear: the excesses of the Sadean villa will signify simultaneously sexual pathology, the genocidal Nazi-fascistic death drive, and the anthropological degradation of Italians in 1970s commodity culture, which for Pasolini is a neo-fascism.

In Pasolini's own comments on *Salò* – which were many – the dehumanization of the victims in the film signifies a reification of human bodies and minds by a culture and economy that makes everything, including human bodies and thoughts, into merchandise – merchandise whose value is determined by the mysterious whims of market forces. To use a term more appropriate to Dante commentary, *Salò* is an allegory of the forces of seduction and petrification, and we might call the pedagogy of the film one of liberation divorced from salvation. It is a film made a few years after Contini, Pasolini's patron philologist, invited Pasolini and Alberto Moravia to offer some commentary on the place of Dante in contemporary culture (see Naldini 290). While Pasolini never wrote the essay for Contini, in a sense *Salò* can be seen as a response to Contini's question about the value of Dante in today's culture and society: Dante furnishes Pasolini with a model of civil poetry, a poetry of the trenches, a way of writing that is engaged, interested, and a poetry that does not cloak the outrage of a maligned and exiled poet. Indeed, the power of Dante's poem – if allowed to survive the petrifications of *dentisti dantisti* – is in part found in his continuing presence as a model of a style of artistic production that combines outrage with engagement, or, to use the Dantesque title from one of Pasolini's last volumes of poetry, *Trasumanar e organizzar*, Pasolini's Dante reveals the necessity to always go 'beyond human' (*trasumanar*) and then 'organize' (*organizzar*).

Let me conclude. I have tried to give a general panorama of Pasolini's work, and the central importance of Dante within it. As we have seen, Dante (especially his *Inferno*) provides the key to understanding the metrical intricacies and plurilinguism of much of his poetry, especially in the *terzine* of many compositions in the *Ashes of Gramsci*. Dante provides the narrative template for modernized versions of the *Inferno*, as seen in the fictions 'La mortaccia' from the 1950s, *La Divina Mimesis* from the 1960s, and *Petrolio* in the 1970s – all remakes of

Dante's *Inferno*, recontextualizing Dante's allegories in the Italy of the economic miracle within the fledgling European Economic Community. Pasolini's famous essays on literature, language, and film found in *Heretical Empiricism* all seem to rest upon his study of Dante's *Comedy*, especially as it is filtered through Contini's stylistic analyses of Dante's plurilinguism. And finally, Pasolini's films, from *Accattone* in 1961 through *Salò* in 1975, are films that, while at times vastly different from one another stylistically and thematically, nevertheless exhibit the filmmaker's indebtedness to Dante. In the months immediately preceding his murder, and while he was making *Salò*, Pasolini chose the disappearance of the fireflies as a metaphor in articles written for the newspaper *Corriere della sera* to suggest to his readers that the economic development of Italy and Europe would not come without a human and environmental price (that is, pollution and corruption), and he once again was counting on his readers' knowledge of Dante's work. After all, the canto of Ulysses – which, as is well known, involves the cautionary tale of how Ulysses used his rhetorical gifts to seduce his men into going beyond proper limits in their fatal *folle volo* – is a canto that is introduced by the image of flames in a valley which take on the appearance of fireflies in the eyes of a peasant off in the distance; and a similar fire will burn and purify the poets of love and seduction in the twenty-sixth canto of *Purgatory*. That is, vain poets and ambitious rhetorical leaders are punished by Dante by the burning fire. And I would love to think that Dante understood that the blinking signals of the fireflies were part of a language of seduction and thus sexual reproduction – precisely the two languages that are so deformed in Pasolini's *Salò*. The flickering lights of the fireflies are the poetic signals making up a natural cinematography of seduction (motivated by an animal instinct), analogous to another all-too-human cinematography of seduction (narrative and sexual), whose corruption is emblematized in *Salò* by the libertines and their storytellers, those hired hands of the entertainment industry.[6]

In his fiction and films – so very often cautionary tales about the powers of seduction and commodity fetishism – Pasolini mourns the disappearance of the fireflies as casualties of modernity. Like Dante, he condemns those responsible for it, and in the process, and again like Dante before him, Pasolini finds he must build narratives that, while they condemn, are in turn self-condemned.[7] Thus Pasolini inherits the form that Dante gave to his fury, *dopo tanto veder*, and uses it to form and burnish his own outrage into the brightly mannered beacon of resistance and independence that his work, and that of Dante before him, continue to represent for their audiences:

> Voglio dire fuori dai denti: io scendo all'inferno e so cose che non disturbano la pace di altri. Ma state attenti. L'inferno sta salendo da voi. È vero che viene con maschere e con bandiere diverse. È vero che sogna la sua uniforme e la sua giustificazione (qualche volta). Ma è anche vero che la sua voglia, il suo bisogno di dare la sprangata, di aggredire, di uccidere, é forte ed é generale. Non resterà per tanto tempo l'esperienza privata e rischiosa di chi ha, come dire, toccato 'la vita violenta.' Non vi illudete. E voi siete, con la scuola, la televisione, la pacatezza dei vostri giornali, voi siete i grandi conservatori di questo ordine orrendo basato sull'idea di possedere e sull'idea di distruggere.[8]

[I want to shout out: I go down into hell and I know things that do not disturb the peace of others. But beware. Hell is coming up to meet you. It's true that it comes with masks and different flags. It's true that it dreams of its uniform and (at times) its justification. But it's also true that its desire, its need to lash out, to assault, to kill, is strong and generalized. Before long the private and risky experience of touching the 'violent life,' as it were, will no longer belong to a single person. Do not delude yourselves. And you are, with your schools, your television, with the calm objectivity of your newspapers, you are the great conservators of this horrendous order of things based on the idea of possessing, on the idea of destroying.]

Notes

1 First published with the title 'Il vuoto del potere in Italia' in *Corriere della sera*, 1 February 1975; reprinted as 'L'articolo delle lucciole' in Pasolini, *Scritti corsari*, 160–8.

2 However, there are notable differences between Pasolini and Contini on the question of Dante's plurilinguism. Pasolini suggests that Dante's apparent *stylistic* plurilinguism (of 'sub-languages' and 'jargons,' as in the Paolo and Francesca canto of the *Inferno*) is in fact betrayed by a 'monolinguism of *tone*': 'Il plurilinguismo di Dante è ben ordinato, ogni lingua, attinta funzionalmente, sta al suo posto' [Dante's plurilinguism is well-ordered, every language, functionally attained, is in its proper place]. See Pasolini, 'La volontà di Dante a essere poeta,' in *Empirismo eretico*, 111. For Pasolini's

discussion of 'free indirect discourse' in Dante, see the essays 'Intervento sul discorso libero indiretto' and 'La mala mimesi,' both in *Empirismo eretico*. For the place of Dante in Pasolini's writings on linguistics, see De Mauro.

3 For a theological explanation of the mystery of God's salvation in this film, see Sitney.

4 For the illuminated manuscripts of the *Divine Comedy*, see Brieger. For an analysis of painterly models in Pasolini's *Decameron*, *Canterbury Tales*, and *Arabian Nights*, see Rumble, *Allegories of Contamination*. For an examination of the influence of Dante and later manuscript illustrators on international film, see Iannucci.

5 On voyeurism, self-reflexivity, and self-critique in *Salò*, see Greene.

6 And it should be noted that, in Italian, the word *lucciola* has many secondary meanings related to the cinema: besides fireflies, the word also could refer to a type of light used in illuminating film sets, or to ushers at cinemas (armed with flashlights guiding patrons through the dark). Furthermore, in slang prostitutes are often referred to as *lucciole*. That is, the term *lucciola* presents a rich set of associations that all have to do with cinema, seduction, and relations of exchange.

7 For an account of the censorship of *Salò* as well as Pasolini's other films, see Betti 213–18.

8 Quoted from Pasolini's last interview (with Furio Colombo) on the evening of 1 November 1975; reprinted in Naldini 410. Pasolini suggested that Colombo entitle the interview 'Siamo tutti in pericolo' ('We Are All in Danger'). The term 'violent life' in the interview refers rather allusively to Pasolini's second novel about the Roman slums, *Una vita violenta*, published in 1959.

Bibliography

Alighieri, Dante. *La Divina Commedia*. Ed. Natalino Sapegno. 3 vols. Firenze: La Nuova Italia, 1985.

– *The Paradiso*. Trans. John Ciardi. New York: New American Library, 1970.

Auerbach, Erich. 1946. *Mimesis*. Princeton: Princeton University Press, 1974.

Betti, Laura, ed. *Pasolini: Cronaca giudiziaria, persecuzione, morte*. Milano: Garzanti, 1977.

Brieger, Peter, Millard Meiss, and Charles S. Singleton. *Illuminated Manuscripts of the 'Divine Comedy.'* 2 vols. London: Routledge and Kegan Paul, 1969.

Contini, Gianfranco. 'Preliminari sulla lingua di Petrarca.' *Varianti e altra linguistica*. Torino: Einaudi, 1970. 169–92.

De Mauro, Tullio. 'Pasolini's Linguistics.' *Pasolini Old and New*. Ed. Zygmunt Baranski. Dublin: Four Courts Press, 1999. 77–90.

Greene, Naomi. '*Salò*: The Refusal to Consume.' In *Pier Paolo Pasolini: Contemporary Perspectives*. Ed. Patrick Rumble and Bart Testa. Toronto: University of Toronto Press, 1994. 232–42.

Iannucci, Amilcare A. 'From Dante's *Inferno* to *Dante's Peak*: The Influence of Dante on Film.' *Forum Italicum* 32. 1 (Spring 1998): 5–35.

Naldini, Nico. *Pasolini, una vita*. Torino: Einaudi, 1989.

Pasolini, Pier Paolo. *Le ceneri di Gramsci*. Milano: Garzanti, 1957.

– *Una vita violenta*. Milano: Garzanti, 1959.

– *La religione del mio tempo*. Milano: Garzanti, 1961.

– *Trasumanar e organizzar*. Milano: Garzanti, 1971.

– *Empirismo eretico*. Milano: Garzanti, 1972.

– *Scritti corsari*. Milano: Garzanti, 1975.

– *La Divina Mimesis*. Torino: Einaudi, 1975.

– 'La mortaccia (frammenti).' *Alì dagli occhi azzuri*. 1959. Milano: Garzanti, 1989. 243–8.

– *A Future Life*. Ed. Laura Betti and Ludovico G. Thorazzi. Rome: Associazione Fondo Pier Paolo Pasolini, 1989.

– *Petrolio*. Torino: Einaudi, 1992.

Rumble, Patrick. *Allegories of Contamination: Pasolini's 'Trilogy of Life.'* Toronto: University of Toronto Press, 1996.

Sitney, P. Adams. '*Accattone* and *Mamma Roma*.' In *Pier Paolo Pasolini: Contemporary Perspectives*. Ed. Patrick Rumble and Bart Testa. Toronto: University of Toronto Press, 1994. 171–9.

Filmography

Pasolini, Pier Paolo, dir. *Accattone*. Screenplay by Pasolini. Arco Film – Cino del Duca, 1961.

– *Mamma Roma*. Screenplay by Pasolini. Arco Film, 1962.

– *Uccellacci e uccellini*. Screenplay by Pasolini. Arco Film, 1966.

– *Decameron*. Screenplay by Pasolini. PEA – Les Productions Artistes Associés (Paris) – Artemis Film (Berlin), 1971.

– *I racconti di Canterbury*. Screenplay by Pasolini. PEA – Les Productions Artistes Associés (Paris), 1972.

– *Salò o le 120 giornate di Sodoma*. Screenplay by Pasolini and Sergio Citti. PEA – Les Productions Artistes Associés (Paris), 1975.

'Non Senti Come Tutto Questo Ti Assomiglia?' Fellini's Infernal Circles

GUIDO FINK

Qual è 'l geomètra che tutto s'affige
per misurar lo cerchio, e non ritrova,
pensando, quel principio ond' elli indige,
tal era io a quella vista nova:
veder voleva come si convenne
l' imago al cerchio e come vi s'indova,
ma non eran da ciò le proprie penne.

[As the geometer intently seeks
to square the circle, but he cannot reach,
through thought on thought, the principle he needs,
so I searched that strange sight: I wished to see
the way in which our human effigy
suited the circle and found place in it –
and my own wings were far too weak for that.]

– *Paradiso* 33.133–9

It is no doubt advisable, before attempting to explore the relationship between Dante's and Fellini's circles, to express one's uncertainty about the qualification of *le proprie penne*. Luckily, *la vista nova*, and the relationship between the image and the circle, are referred in *Paradiso* 33 to something much more complex, no less than the mystery of incarnation, while the less formidable theme of Dante's influences on Fellini's cinema has been already and quite persuasively recognized and described by, among others, Barbara K. Lewalski, Peter Bondanella, John Welle, Ben Lawton, and Amilcare Iannucci.[1] Even Pier Paolo Pasolini, while emphasizing the importance of Fellini as total auteur of *La dolce vita*, mentioned the transformation of the various actors ('the excellent Mastroianni and stupendous Anita' becoming 'another Mastroianni' and 'another Anita') as well as the process of violent, total reinvention and amplification with which actors or 'characters taken from reality' (e.g., actress Laura Betti, writer Leonida Repaci, artist Anna Salvatore, etc.) were being 'grafted into the complicated organism of Fellinian language' (see Pasolini). Similar words must have been used several times by Dante's contemporaries in the comparison between the spirits met by the Florentine in his poem and the real or mythical figures with whom they were familiar.

A *similarity* of some sort between Dante's and Fellini's worlds (which is something quite different from mere *influence*, the latter being just a sort of heredity or dim remembrance) has been already suggested, within the series called *Block-notes di un regista*, by such an expert in both fields as Professor Jacqueline Risset. 'Ma non senti come tutto questo ti assomiglia, Federico?' [Don't you find it similar to you, to your work, Federico?], Ms Risset asks, while the director himself seems hesitant before accepting the proposal to make a movie out of Dante's poem (see 'L' Inferno' in Tornabuoni 79). In this draft, which is all that remains of a very vague project, Fellini is desperately resisting the pressures of various odd characters (ignorant producers, mellifluous press agents, legal representatives of mysteriously powerful television companies) who are consistently trying to lure him into signing a rich fat contract for this movie he doesn't really want to make: 'All my life I have been pestered by these extravagant offers. You can't say no: you are Italian, Dante was an Italian, and Americans appreciate your work ... A great serial, thirty-three episodes, sold all over the world! Absolutely terrific!' Thirty-three episodes, not ninety-nine or one hundred: it is quite clear the project was to be limited to a film or television adaptation of *Inferno*. Finally, feeling like a puppet in the hands of these anxious, overexcited entrepreneurs, the director actually becomes a puppet, a wooden male doll propped on an armchair. Yet, he cannot avoid being tempted: for instance, why not have 'Caron dimonio con gli occhi di bragia' [the demon Charon, with his eyes like embers (*Inf.* 3.109)] as the old mad beggar who lived on an abandoned boat on the beach of Rimini? Couldn't he shout to the kids of Rimini, on a foggy day, the famous threat 'Guai a voi, anime prave!' [Woe to you, corrupted souls! (*Inf.* 3.83)]? Later on, while at the University of Rome he is listening to an incomprehensible madman lecturing on Dante and psychoanalysis, Professor Risset whispers to him the already quoted words: 'Ma non senti come tutto questo ti assomiglia, Federico?' [Don't you find it similar to you, to your work?].

Being similar – not different, yet not identical – is a tricky concept, not only in this context. According to Michel Foucault (40), for instance, each case of similarity is at the same time what is most evident and what is most mysterious. Despite obvious differences, Dante and Fellini, in any case, may have had something in common. Both, for instance, seem to take great pleasure in transferring into their fictional works real people the authors have met or heard about. Moreover, both have their Virgils and their Beatrices, even if Fellini tends to kill off his *maestri e duchi* (the French critic-consultant in *Otto e mezzo*), or have them commit suicide (Steiner in *La dolce vita*), and to look at his redeeming figures (the young servant on the beach at the end of *La dolce vita*, the girl at the fountain in *Otto e mezzo*) from a distance, with hopeless nostalgia. We might even say that his pilgrimages are not voyages to, but voyages from, Beatrice. Again, both tend to be highly self-reflexive, as amply shown by such films as *Otto e mezzo*, *Roma*, or *Intervista*, and by Dante's frequent addresses to his own memory or artistic skill, such as the famous one at the beginning of *Inferno* 2.[2] Finally, they are both interested in, and critical of, Catholic religion as practised and understood in their times. Of course, Dante could and would never express himself about his own religion as Fellini did, when he stated that he could not escape 'from the amniotic sac of Catholicism,' and that even if he was not 'greatly attracted to rebellion,' yet he felt grateful to Catholicism for giving him 'that roguish streak of rebelliousness that redeemed him.' 'Catholic ritual,' he actually said, 'acts as a stimulant: it lends a subtle and disturbing pleasure to breaking the rules and infringing the prohibitions that it sets.'[3] But a contemporary non-Catholic critic, Harold Bloom, feels quite authorized to call Dante highly blasphemous, while placing him at the centre of his personal Western canon. Dante's poem is above all a prophecy and 'takes on the function of a third Testament, in no way subservient to the Old and the New,' while Dante 'never acknowledges that the *Comedy* must be a fiction, his supreme fiction' (Bloom 73). And if, to Bloom, Dante's outstanding characteristic as a poet and a person is first of all pride rather than humility (something we could never refer to Fellini's self-effacing fictional persona), yet other aspects that Bloom finds in Dante (originality rather than traditionalism, exuberance rather than restraint) may be easily attributed to the author of *Giulietta degli spiriti* and *Casanova*.

There is another aspect, in any case, that may be relevant in a discussion about the difference and the similarlity between Dante and Fellini: their obvious tendency to structure their work in circles. The naïve, wide-eyed streetwalker in *Nights of Cabiria*, Marcello in *La dolce vita*, Ascilto and Encolpio in *Satyricon*, and the title hero in *Casanova* are consistently following a more or less circular route that apparently brings them back, after many stops and stations and meetings and delusions, to their starting point, while Dante the pilgrim somehow reverses the downward direction of the first *cantica* in order to climb the sacred mountain of Purgatory and to ascend one heaven after the other until, presumably, he comes back a very different and more mature human being. Also, we should bear in mind that at the end of each episode or encounter (e.g., the movie star, the pilgrimage, and the fake 'Oscar' for Cabiria; Maddalena, Sylvia, and Steiner for Marcello), the Fellini hero is deceived or betrayed, while Dante the pilgrim keeps moving forward, even if moved or shocked. In a way, Dante leaves behind all the figures he meets, except, of course, Beatrice, while Cabiria is in each case abandoned and Marcello may well feel, even if not literally, left behind and condemned to his mediocre routines. Within each circle, on the other hand, both the poet and the modern filmmaker often seem interested in breaking up the usual narrative and/or visual pattern with sudden changes, apparitions, abrupt disappearances. *Inferno* 10 is certainly one of the most evident examples in Dante, with all the swerving from Farinata to Cavalcante and vice versa, generally announced by such verbal signifiers as *subitamente, allor surse, di subito rizzato*, so well analysed by Eric Auerbach in a famous chapter of his *Mimesis*. The sudden apparitions in Fellini's films of such icons as the title hero in *Lo sceicco bianco* or the gorgeous star Sylvia in *La dolce vita* (it does not really matter if the former is supposed to be frankly satirical, while the latter is only partly so) do create a sort of epiphany, an apparently reverent suspension in the filmic narration, later to be resumed when they sooner or later fade out, or suddenly disappear, with a lack of apparent explanation that was structurally quite novel within the usual patterns of cinematic narration at the time. One can also think of at least one case of sudden swerving in Fellini's work, when Guido, in one of the daydreaming sequences of *Otto e mezzo*, receives a frankly erotic kiss by his mother, who, as we see at the end of the kiss, is no longer his mother but his wife, Luisa.

Are such dreams, visions, and apparitions truly infernal? Yes and no, we should probably answer, or, better yet, not always, not entirely. 'Don't you know that La Saraghina is the devil?' the shocked Father

Confessor asks of blushing, confused little Guido in one of the child-hood reminiscences of *Otto e mezzo*. Yet, the dark, gigantic, dishev-elled female, who lives in a grotto near the sea, and is always ready to lift her skirt for a few pennies in front of the pupils of the nearby Catholic boarding school (a figure that Fellini draws from his adoles-cent experiences, and perhaps from a famous episode in Thomas Wolfe's autobiographical novel *Look Homeward Angel*) does not really convey infernal connotations. Her distant gaze is sad, mournful, more reminiscent of a Mother Earth figure than of a she-devil. In the justly celebrated preface to the publication of four scripts of Fellini's films, Italo Calvino perceptively remarked that Fellini could go quite far in the description of physical repulsion, but would always stop short about moral repulsion, while he was always ready to redeem what could be monstrous and to present it as part of human nature, with a sort of indulgent, sensual complicity. 'Both the lazy province of *I vitelloni* and the movie-making underworld of Rome,' he wrote, 'are circles of Hell, but may be at the same time enjoyable lands of cockaigne' (Calvino xxiv). Also, when reading Dante (as Bloom mali-ciously points out), we are not supposed to question the reality of his vision; but when watching a Fellini film, we are encouraged to look at it, not as the representation of something real (hence his break with neo-realism), but as a vision, a dream, even if, of course, Fellini was always in control of his dreams and reveries, although sometimes pretending (as in *Otto e mezzo*) that he was not.

The oneiric quality of Fellini's cinema became, of course, more and more evident in his mature work – but it was already perceptible from the very beginning. The Roman journey of the newlyweds in the first picture that was completely his own, *Lo sceicco bianco*, quickly degener-ated into a double parallel nightmare for both the authoritarian Ivan and the wide-eyed Wanda, equally shattered by the encounter with the miserable stuff their contrasting dreams were obviously made of; and rarely would his pathetic characters be visited by ghosts and appari-tions who finally proved benevolent, as happens to the title heroine in *Giulietta degli spiriti*. *Otto e mezzo* marks, not only in this sense, a turning point, an attempt to move up from dreams (or nightmares) to what Bachelard calls the *reverie*: 'reveries ... which help us to descend so deeply within ourselves that they rid us of our history'; 'by dreaming of childhood, we return to the lair of reveries, to the reveries that have opened up the world to us' (Bachelard 99, 102). When adopting the magnifying lens of his childish vision, Fellini, in any case, could create his more memorable epiphanies, like the passing of the *Rex*, the luxurious liner, in *Amarcord*: no doubt one of the few scenes in modern cinema that have been capable of conveying a sense of the sacred – not marred, actually increased, by the gentle, tender irony of the parallel adult gaze of the narrator.

Visions of Paradise are, of course, outside the province of this paper, as would be the ascent to Purgatory of Zampanò and Augusto, the belatedly repentant heroes of *La strada* and *Il bidone*, whose eventual redemption seems to be granted thanks to what Dante's devils contemptuously called *lagrimetta*, without the complex negotiations described by Stephen Greenblatt in his recent and fascinating book *Hamlet in Purgatory*. If we want to meet a real, unrepentant devil in Fellini's cinema, we have to move to *Toby Dammit*, Fellini's contribution to an ill-advised omnibus picture revisiting three Edgar Allan Poe stories called in Italy *Tre passi nel delirio* but available in English-speaking countries in a horrendously dubbed French version called *Spirits of the Dead*. It is, of course, a little devil, one *piccolo diavolo*, as Roberto Benigni would call it; and it has the dangerously captivating looks of a blonde, slightly mischievous little girl, not so different from the little Cupid who mocked the manic puritanism of Fellini's Dottor Antonio in another, deservedly more successful omnibus film, *Boccaccio '70*.[4] *Toby Dammit* is, of course, a joke, exactly as the original Poe story, called *Never Bet the Devil Your Head*, poking fun at the Transcendental credo of the Bostonian intellectual leadership of the times:[5] it may be significant that it turns out to be the only disturbing and upsetting episode in the whole picture, while those by Malle and Vadim, elegantly but vainly trying to bring to the screen Poe's horror and his explorations of the theme of the double (*William Wilson, Metzengerstein*), ring desperately hollow and are inferior to the less pretentious efforts coming from the Roger Corman factory. Moving the time and place from nineteenth-century Massachusetts to the Roman filmmaking milieu, Fellini presents Toby as a burnt-out and self-destructive British movie star, who accepts to star in an Italian picture, a project described as the first Catholic western, written by a Vatican personality and to be directed by two Marxist brothers (an obvious parody of the Tavianis), whose intention is to celebrate Jesus as the eternal Prairie man, 'something between Dreyer and Pasolini, with a touch of Fred Zinneman.' Yet, in this little and deliberately playful spoof, the infernal connotations are deeply disturbing from the very beginning, which presents Toby's arrival at the Roman airport of Fiumicino, the 'glass coffin,' where we see a group of nuns whose clothings are flying around in a sort of all-pervading *bufera infernal*, mysterious Moslems ominously reciting their mournful prayers, and soon after, during the taxi ride toward Rome, horrendous scenes of bloody car accidents with dead or dying animals lying on the cluttered *autostrada*. This kind of horror without redemption, entirely new in the Fellini canon, may be partly due to the fact that *Toby Dammit* is the director's first collaboration with Bernardino Zapponi, a writer whose interest in the occult and the uncanny would soon lead Fellini to visit more ghostly and dismal *circles*, from which no salvation will be in sight except in death (e.g., the Villa of Suicides in *Satyricon*) or in a return to the preconscious world of the Mothers (*Casanova*). Quite different from the witty satirical talent of Ennio Flaiano (whose contribution is so lively and perceptible in early Fellini, up to *La dolce vita*) or from the poetical reveries of Tonino Guerra (*Amarcord*), Zapponi is probably responsible for the most morbid, uncanny overtones of this little horror story, and of its cruel, repellent description of Roman movie-making, involving and desecrating even a beloved icon like the old comedian Totò: it is a truly infernal world, from which the title hero can only escape following the deceptive invitation of a little Beatrice turned she-devil, and driving his red Ferrari to his death.

But Zapponi is not among the collaborators to the script of the even more disturbing *Prova d'orchestra*, perhaps the most bitter and desperate of Fellini's films and one of my all-time favourites. It is apparently another little, almost playful film, made with a small budget for Italian television and entirely set in a concert hall during rehearsals, but it depicts a world where there is no need of the Devil since, as Jean-Paul Sartre would put it, 'l'enfer, c'est les autres' [Hell is other people (*Huis Clos*)]. Superficially misunderstood by various critics as a pamphlet against the 'revolutionary' generation of the 1960s and a plea for duty and obedience in society as well as in artistic creation, this bitter parable goes well beyond what may have initially been the director's confused reaction in the terrible days of the assassination of Aldo Moro, the president of the Italian Christian Democratic party; it actually expresses the author's inner contradictions between the need for order and the seduction of chaos, the artist's intimate longing toward loneliness and the need for the collaboration of the Others, as interpreters or members of the audience: a desperate, unsolvable conflict between the equally unacceptable answers provided by anarchy (the loud, violent, vulgar, and sterile revolt of the musicians) and Power (the supernatural intervention of an angry God, or the directions of the German conductor, whose words become more and more similar to Nazi proclamations). Perhaps the best definition of this little but shattering picture has been given by the Italian historian Carlo Ginzburg, who spoke of the director's view of his and our brethren as seen with both 'passion and repulsion' in a private letter that Fellini saved and was later to be published (Tornabuoni 92).

Yet it may be significant that at the end of the movie, so full of sound and fury, we are to hear not only the mad director's screams but Nino Rota's music, finally delivered in its beauty and sweetness, as if the whole parable had been just a necessary preparation, an invitation to forget our selfish mediocrity and to join forces in the search for safety ('Le note salvano noi,' shouts the conductor in his bad Italian: musical notes do save us). Is there, somewhere hidden behind the Inferno of our daily life, the consolation of new glimpses of a possible Heaven, such as had been provided in *Amarcord* by the passing of the *Rex*? This reminds us, after all, that even in the latest, equally bitter, but perhaps less satisfactory films made by Fellini (*Ginger e Fred* or *La voce della luna*), music, even if, unfortunately, no longer entrusted to the marvellous Rota, turns out to be a partial remedy against the mediocrity and vulgarity of modern life and society: in both cases, dance provides moments of enchantment and forgetfulness, brief parentheses in the all-pervading decay of a world that does not deserve to be saved and perhaps does not really want to be. Or, to put it in another way, and to go back to the words of the other explorer of Heaven and Hell, Fellini may have felt at the end of his career and of his life that *la navicella* of his *ingegno* was no longer, alas, spreading its sails: that, actually, it could and perhaps would be destroyed, exactly like the luxurious *Gloria N*, at the end of *E la nave va*, finally surrendered with the motley crew of its doomed and weird passengers to a destructive terrorist attack. But once again, shouldn't we be somehow relieved and gratified by the fact that on a small lifeboat, a solitary witness, a mediocre journalist with the sole company of a fantastic animal, survived and was spinning the wheel of his ancient camera? In a way, even the ultimate destruction was thus recorded on the roll of film, the ultimate circle.

Notes

1 Barbara Lewalski discusses the purgatorial nature of Fellini's work; Peter Bondanella (118–20) compares the death of Augusto, at the end of *Il bidone*,

with the *lagrimetta* that redeemed Buonconte da Montefeltro, as related in *Purgatorio* 5; John Welle convincingly connects the recurrence of the motif of greetings and salutations in *La dolce vita* and in Dante's work, particularly in *La vita nuova*; Ben Lawton points out the relevance of Italian literature, both high and popular, in Fellini's cinema; and Amilcare Iannucci devotes particular attention to the Dantesque aspects in Fellini's (and in Pasolini's) cinematic work.

2 'O mente che scrivesti ciò ch'io vidi, / qui si parrà la tua nobilitate' [O memory that set down what I saw, / here shall your excellence reveal itself (*Inf.* 2.8–9)]. This gives a more personal and self-reflexive quality to the traditional invocation to the Muses in the preceding line.

3 Costantini 117. Perhaps it should be remembered here that when Italian leftist critics, who were more or less oriented toward Marxism or quite faithful to the literal dogmas of neo-realism (the most influential one at the time being Guido Aristarco, the editor of *Cinema Nuovo*), were rejecting *La strada* or *The Nights of Cabiria* as too overtly mystical, the Catholic Church of the time, with few exceptions, was rather unanimous in condemning Fellini's work as 'sinful' and blasphemous. *La dolce vita,* in particular, was the occasion of a nationwide scandal that turned out to be a sort of *rite de passage* for Italian cinema and Italian society at large between the end of the 1950s and the beginning of the 1960s. After the first screening at the Capitol Cinema in Milan, the director himself was assaulted, insulted, and spat upon by a mob loudly accusing him of being 'a Communist pig.' The Church and the rightist political parties attacked the movie, retitled 'The Disgusting Life' in the Vatican paper, both in Parliament and in the press. Fellini asked for an appointment with Cardinal Montini, the future Pope Paul VI, and vainly sought forgiveness for the Jesuit father Nazareno Taddei, who had praised the movie in a magazine and was severely punished for this (see Tornabuoni 370; Costantini 56–61). Even the author of these notes could tell a few colourful anecdotes about what happened to him when he inadvertently accepted to lecture on *La dolce vita* in the Catholic region of the Veneto.

4 Most likely *Boccaccio '70* was successful thanks to de Sica's crowd-pleasing novelette, *La riffa*, obviously inferior to Fellini's witty and surrealistic *Tentazioni del dottor Antonio* and to Visconti's wonderful, incredibly under-rated *Il lavoro*, adapted from a Maupassant story. This gem was, among other things, a subtle yet affectionate parody of the Antonioni canon and of the affluent society usually portrayed by the author of *L'avventura* and *La notte*. The Italian original version of *Boccaccio '70* also included Monicelli's

Renzo e Luciana, a modern rewriting of Manzoni's *Promessi sposi* set in the industrial Milan of the so-called 'economic miracle,' and mysteriously excised in the editions for the foreign market.

5 In the Poe original, Toby is doomed to be one of the damned because his left-handed mother had been slapping him from the left to the right, contrary to the natural movement of the globe.

Bibliography

Auerbach, Eric. *Mimesis: The Representation of Reality in Western Literature.* Trans. Willard R. Trask. Garden City, NY: Doubleday, 1957.

Bachelard, Gaston. *The Poetics of Reverie: Childhood, Language, and the Cosmos.* Trans. Daniel Russell. Boston: Beacon Hill, 1961.

Bloom, Harold. *The Western Canon: The Books and School of the Ages.* New York: Riverhead Books, 1995.

Bondanella, Peter. *The Cinema of Federico Fellini.* Princeton, NJ: Princeton University Press, 1992.

Calvino, Italo. 'Autobiografia di uno spettatore.' In *Quattro film*, by Federico Fellini. Torino: Einaudi, 1974.

Costantini, Costanzo, ed. *Conversations with Fellini.* Trans. Sohrab Sorooshian. San Diego: Harcourt, Brace, 1995.

Foucault, Michel. *Le parole e le cose: Un'archeologia delle scienze umane.* Trans. Emilio Panatescu. Milano: Rizzoli, 1978.

Greenblatt, Stephen. *Hamlet in Purgatory.* Princeton, NJ: Princeton University Press, 2001.

Iannucci, Amilcare. 'From Dante's *Inferno* to *Dante's Peak*: The Influence of Dante on Film.' *Forum Italicum* 32.1 (1998): 5–35.

Lawton, Ben. 'Fellini and the Literary Tradition.' *Perspectives on Federico Fellini.* Ed. P. Bondanella and C. Degli-Esposti. New York: G.K. Hall, 1993. 191–202.

Lewalski, Barbara. 'Federico Fellini's Purgatorio.' *Federico Fellini: Essays in Criticism.* Ed. P. Bondanella. New York: Oxford University Press, 1978. 113–20.

Pasolini, Pier Paolo. 'The Catholic Irrationalism of Fellini.' Trans. Frank and Pina Demers. *Film Criticism* 1 (1984): 64–73. Rpt. in *Perspectives on Federico Fellini.* Ed. Peter Bondanella and C. Degli-Esposti. New York: G.K. Hall, 1993. 101–9.

Tornabuoni, Lietta, ed. *Federico Fellini.* Milano: Rizzoli, 1995.

Welle, John. 'Fellini's Use of Dante in *La dolce vita*.' *Perspectives on Federico Fellini.* Ed. P. Bondanella and C. Degli-Esposti. New York: G.K. Hall, 1993. 110–18.

Dante and Canadian Cinema

JOHN TULK

Canadian cinema, like the cinema of other countries, has two broad periods, the silent one from 1896 down to 1929 and the sound one extending from 1929 to the present day.[1] The silent period sees, at its outset, the appearance of documentary films, which were then followed, especially after 1912, by a proliferation of fiction films, especially wilderness and adventure stories, filmed by numerous studios located in very unlikely places from Halifax to Victoria. The sound period witnesses the intervention in film of government, first in 1939 with the foundation of the National Film Board of Canada under the leadership of John Grierson, and then, much later, in 1964 with the creation of the Canadian Film Development Corporation, which changed its name to Telefilm Canada in 1983. The National Film Board has acted as a kind of film school for budding Canadian filmmakers. At first it fostered English-Canadian and male film talent, and developed such directors as F.R. 'Budge' Crawley, Sidney Furie, and Don Owen. Then the NFB created French and woman units, which led to the cultivation of French-Canadian and women filmmakers who have made their mark with a number of uniquely Canadian film contributions, from Michel Brault's *Les raquetteurs* (1958) to Denys Arcand's *Jésus de Montréal* (1989), and from Bonnie Sherr Klein's *Not a Love Story* (1982) to the teenage female collective's (Beverly Brown, Morgan Gage, Amber Goodwyn, Karen Shamy-Smith) *Salt* (2000). The Canadian Film Development Corporation of Canada has played a very different role, providing funding to stimulate independent production in the private sector. It has helped finance many commercially and critically successful films and flops, but has unwittingly, in the process, attracted the movie moguls from the south, who have conferred on major Canadian cities not only a curiously American filmic character but also the dubious sobriquet of Hollywoods of the North. Finally, Canadian sound cinema saw the beginnings in the late 1960s of Canadian experimental or avant-garde film. Its forebears were visual artists such as Jack Chambers and Michael Snow, while its numerous present-day practitioners include Al Razutis, David Rimmer, Richard Kerr, Mike Hoolboom, and Bruce Elder. Together, these experimental filmmakers have established Canada as an international leader in this milieu and have provided 'Canada's foremost contribution to contemporary cinematic discourse' (Feldman, *Take Two* 246).

Throughout this history, one presence is pervasive and enduring, the presence of Dante. In fact, Dante has been appropriated by Canadian filmmakers for all of the reasons he was appropriated by filmmakers of other countries. This is true of both good and bad films. Thus, he has been used to bestow authorial significance on a particular filmmaker's work, as with Eric Nicholas's 1996 *River Rats*, a rather sophomoric crime caper, which opens with a quote from *Inferno* 10 and proceeds to an extended and juvenile discussion of bodily bowel movements. Or again, he has been used to lend plot, structure, or mood, as in Nicholas Campbell's 1999 *Boozecan*, 'a slice-of-life sleaze film' (Files 34) which takes us on a downward journey through the seamy and infernal underbelly of Toronto's illegal after-hours drinking clubs and which introduces us to a host of lost souls who represent gripping vitality and criminal depravity. Or, again, he has been used to develop character as in Carl Bessai's *johnny* (2000), the first Canadian film shot according to the stark dictates of Dogme 95.[2] Its utterly realistic squeegee kid hero is a Mephistophelian demon who gets off enticing his fellow squeegee kids to do evil and who devours them as they freely surrender to his will. Finally, Dante has been used to impart a particular type of allegorical meaning to a film or suite of films, such as Paul Almond's profound 'Bujold trilogy' (*Isabel*, 1968, *The Act of the Heart*, 1970, and *Journey*, 1972), which, like Dante's poem, was undertaken to 'profit a world that lives badly' and which deals with the difficulties of attaining 'spiritual reality' in a modern urban setting that is resolutely materialistic.

Perhaps, however, the major way in which Dante has engaged Canadian filmmakers has been with respect to the pivotal issue of vision. In this brief paper, I do not have sufficient space to do adequate justice to all of the Canadian films which could be brought together under this banner of vision. Instead, I propose to concentrate on select sets of scenes from two English-speaking Canadian films, one silent and one sound, each very different from the other, each dealing with vision in a markedly different manner, and each corresponding to different aspects of Dante's vision as raised in the *Commedia*. In so doing, my approach will be that of an amateur, I being neither a professional film critic nor a Dante scholar. But I am an amateur in the fullest sense of the term, having a profound love of Dante and of cinema. My methodology will not be intertextual, that is, laying texts side by side and examining direct echoes of one in the other, but rather interdiscursive, comparing two works, albeit in different media, one of which, consciously or unconsciously, makes use of the other, which is clearly engraved in the public imagination. Thus I propose opening up the texts, looking underneath, to determine what is really happening: what is the vision of this particular filmmaker; how does this vision unfold in the particulars of this filmmaker's work; and how does this filmmaker's vision correspond to aspects of Dante's vision as revealed in the *Commedia*?

Back to God's Country was released in 1919. The film was directed by David M. Hartford and produced by Ernest Shipman, so-called 10 per cent Ernie, who was an extraordinary entrepreneur in the early Canadian entertainment business (Morris, *Embattled Shadows* 99 ff; Feldman and Nelson 14 ff). The screenplay was adapted from a short story by adventure writer James Oliver Curwood and was written by Nell Shipman, wife of Ernie, who was also the star of the film (Morris, *Embattled Shadows* 100 ff) and a pioneering talent in early silent cinema.[3] The movie was shot largely on location, in the wintry wilderness north of Great Slave Lake, under very harsh conditions. Cast and crew had to face extreme cold (the original male lead, Ronald Byram, caught pneumonia and died) and unprecedented technical problems (Walker and Walker, 'Danger' 34–42). But Ernest managed to bring the shoot to successful completion and used his considerable marketing skills to sell the film to the largest possible audience. He developed, for example, the tantalizing slogan 'Don't book *Back to God's Country* unless you want to prove that the nude is not rude,' a slogan derived from a scene in the film which shows Nell diving nude into a pool of running water close to her cabin. When released, the movie was an instant critical and popular success, returning more than three million dollars to its backers, a yield of 300 per cent, and making it proportionately the most successful Canadian movie of all time.

The movie recounts the story of Dolores Le Beau (Fair or Good). She lives happily in a pristine forest with her father. Into her life comes consummate evil in the person of Rydal, who rapes her, kills her father, and escapes unrepentant. Rescued by her fiancé, Dolores marries, moves to the city, and from there undertakes a sea journey to the northern wilderness accompanied by her husband. Complications ensue: the captain turns out to be Rydal; her husband is seriously injured; there is no doctor and the ship is frozen in for the winter. Refusing to yield to Rydal's continuous lewd advances, Dolores escapes with her husband on a sled across the barren terrain, accompanied by her faithful dog Wapi and hotly pursued by Rydal. She eventually makes it to safety, and Rydal perishes in the frozen North.

This melodrama is infused by Nell Shipman with a poetic vision of good and evil which is epic and which is, I believe, ultimately traceable to Dante. Dante's vision of the realms of the afterlife is, of course, unique. Nowhere is this uniqueness more apparent than it is with respect to Purgatory and the Earthly Paradise, the scene of the fall of humankind from grace. Dante literally rips Purgatory out of the infernal subterranean abyss to which it had been confined and turns it into a mountainous realm of repentance located in the southern hemisphere. Moreover, he makes the Earthly Paradise the crowning pinnacle of the Mountain of Purgatory (Iannucci, 'Dante's Limbo: At the Margins of Orthodoxy'). In so doing, he displays a deft strategy for structuring the pilgrim's journey of salvation. First, Dante establishes a strict polarity between the realm of evil and the realm of goodness, which are figured as two distinct realms. Evil is in Hell, a realm located in the northern hemisphere and a realm, especially the lower one descends, of extreme cold, darkness, cacophony, and dissonance. Good, on the other hand, is situated in Purgatory and, especially, in the Earthly Paradise at its top. These realms are located in the southern hemisphere and are places of warmth, light, euphony, and harmony. Secondly, in order for the pilgrim to reach the Earthly Paradise, he must first travel through the realm of evil, for only the soul which resists evil can enter the Earthly Paradise. Thirdly, whereas the Earthly Paradise had been viewed as a place long vanished, Dante brings it vibrantly to life (cf. *Purg.* 28–33). It is a divine forest, the last refuge of goodness before the celestial realm, and God's very imprint suffuses it: a lovely woman, Matilda, a figure of the golden age of earthly felicity, is its guardian; light shines and gentle winds blow; its stream is the purest water imaginable; and here the human and nature are one. It is, in short, God's country, and Dante's journey to it, the scene of the fall, is richly symbolic: it is the last stopover before the ascent through Paradise, and in coming to it Dante signifies that he is nearing his true and heavenly home.

This afterlife vision of Dante is a mirror vision of *Back to God's Country*, which likewise is imbued with two distinct realms. At the film's outset, we are introduced first to the realm of God's country. It is a blessed forest, located in the southern hemisphere, and has all of the trappings of Dante: pure water and light, gentle winds and sounds. Most importantly, Dolores is figured as a Matilda figure, the forest's guardian, an innocent person with preternatural gifts who has a quasi-mystical relationship with all of the beasts of the realm. But into her forest comes the archdemon of evil, and she is driven out. Now she journeys to the realm of evil in the northern hemisphere, a realm of icy cold, cacophony, and dissonance (all of the film's shots of the North are in extreme darkness, and everything is desolate, the cold and ice ever present). It is only when Dolores refuses to give into evil and flees from it that she is brought to safety and is able to return to God's country. The symbolism at the end of the film is as profound as Dante's: Dolores is saved and, like Dante, has a vision of her return to the forest, which then becomes a reality; Rydal, on the other hand, perishes in the realm of evil by plunging headlong into an icy grave, which engulfs him forever and which he shares with Dante's Lucifer, who is portrayed as a giant encased in the ice.

Back to God's Country is one of the few silent Canadian films to have survived (it was lovingly restored by Bravo television in 1997). It is memorable for a number of reasons: its length (it was an eight-reeler), its epic scope, its incredible sets, its remarkably daring scenes, and, above all else, its Dantean-inspired universal vision of good and evil.

Illuminated Texts was produced in 1982 by R. Bruce Elder, teacher and author, a most vocal critic of the Canadian film establishment, and one of the most pre-eminent of Canadian experimental filmmakers.[4] *Illuminated Texts* is one small filmic element of the massive film cycle *The Book of All the Dead*, a cycle of films of the first quarter of Elder's life that takes over forty hours to view in its entirety.[5] As Elder has made abundantly clear ('Dante and *The Book of All the Dead*' 1ff), the major inspiration for *The Book of All the Dead* is Dante's *Commedia*, myriad fragments of which have been scattered throughout the cycle. Both in *Illuminated Texts* and in the cycle as a whole, Bruce Elder shows that he shares much in common with Dante. Both work in the epic tradition (Dorland 27), a tradition which begins with Homer and continues through Dante to Milton, Blake, Joyce, and Pound, another author of major significance for Elder. Both, in their respective arts, create visions of entire worlds: Dante, a poetic vision of the three realms of the afterlife; and Elder, a filmic vision of the unfolding of history leading to the world of modernity and technocracy (MacDonald 20; Dorland 22 ff). Moreover, in constructing these visions, both Dante and Elder share a *modus operandi*. First, both have a preconceived plan for the overall structure of their worlds' unfolding. Dante lays bare this plan in the prologue to the *Commedia*, *Inferno* 1, and Elder has admitted to having a sense of the progression of his cycle from the beginning and to have known the general shape before he began (Dorland 26–7). Secondly, both artists elaborate their visions with a dazzling and encyclopedic display of erudition. The *Commedia* and *The Book of All the Dead*, especially *Illuminated Texts*, are the products of a lifetime of learning, and both are constructed from a plethora of diverse sources with the result that the seamless interplay of all these sources constitutes a veritable polysemy and testifies to the eclectic retention of both artists' dynamic intellects (cf. Feldman, 'Bruce Elder's *Illuminated Texts*' 45). Finally, in their respective works, both Dante and Elder employ a mixed style, which intersperses scenes of daring reality and gross parody, as the appropriate vehicle for driving their respective visions home.

Illuminated Texts is Elder's *Inferno* (see Bart Testa's essay in this volume). But rather than a gradual spiral and downward journey, *Illuminated Texts* is a frenetic leap forward through history and time to the age of modernity and technocracy (Feldman, 'Bruce Elder's *Illuminated Texts*' 45; Testa in this volume). Employing philosophical models provided by George Grant and literary ones afforded by Northrop Frye, *Illuminated Texts* points to the Christian myth of the Fall and charts the movement from paradise to apocalypse, or, in the formal terms of the film, from plenitude to fragmentation. Divided into eight principal parts, *Illuminated Texts* is not narrative in the normal and narrow sense of the term, but uses images, both natural and computer-generated, voices, words, and sounds, many again generated by computer, and moves from depictions of a natural world, pure and unsullied, to those of a corrupted world, which gain horrible momentum along the way and which lead to the fragmentation of both society and the individual, as exemplified by the monadic texts of Sartre and Lacan, among others, which now occupy the film. These texts are shaped into a poetic narrative and 'provide the climax for the film's revelation of a world confronted by the horror of where its own collective history has led' (MacDonald 20). Thus, *Illuminated Texts* culminates in disturbing images of the most incomprehensible of all incomprehensible human acts – the extirpation, the annihilation, the genocide of an entire race –

the Holocaust, accompanied by the text, in increasing frequency, of the question of a child who is about to be killed but who is told she is going to join her mother: 'Is it far?' The final shots of the film are a veritable bombardment of the senses and leave one drained, violated, alone, and ultimately forgotten as the individual self surrenders to the atrocities the collective self has wrought.

In addition, these final shots show us how completely Elder has absorbed Dante. They take us to the heart of vision, both Dante's and Elder's, and explore its ontological and epistemological status. In this respect, I should like to bring together Elder's culminating vision in *Illuminated Texts* and Dante's culminating vision in the *Commedia*, the former a vision of pure horror, the latter a vision of pure joy. Having prepared us since canto 1, Dante in the final canto of the *Paradiso* sets out to present his vision of the reality of the experience of the Godhead (*Par.* 33.55ff). This is the poem's culminating experience and one which taxes all of Dante's powers as a poet (cf. Singleton 571ff). There are a number of elements that stand out in Dante's poetic description of his vision. The first is that the poet is about to present an incomprehensible and inexpressible object, the very vision of God. The second is the seeming inability of the poet to capture that object given the incommensurate distance between the dazzling vision itself and Dante's meagre abilities as a poet and, closely related, between the seen and the remembered. Dante therefore begins with a modesty *topos* claiming that his speech is not up to the experience ('Da quinci innanzi il mio veder fu maggio / che 'l parlar mostra') [From that point on, what I could see was greater / than speech can show (*Par.* 33.55–6)] and that his memory is poor. To reinforce the latter, Dante complains that he can remember so little of the recent experience, whereas the famed exploits of Jason and his Argonauts are remembered twenty-five centuries later ('Un punto solo m'è maggior letargo / che venticinque secoli a la 'mpresa / che fé Nettuno ammirar l'ombra d'Argo') [That one moment brings more forgetfulness to me than twenty / -five centuries have brought to the endeavor / that startled Neptune with the Argo's shadow! (*Par.* 33.94–6)]. The third point, however, is that this modesty does not stop the poet, as the following description of the Godhead as three circles discerned within a single light makes perfectly clear (*Par.* 33.115 ff), a description which is both theologically and poetically impeccable. The fourth is that Dante *qua* poet, in order to present his object of experience poetically, must first internalize the object and be transcended by it. Dante's sight, he tells us, becomes rarefied, and he becomes altered and is able to penetrate the Light more deeply ('ma per la vista che s'avvalorava / in me guardando, una sola parvenza, / mutandom'io, a me si travagliava') [but through my sight, which as I gazed grew stronger, / that sole appearance, even as I altered, / seemed to be changing (*Par.* 33.112–14)]. Thus does Dante move from seeming hesitation to poetic description and bridges the gap between the reality and the retelling, between the inexpressible and the expressed, between sacred truth and poetic approximation.

In a totally analogous manner, having prepared us gradually, Elder sets out at the conclusion of *Illuminated Texts* to present the culminating vision of the work, the Holocaust. The object to be presented, like Dante's, is incomprehensible and inexpressible. Elder, too, is aware of his meagre abilities as a filmmaker and so begins, like Dante, by suggesting he is doomed to failure, a failure suggested by the very pyrotechnic film sequences which precede and which seem to signify the end, not only of this film, but all film. But Elder, like Dante, continues and succeeds in conveying through the film's closing images the reality behind the incomprehensible. In so doing, Elder must first, like Dante, internalize and be transcended by his object. This is suggested by the image of Elder himself accompanying the closing shots, which show him as a ghostly image refracted off the wall of a concentration camp, absorbing, becoming the image. Thus does Elder move from stasis to filmic description and so bridges the gap between the inexpressible and expressed.

What makes this vision possible for both Dante and Elder? I feel that the answer once again highlights how much Dante and Elder have in common. Dante's *Commedia* is about suffering leading to consummate joy. Elder's *Illuminated Texts* is about suffering, but later parts of his cycle, *Exultations*, *Burying the Dead*, and *Et Resurrectus Est*, are also about discovering the joy of divine love. Images of suffering permeate Dante's work as they do Elder's. *Illuminated Texts*, in fact, links the personal suffering of the filmmaker and the collective suffering of humankind. Such visions of suffering are shared, can only be shared, by two individuals who have known the pain of suffering and the joy of release. Both Elder and Dante bring to their work the perspective of the suffering exile. In fact, an interview which Elder gave *Cinema Canada* in 1985 (Dorland 22–6), and which highlights his exile and his suffering, reads almost verbatim like the similar account of Dante's vicissitudes in the *Convivio* (3.4–5). In these passages, both men reflect on their exile, Dante from his beloved Florence, Elder from the established film community, and on the cost of that exile to them and their works. In other words, what accounts for the vision of Elder and Dante is suffering, which allows them to penetrate deep inside themselves and convert the images they find there in perception into the images of their imagination and, ultimately, thought. Out of this process comes vision. This vision represents the spiritual education that is the *Comedy* and *The Book of All the Dead*, a spiritual education that is

> the growth towards the insight that all that is given in experience truly is a gift; and we must have faith that though some of our experiences, like nightmare monsters wrought in the dark, may seem like cruel repayments for our efforts to find God, even such cruel succubi turn out to disclose the Be-ing of Goodness, if we wait long enough. Consciousness of the significance of the particular is enlarged until, at last, the poetry of experience is awakened, and, an emotional experience is called forth that awakens one to our oneness with our circumstance, i.e., that which stands around us. (Elder, 'Dante and *The Book of All the Dead*')

Notes

1 Overviews of the history of Canadian cinema are provided by Canadian Institute; Clandfield; Feldman; Feldman and Nelson; Knelman; Morris; Pratley; and Rist. Individual aspects appear in Canadian Film Institute; Evans; and Leavey. A useful collection of film documents is assembled by Fetherling. Canadian experimental film is explored by Elder, *Image and Identity*; Glassman; Hoolboom; Jonasson and Shedden; Lowder; Shedden; and Testa. The industry side of Canadian film is covered by Beattie; Globerman and Vining; Magder; and Posner. The history of Quebec cinema is treated by Coulombe and Jean; Donohoe; Garel and Pâquet; Lever; Marsolais; Pageau and Lever; and Véronneau and Handling. The National Film Board of Canada maintains a web site (*http://www.nfb.ca*), as does Francocine, whose web site (*http://www.francoculture.ca/cine/*) is devoted to French-Canadian cinema and film. Finally, Donald Brittain's documentary film *Dreamland*, which is available from the National Film Board of Canada, is a nostalgic look at Canadian movies from 1895 to 1939.
2 Dogme 95, which established the genre of dogma film, was developed by a Danish collective founded in 1995 by directors Lars von Trier (*Idioterne* or *The Idiots*) and Thomas Vinterberg (*Festen* or *The Celebration*). Dogme 95 is a

reaction to Hollywood-style filmmaking and presents a series of rules which are known as the 'vow of chastity.' The rules, quoted from the Danish collective's web site (*www.dogme95.dk*), include the following: (1) shooting must be done on location; (2) the sound must never be produced apart from the images or vice versa; (3) the camera must be hand-held; (4) the film must be in colour; (5) optical work and filters are forbidden; (6) the film must not contain superficial action; (7) temporal and geographical alienation are forbidden; (8) genre movies are not acceptable; (9) the film format must be Academy 35 mm; (10) the director must not be credited.

3 Nell Shipman has become the focus of much recent research. Besides her autobiography, *The Silent Screen and My Talking Heart*, there are studies of her life and work by Armatage, Everson, Foster, Slide, Smith, and Walker and Walker. There is also a web site (*www.utoronto.ca/shipman*) dedicated to her life and work.

4 Elder is a professor at Ryerson Polytechnic University. He has published extensively and is the author of a key text on Canadian culture and avant-garde film, *Image and Identity*. Elder rarely minces his words. He was involved in a major controversy in 1985 over his essay 'The Cinema We Need,' which appeared in *Canadian Forum*. His position was heavily criticized by Piers Handling and Peter Harcourt in *Cinema Canada* (July-Aug. 1985). His rebuttal also appeared in the same issue. His films have been screened, among other venues, at New York's Museum of Modern Art, Berlin's Kino Arsenal, the Centre Pompidou in Paris, the San Francisco Cinematheque, and Hamburg's Kino Metropolis. Retrospectives of his work have been presented by Anthology Film Archives in New York, Il Festival Senzatitolo in Trento, Images '97 at Toronto, and the Antechamber in Regina. The recipient of numerous awards, including a Genie, Elder was honoured by the Art Gallery of Ontario in 1985 with a major homage, which concluded with the Canadian premiere of his just-completed eight-hour film *Lamentations*.

5 All of the filmic elements of the massive cycle are catalogued by the Canadian Filmmakers Distribution Centre and may be ordered through their web site (*www.cfmdc.org*).

Bibliography

Armatage, Kay. 'Nell Shipman: A Case of Heroic Femininity.' *Gendering the Nation: Canadian Women's Cinema*. Ed. Kay Armatage et al. Toronto: University of Toronto Press, 1999. 17–38.

– 'The Silent Screen and My Talking Heart.' *Journal of Social and Political Theory* 14.1–3 (1990): 12–17.

Beattie, Eleanor. *The Handbook of Canadian Film*. Toronto: Peter Martin Associates, 1977.

Canadian Film Institute. *The First Fifty Years*. Ottawa: Canadian Film Institute, 1985.

Canadian Institute. *Canadian Film*. Toronto: Canadian Institute, 1994.

Clandfield, David. *Canadian Film*. Toronto: Oxford University Press, 1987.

Cori, Howard. 'The Irony of the Blockbuster.' *Weekend Post*, 6 Aug. 1999, p. 4.

Coulombe, Michel, and Marcel Jean, eds. *Le dictionnaire du cinéma québécois*. Montréal: Boreal, 1991.

Donohoe, Joseph I., Jr, ed. *Essays on Québec Cinema*. East Lansing: Michigan State University Press, 1991.

Dorland, Michael. 'Bruce Elder, *Lamentations* and Beyond.' *Cinema Canada* 124 (Nov. 1985): 21–7.

Elder, Bruce. 'A Vindication.' *Cinema Canada* 120–1 (July-Aug. 1985): 32–4.

– 'Dante and *The Book of All the Dead*.' Talk delivered to the Dante and Cinema Conference, University of Toronto, 1 April 2001. Unpublished.

– *Image and Identity: Reflections on Canadian Film and Culture*. Waterloo, ON: Wilfrid Laurier University Press, 1989.

Evans, Gary. *In the National Interest: A Chronicle of the National Film Board from 1949 to 1989*. Toronto: University of Toronto Press, 1991.

Everson, William K. 'Rediscovery: The Films of Nell Shipman.' *Films in Review* 40.4 (April 1989): 228–30.

Feldman, Seth. 'Bruce Elder's *Illuminated Texts*.' *Cinema Canada* 92 (Jan. 1983): 45.

– *Take Two*. Toronto: Irwin, 1984.

Feldman, Seth, and Joyce Nelson, eds. *Canadian Film Reader*. Toronto: Peter Martin Associates, 1977.

Fetherling, Douglas, ed. *Documents in Canadian Film*. Peterborough, ON: Broadview Press, 1988.

Files, Gemma. 'Intoxicating Boozecan.' *Eye*, 21 Oct. 1999, p. 34.

Foster, Gwendolyn. *Women Film Directors: An International Bio-Critical Dictionary*. Westport, CT: Greenwood Press, 1995.

Garel, Sylvain, and André Pâquet. *Les cinémas du Canada*. Paris: Centre Georges Pompidou, 1992.

Glassman, Marc. *The Displaced Narrator*. Toronto: The Funnel, 1985.

Globerman, Steven, and Aidan Vining. *Foreign Ownership and Canada's Feature*

Film Distribution Sector: An Economic Analysis. Vancouver: The Fraser Institute, 1987.

Handling, Piers. 'The Cinema We Need?' *Cinema Canada* 120–1 (July-Aug. 1985): 29–30.

Harcourt, Peter. 'Politics or Paranoia.' *Cinema Canada* 120–1 (July-Aug. 1985): 31–2.

Hoolboom, Mike. *Inside the Pleasure Dome: Fringe Film in Canada.* Toronto: Gutter Press, 1997.

– *Tales of the Bizarre and Unexplained: Fringe Film in Canada.* Toronto: Pages Books, 1996.

Iannucci, Amilcare A. 'Dante's Limbo: At the Margins of Orthodoxy.' *Dante and the Unorthodox: The Aesthetics of Transgression.* Ed. James Miller. Forthcoming.

Jonasson, Catherine, and Jim Shedden, eds. *Recent Work from the Canadian Avant-Garde.* Toronto: Art Gallery of Ontario, 1988.

Knelman, Martin. *This Is Where We Came In: The Career and Character of Canadian Film.* Toronto: McClelland and Stewart, 1977.

Leavey, Peggy Dymond. *The Movie Years: A Nostalgic Remembrance of Canada's Film-Making Capital, Trenton, Ontario, 1917–1934.* Belleville, ON: Mika Publishing Co., 1989.

Lever, Yves. *Le cinéma de la Révolution tranquille: De Panoramique à Valerie.* Montréal: Y. Lever, 1991.

– *Histoire générale du cinéma au Québec.* Montréal: Boreal, 1995.

Lowder, Rose, ed. *The Visual Aspect: Recent Canadian Experimental Films.* Avignon: Éditions des Archives du film expérimental, 1991.

MacDonald, Scott. 'Text As Image in Some Recent North American Avant-Garde Films.' *Afterimage* 13.8 (March 1986): 9–20.

Magder, Ted. *Canada's Hollywood: The Canadian State and Feature Films.* Toronto: University of Toronto Press, 1993.

Marsolais, Gilles. *Le cinéma canadien.* Montréal: Éditions du Jour, 1968.

Morris, Peter. *Embattled Shadows: A History of Canadian Cinema, 1895–1939.* Montreal: McGill-Queen's University Press, 1978.

– *The Film Companion.* Toronto: Irwin, 1984.

Pageau, Pierre, and Yves Lever. *Cinémas canadien et québécois.* Montréal: Collège Ahuntsic, 1977.

Posner, Michael. *Canadian Dreams: The Making and Marketing of Independent Films.* Toronto: Douglas and McIntyre, 1993.

Pratley, Gerald. *Torn Sprockets: The Uncertain Projection of Canadian Film.* London: Associated University Press, 1987.

Rist, Peter Harry, ed. *Guide to the Cinema(s) of Canada*. Westport, CT: Greenwood Press, 2001.

Shedden, Jim, ed. *Presence and Absence: The Films of Michael Snow, 1956–1991*.
Toronto: Knopf, 1995.

Shipman, Nell. *The Silent Screen and My Talking Heart: An Autobiography*. Boise,
ID: Boise State University Press, 1988.

Singleton, Charles. *The Divine Comedy. Paradiso. Commentary*. Princeton:
Princeton University Press, 1975.

Slide, Anthony. *Early Women Directors*. New York: Da Capo, 1984.

Smith, Judith. 'Nell Shipman: Girl Wonder from God's Country.' *Cinema
Canada* 51 (Nov./Dec. 1978): 35–8.

Testa, Bart. *The Avant-Garde and Primitive Cinema*. Toronto: The Funnel, 1985.

– *Back and Forth: Early Cinema and the Avant-Garde*. Toronto: Art Gallery of
Ontario, 1992.

– *Spirit in the Landscape*. Toronto: Art Gallery of Ontario, 1989.

Véronneau, Pierre, and Piers Handling, eds. *Self Portrait: Essays on the Canadian and Québec Cinemas*. Ottawa: Canadian Film Institute, 1980.

Walker, Joseph, and Juanita Walker. 'Danger in God's Country.' *American
Cinematographer* 66.5 (May 1985): 34–42.

– *The Light on Her Face*. Hollywood: ASC Press, 1984.

Dante and Cinema: Film across a Chasm

BART TESTA

Dante and cinema? The *Commedia* and cinema? The discussion hardly has begun, but several film artists have already spoken first, and spoken of an abyssal chasm of time. These hazardous notes concern three 'artist's films' by Stan Brakhage, Michelangelo Antonioni, and Bruce Elder.[1] The first hazard is that these notes cannot be remotely responsible to the immense reserve of philological and interpretative scholarship on Dante. Another is referring to 'artist's films' (Brakhage's coinage), a term without critical currency in cinema studies, where such works are slotted as 'avant-garde' or 'experimental' cinema. But that draws a genre ghetto around films, and such definitions are not at issue here. In any case, these films – not 'a cinema,' but single films – do have a relation of radical otherness to the movie industry. It is in this place of alterity that the abyss of time, of history, between Dante and cinema opens initially to view.

Among the classic texts of the Western canon, Dante must seem most remote to filmmaking. The lyric poet who wrote the great epic of medieval Catholicism, Dante could not be further removed in his forms and sensibility, compositional élan, cosmology, and (especially) in the poet's completeness, from the modernity to which cinema belongs. I am not just referring to the fables promulgated by our media theorists. These fables of film technology tell us that a fragmented and phenomenalist visual culture, secularism, and the languages of instrumental reason determined cinema's invention and all that flowed across our century's screens since. These fables are true and their truth militates against the very idea of Dante as plausible in cinema. Nonetheless, even if we could fantasize some reform that would free filmmaking from these techno-cultural determinations, there is an epochal abyss between the poet and film still older, denser, deeper, and darker than the meaning of 'modern media.' A chasm was cut out of European time at the Baroque, the age of Shakespeare, of Milton, of Bernini, and Velasquez. In film, it halted even Sergei Eisenstein – the great self-primitivizing artist of classic film history – and held him forever in the Baroque Mexico that formed his later, 1930s imaginary, as we can vividly see in his masterful film of ancient Rus, *Ivan the Terrible*, fifteen years on. Consider, too, the post-war European filmmakers who resist the magnetic modern literary realism of Dickens and Balzac, Verga and Zola, that gave us Hollywood and socialist realism, French poetic realism and Italian neo-realism alike. For instance, recall Bergman and Tarkovsky attempting to traverse the chasm and their results, the most vivid religious film-works of a modern Baroque: *The Seventh Seal* and *Cries and Whispers*, *Andrei Rublev* and *Nostalghia* – extraordinary and beautiful films, but suggesting to us no prospect for Dante and cinema. There are, nonetheless, a rare few; Carl Theodore Dreyer and Robert Bresson, northern Europeans both, Protestant in spirit, strict modernists in style, slip beneath the bar of the Baroque. The only other filmmaker of the post-war era for whom such candidacy is plausible, if only for his willing it so titanically, and because of his intense 'linguistic' saturation, is Pier Paolo Pasolini. But the discussion of these filmmakers and Dante has hardly begun – and only with Pasolini is the name of Dante even brought up (Sitney, '*Accattone*' and *Vital Crises* 173–84).

Dante and cinema, then?

The films drawing me to this question in these hazardous notes do not belong to the tiny catalogue just enumerated. These films do not envision Dante crossing the abyss of time to us. They do not try to bridge time or to 'reconstruct' the Dantean text in modern terms. Instead, Brakhage's *The Dante Quartet* (1987), Antonioni's *Il deserto rosso* (1964), and Elder's *The Book of All the Dead* (1978–96) exacerbate their modernity, and they make the abyssal chasm between us and Dante, between his poem and their films, the issue. They do so by making time itself their problem.

Perhaps, to begin with Brakhage, one should speak initially of an imaginary, or reimagined, Dante, a Dante of space. Brakhage's Dante is imagined within the intensities of a single subjectivity. *The Dante Quartet* proposes to its viewers Brakhage's vaunting ambition of imaging the *Commedia* paradoxically: as an artist's interiority that can be known again, but for the first time, as kin to Dante's. The film is extremely compressed, just eight minutes. It is in four parts, divided by titles handwritten on the screen, by frame format, and by imagery; there are two for 'hell' and one each for 'purgatory' and 'heaven.' Each frame is an 'abstract' hand-painted directly on the celluloid surface, using various stocks, from IMAX 70 mm, to 35 mm and 16 mm, and then the whole printed on 35 mm.[2] The images, in full-sized projection, possess tremendous vividness and depth and texture. The effect seduces the viewer's imagination instantly, so that each shot seems like an interior landscape streaming over the screen. In his brief published statement on the film, Brakhage writes that the film

> demonstrates the earthly conditions of 'Hell,' 'Purgatory' (or Transition) and 'Heaven' (or 'existence is song,' which is the closest I'd presume upon heaven from my experience) as well as the mainspring of/from 'Hell' (Hell Split Flexion) in four parts which are inspired by the closed-eye or hypnagogic vision created by these emotional states. ('Note')

That Brakhage can claim his film 'demonstrates' the 'earthly conditions' corresponding to the sacred poem speaks from Brakhage's belief that Dante's work also speaks of interior conditions of the poet's soul, and he implies that these have been unfolded into the epic form of the *Commedia*. Film might, then, speak of the same inner conditions in Brakhage's own 'earthbound' self and give rise to a work that is a plausible analogon of the poem. Another notion Brakhage broaches in this text might be regarded as methodological: 'hypnagogic vision created by these emotional states' explains why such an analogon appears possible to the film artist's envisioning. *Behind* our eyes is a vision of the emotions so dense and complex it may be said to compress hell, purgatory, and heaven within us, and the artist can make that vision manifest in film. To suggest why Brakhage could proffer this explanation requires we accept, as a preliminary, this artist's aesthetic – or the essential myth of it.

The radical daring of Brakhage's making a film earnestly entitled *The Dante Quartet*, and the significance of the ambition, might be adumbrated by recalling that Dante signifies to us a totality. A whole civilization in all its dimensions is in the *Commedia*. This recognition gives rise to the certainty the poem forms in us that it is true epic. From this angle, Brakhage's ambition must appear ridiculous, and a dire requirement the modern artist's sets himself, that a whole civilization must be made both to rest upon and arise anew from his solitary subjectivity, seems desperate, and in a characteristically modern way. Yet, Dante was also a lyric poet, for all that happens in his poem occurs to him. The panorama of the epic is also the single event of the poet's spiritual experience, his vision, his redemption. All that is spoken in the poem is the event spanning a liturgical week, the Easter Week of 1300. That radically abbreviated temporal arc of the *Commedia* is the symbol of Dante's lyric. What permits Dante this symbol is Neoplatonic temporality. The unity of time, *sub specie aeternitatis*, and the final unreality of historical narrative, or concatenate time, when posed against the vision of *Paradiso* are the features of the epic-lyric duality of the poem in another angle. It is a duality resolved in the totality of a narrative enfolded by another order of time, the time of sacral order itself. And, guided by Virgil and then by Beatrice, the poet traverses this order as a totality. This is the order, as critics say, of Augustinian time; narrative history is the *saecula senescens* enfolded by divine time (Voegelin, *Science* 92–3; *Ecumenic* 178). Dante reaches that order in his vision of the *Paradiso*. Hence, in the poem's progress, the narration leads the reader toward and through a vast unfolded *spatialized* moment. There are many stories and characters, but the poet passes through them as a vast dilation of space, and, so, while there are episodes, the poet's traversal does not move to historical-narrative time. It unfolds as journey in space, a totality around a centre, not of succession. The poem's vast volume is a synchrony.

The first impact *The Dante Quartet* has on its viewer, as I said, is its vast spatiality and film-space as an intense mobility, as if we were imaginatively rocketing through a landscape. This is not, however, the perspectival space of narrative painting. The imagery is a space of layers and events that emerge out of and merge with a wide and vast spatial tumult that stills and moves, converges and severs from a whole never quite grasped. The visual composition of *The Dante Quartet* produces an 'all-at-once' temporal effect, a cinematic synchrony, despite its great variety and extraordinary sense of motion.

A film must materially proceed through the passage of frames past the projector light, but Brakhage's composition thwarts that material effect of a successive time-line of frames through music-like editing and the highly complex painted-on-film spatiality that plants the viewer firmly 'in the moment.' The taut dynamism of visual forms halts in a streaming image – Brakhage calls it 'moving visual thinking' – here of tumult and finally of the paradoxically mobilized stasis of light and colour. In all this, Brakhage inherits the radical intentions of abstract expressionists; his films reinvent these American modernist painters' pioneering 'overall effect.' Instead of the subordinating play of figure and ground, of movement of the viewer's eye from motif to motif – that is, the narrative of visual relations, the working of *istoria* painting absorbs in the Renaissance and fully internalizes in the Baroque – Barnett Newman, Jackson Pollock, and Mark Rothko tangle motif into 'painterly' dynamism that moves the eye materially to different, interior rhythms. This mode of painting is characterized by a spatialized temporality of a terrible intensity, of an intensity *inside* the moment of maximum torsion of visual forms – the skein of Pollock's 'drip paintings,' the single tear or 'zip' of Newman's *Stations of the Cross*, the frame-volume-light dialectic of Rothko's stilled volumes of colour.

This American painting speaks a totalism that is describable formally but, finally, unnameable and radically resistant to paraphrase. Hence the notorious rumour that it is 'about nothing' (Krauss 237–8). The deep interpretive problem, from the start (the 1940s), was not really 'abstraction' but what E.A. Carmean, Jr, terms 'the subjects of the artist' (30–9). These painters repeatedly denied that their works were abstract, and they often named and described them in religious or mythic terms, in the cadences of epic, in their quest for recovering the arche-language of visual forms. This was an art that sought to cross the abyss of history to recuperate primal visual truths, whose historic names are clothed in classical, biblical, or primitive languages, but this was art made in the belief that the artist can slip under, can detour around, linguistic representations, worn down by modern historicism, through which we recall them.

Heir to this tradition in film, Brakhage's solution to the problem of 'the subjects of the artist' was to declare for the subjectivity of the artist, an argument drawn from modern American poetics, and especially from the poet Charles Olson (Sitney, *Visionary* 173–200; Elder, *Brakhage* 351–61 and passim). To read his note to *The Dante Quartet* in light of theorization in his *Metaphors on Vision* leads us to recognize that Brakhage believes that 'emotional states' produce in the body effects that, in the eyes, are registered as 'hypnagogic' or closed-eye vision. Brakhage's claims for the truth of closed-eye insight that such internal visual experiences generate are that they permit the artist to produce filmic rhythmic forms and imagery that are new analogues of great poetic works. The filmic equivalent of the 'all-at-once' effect in *The Dante Quartet* arises from interior states of hell, purgatory, and heaven – or 'song' (i.e., the dissolution of emotion into an ecstasis of music/rhythm) – that possess the film artist in a lyrical register, and that yield the film in colour and light and form and rhythm.

For Brakhage, then, the internal experience of the subject permits a lyric recuperation of a Dantean totality to arise from the most intimate springs of Brakhage's own art-making – his body, his eyes, his emotions, his hand-to-celluloid (these regarded as a taut unity) – and so the *Commedia* arises 'again' and yet for the 'first time' in *The Dante Quartet* because what was *in* Dante arose to articulation in the *Commedia* without deviation; and what arises in the modern artist by living and attending in his art can be the analogous because these experiences are always already there in us. In this conception, the epic collapses onto the lyrical and Brakhage's film is not remaking or interpreting Dante in its articulation, but its radical compression projects the total inner space whence the epic poem arises. The images of *The Dante Quartet*, like those of Rothko, Pollock, and Newman, are, therefore, redolent of vast interior landscape because they seek powerfully to impose on the viewer a sense of a totality of visual space, of all possible inner space, of a spiritually charged virtuality. Here, as Newman says, 'It happens.'

For all that severs us from Dante, such is our culture's virtually subcutaneous, even atavistic, sense of the *Commedia* – this spatialized totality. Beyond this, what comes to expression in Brakhage's film is not an analogue of what *signifies* in the poem, not the representation, the symbolism, the compositional system, and surely Brakhage's film is not adaptation of themes or doctrines. But the analogue is a making manifest of the intensity of experience immanent in the poem and now immanent in film. Analogue of what happened there, in the poem, *The Dante Quartet* condenses into eight visionary minutes what unfolded as great epic. This is the myth of Brakhage's aesthetic brought to bear on this film.

In the same note quoted above, Brakhage remarks the film was made over six years and after '37 years of studying *The Divine Comedy*.' What did he learn from that study? Brakhage drew upon poets and ways of reading poetry, to forge the Brakhagian myth of filmmaking (Elder, *Brakhage* passim). That myth criss-crosses American modernist poetics with the myth of abstract expressionism, and both share the ambition of American mythopoesis (Sitney, *Visionary* 153–62, 195–227), which I have just roughly sketched. This mythopoeic project in American art and literature possesses an ethic and a pathos. The ethic is individualist and Pascalian: the artist wagers that he or she can, in solitude, come to be within range of the kind of totality that the most ancient myths and texts embody. Dante is one such range. The wager falls on what wrestling the art medium the artist seizes (or seizes him, for this is the

Augustinian ethic of vocation revisited) demands of him or her. And what 'it' will happen, the wager made, will happen despite a modern culture that has lost the capacity otherwise to know, imagine, or remember, much less speak again, what Dante is.

A way to read Dante in this light is remotely plausible. Not everything Dante expressed was owed to a richly differentiated symbolism of the culture in which he lived. Dante did not write the *Commedia* wholly out of himself and his genius arose within the condition of an order and knowledge, and his poem, in this sense, was given to him to write by the tradition available to him.[3] Nonetheless, the limit to that tradition is, in a paradoxically humbling way, enunciated in the *Paradiso* when Beatrice says that all that has come before is an illusion, a sort of story tailored to human consciousness unprepared to receive the true vision. The poet testifies to having the true vision now and that it recapitulates the whole long epic. But he cannot write that recapitulation. His poem (in a way) collapses into a luminous noetic experience given to him alone, collapses into the transcendental intensity of a lyric kind that cannot be spoken.

The pathos: the wager that abstract expressionists made, and that Brakhage makes today, is that by giving themselves to art-making, conceived as a privileged access to the self that does not otherwise know itself, the artist can again imagine a totality properly analogous to a work like Dante's *Commedia*, and accede to that noetic intensity from which the panorama of the poem arises. Brakhage cannot imagine Dante's mystical vision in *Paradiso*, as his note freely admits. It is not given to him any more than the medieval culture of the poem is given again. He bets nonetheless that he has imaged its spatialized time truly, however, and he paints its analogue on film. This wager is what moves us to the film and its truth, whether we accept the myth of his art or not. The pathos of this wager runs through the whole of the problem of the 'subjects of the artist' in abstract expressionism. Its mythopoeic intensities are not a search for a symbolic armature, for a recovery of the whole in articulate form. Critics may read Newman's 'zips' in *Stations of the Cross* through the lens of a theologized existentialism (Polcari 197–202) or even a 'remystifying' Gnostic theology (Taylor 83–95), or regard Rothko's luminous canvases as a tragic light emanating from the tension of the divine and human – but these efforts are rightly suspect. There is a dilemma here, hence the pathos. Such a symbolism – like the cross attributed to Newman's *Stations of the Cross* – if achieved in the art's making, would potentially join it to tradition, but only once again in order to subject this art to modern historicism, and reduce it to 'iconography.' Then, it becomes illustration. If not this option, the effort constantly threatens collapse into solipsistic delusion, into a type of internal cruelty that putatively destroyed Rothko (Bersani and Dutoit 139–45). The subjectivizing of the arche-language and mythic primals in this way, toward the intense condensation of classic epics to the inner point of the artist, is a monstrous prospect, a wager with grave dangers. This is the pathos that arises from the ethic of focusing a classic tradition onto the single sensibility, onto a solitude, that of the artist.

Brakhage's 'all is song' offers the equivalence of the musical form of the work itself and a brief liberation into contemplation. *The Dante Quartet* reaches this kind of heaven, for really watching *this* behind our eyes witnesses final bliss, again for the first time what Dante's vision was. If we can even imagine it. The filmed moment is only minutes long, however, and it is materially made. It is a hopeful fiction. It is not heaven (Brakhage admits) but a cinematically made intimation. It witnesses to Brakhage's immense vitality that he can admit the dilemma into his art, and he can do so without irony and without breaking himself on it. Now, this pathos also exemplifies the impossibility of Dante and cinema. The wager taken, *The Dante Quartet* is one of precious few works of American cinema one can place beside Newman's *Stations of the Cross* without embarrassment. And it is a great modern Dante film. But it must also be regarded, like Newman's series, to manifest the deprival of all Dante represents of cosmology, authority, symbolism, and noetic experience not our own. The abyss that opens between him and modern artists opens as well across the iconoclastic expanse of those paintings, across the rapture of this Brakhage film. It falls to Brakhage to meet that deprival by wagering on the fragility of a solitude – however expansive – by making of something earnestly entitled *The Dante Quartet*.

There is another kind of intensified solitude, another pathos, and another, diametrically different cinematic time in Antonioni's *Il deserto rosso*. Should we regard *Il deserto rosso* as Antonioni's *Inferno*? A strong temptation. The film begins with an infernal image: a smokestack in close-up emitting poisonous yellow smoke. The grating, pulsing thunder of industry that accompanies it is an appalling sound. The sequence proceeds to show a woman stumble confusedly along a ditch, and then she stares – we see her in close-up – out over a poisoned landscape, the camera panning so close to the smoking grey sludge of it that her vision fills the frame. The images are of Ravenna, where Dante was exiled and where the final cantos of the *Paradiso* were composed. The location for two of the film's important scenes is the Via Alighieri, whose terminus is Dante's grave.

But the temptation should be resisted. The *Inferno* would be, in a way, too reassuring a final comparison for this Antonioni film. Surrounded by ecological catastrophe, the woman of that first sequence (she is Giuliana, the heroine) would seem on this reading a consciousness passing through, holding encounters with damned spectres, and the film's images would attenuate into a secular equivalent of a diorama of hell. We can readily, and with some legitimacy, interpret *Il deserto rosso* just this way, perhaps because its *mise-en-scène* has expanded – by metastasis – to become commonplace in our contemporary cinema. Such an account of *Il deserto rosso* would, nonetheless, be impoverished. As imposing as its lurid spaces are to our eyes, it is a film of time. Giuliana is not a consciousness passing ghostly through the film's *mise-en-scène*. She suffers and struggles, and comes to realization for us as subject in process.

Giuliana is married to an engineer, Ugo, who is not at all uncaring (though irrelevant), has a son, Valerio, who puts her through a cruel trial of separation; and she takes a lover, Corrado, who tempts her, and thereby finally strengthens her. If much of the film does concern encounters with ruined ghosts (and a major imagistic passage is devoted to this [Arrowsmith 99]), and if Corrado can be convincingly assimilated to Dante's Ulysses (Sitney, *Vital Crises* 214–15), Giuliana also encounters other, much more ambiguous figures like herself – a worker, his wife, people on journeys – struggling to go or stay somewhere. She is not wholly alone, despite her solitude; Antonioni has singled her out from a procession of souls, without Giuliana realizing it.

In taking the film to be *Purgatorio*, I want to emphasize that the filmmaker has recognized that Dante's poem in this canticle exists in time in a way the *Inferno* and *Paradiso* do not. Purgatory's souls are in motion, here tangent with earthly temporal experience. Giuliana is likewise, though unwillingly, painfully, moving in time and in spiritual trial and tribulation; she is in motion, however hesitant. Antonioni takes her drama as the centre of the film, as exemplary of historical time, of the time of transition, between a lost paradise, which figures in Giuliana's 'Sardinian fantasy' and in her inchoate desires and fears, and what now seems hell itself.

As he does in all his films, Antonioni places his protagonist in an 'in-between' time, suspended between a past that has departed and a future that is not yet arrived (Antonioni 82–4, 283–98). However, the modern execration of this 'between' is that one lives before uncertain destination – the order of time is unknown to modernity – and it is carried under the burden of a terrible sense of loss, the loss of earthly paradise, which appears under the confusing guise of fantasy. In William Arrowsmith's rich formulation:

> Antonioni explores this perennial fantasy of the paradisal worlds which contains so much of us that we are constantly in danger of thinking it our true selves, what we once were before being expelled from the bright Garden of Being. Philosophically, its power and appeal are in our bones as the old human hunger of 'Becoming' for 'Being.' It is Plato's sun, Spinoza's God, or Heidegger's dasein. Erotically, it is Freud's 'oceanic feeling,' the warmth and security of the womb. Culturally, it is animistic feeling – the individual's absolute 'oneness' with nature and society, so irresistible to those who fear that they have fallen out of culture into mere fragmentary existence, that nature and the 'gods' are dead. Politically, it is the appeal of millennialism in any form, the ideal past projected as the future. (89)

Antonioni resists this fantasy. Dante enfolded purgatorial time by hell and paradise. Antonioni, confronting the chasm between the poet and the modern, finds this impossible, and there are two consequences: he folds both hell and heaven into his purgatory as images isolated, framed, emphatically beautiful, made compositionally atemporal. But, otherwise, time in his film is presented, I want to say, naked and accented, made into the form of painful suspension. This is the case at the film's most intimate level. The shooting and cutting in *Il deserto rosso* is the opposite of *The Dante Quartet*; time hangs suspended between moments of dramatic or spatial crystallization. The pauses and *longeurs* – so notorious an aspect of Antonioni's de-dramatized filmic narration – here inscribe the purgatorial suspension of Giuliana into every sequence, determine every measurement taken of the transitions between shots. *Il deserto rosso* is a film of pained intervals.

But this is hardly to suggest a signifying equivalence or analogy between Dante and Antonioni. The allusions the filmmaker weaves into his film instead propose to us a chasm of imagining that, by the end, becomes abysmal. Let me offer two examples. P. Adams Sitney, who has lucidly explored the Dantean motifs of *Il deserto rosso*, remarks,

> [Dante's] image for the earthly paradise, Eden at the summit of the mount

of Purgatory, turns on a simile to the once beautiful harbour of Ravenna. Dante described the pine forest in *Purgatorio* 28 (ll. 7–21) thus:

A sweet breeze that had no variation itself
was striking on my brow
with the force only of a gentle wind,
by which the fluttering boughs
all bent freely towards the quarter
where the holy mountain casts its first shadow;
yet were they not so deflected from their upright state
that the little birds among the tops
ceased practicing their arts,
but singing greeted the morning hours
with full joy among the leaves,
which kept such a burden to their rhymes
as gather from branch to branch
through the pine forest on Chassi's shore
when Aeolus lets forth Sirocco.

Chiassi was the port of Ravenna. The Edenic locus has become the centre of oil refineries at the mouth of the Po. The very factory Ugo directs is surrounded by pines, but the film makes abundantly clear that Dante's Arcadian site has become a phantasmagoria of foul pollution. (*Vital Crises* 213–14)

At the very end of the film, Giuliana returns to the smokestack with her small son, Valerio, and in the final dialogue explains:

Valerio: Why is the smoke yellow?
Giuliana: Because it is poison.
Valerio: Then, if a bird flied into it, he dies.
Guiliana: Yes, but the birds have learned not to fly through there any more. (cited in Sitney, *Vital Crises* 217)

This is the image of an earthly paradise lost, of the lost Chiassi that could become so exquisite an imagery for Dante. This final speech acknowledges the abyss that history has opened in space – in this case, a particular spot. The moment of meditation on the site – at the same place on earth, complete with the birds, but substituted for their song the clang of machinery – announces the irrecoverable character of that place as a resource for the artist. History has turned the world into deprival. Yet, Giuliana can still be heard here, Sitney says, 'catechizing her son.' She has come to where the film opens to acknowledge the purgatory of our modernity, and this speech follows, after an ellipsis, directly on another, spoken to an uncomprehending Turkish sailor, in which she declares, 'I have to think that all that happens to me is my life.'

It is sometimes asked whether the *Commedia* was written retrospectively, after Dante's possession of his vision, so that he knows where he will arrive and is already the enabled poet who can write *Paradiso*. Or, is Dante writing the poem as he advances spiritually and taking *his* wager that he will become the artist who can finish his poem? It is Gilson who advances the former view and modern commentators who emphasize the latter. For Gilson, Dante is the great philosophical poet and his poem is a great compendium written with a supreme confidence in the tradition, and this goes to the sacred sense of time and order and the mystique of noetic experience. For modern interpreters, Dante is much more a poet who struggles through acts of consciousness and creation, and so he writes in biographical time and the struggle of consciousness becomes the sense of the *Commedia*. In a way, Brakhage's wager in making *The Dante Quartet* accents, despite everything that places him within a modern conception, Gilson's sense of Dante writing *sub specie aeternitatis*, that the artist is *now* capable, at least of making the wager. Antonioni's ascetic conception is more purely in the modern mode: Giuliana's time is her biographical time, a purgatory suspended between the hell that séems to surround her and the paradise she fantasizes.

There are two solitudes at stake. The time *between* leaves us suspended in history, an 'epic' solitude that pulls us from the spaces that (we imagine) once grounded us, modernity's axial point at the 'retreat and return of origin' (Foucault, *Order of Things* 328–40). The solitude of Giuliana herself, however, is the aspect of this collective narrative (Arrowsmith 87) that impresses us. We find her, in the film's fourth sequence, in a small empty shop on the Via Alighieri, an old street where history does not intrude, which is perhaps why we find her there alone. Corrado visits her. It is only their second encounter. Distressed and moving anxiously around the room, hugging walls, Giuliana worries that Ugo has told Corrado that she may have attempted suicide (Ugo has not), and Corrado, trying to become better acquainted, launches into a suggestive abridgement of his life story (and his role as the film's Odysseus, as Sitney shows, begins here, with his lies and tales of restless travel). As the fragmented conversation proceeds, Giuliana passes beneath two large rectangular patches of paint – samples on a wall of the unfinished shop. They are an allusion to Rothko and recall that Antonioni wanted first to name the film 'Blue and Green,' the colours in this film of fantasized spiritual rest and spiritual motionlessness. The Rothko wager is reshaped as the film proceeds, as Giuliana's fantasy of paradise, which she narrates gently to her son, Valerio, who is temporarily bedridden. The fantasy places her, refigured as a young girl, outside history in a lovely cove; and there she encounters a ship that approaches and mysteriously retreats; then she hears voices and becomes aware that the rocks surrounding her are like flesh. Who is singing? she asks. Everything.

Interpretations of this sequence abound, but here we might regard it, as Arrowsmith's remark above suggests, as a parody in pathetic earnest of *Paradiso*. A parody, because we recognize Giuliana is telling this tale to comfort herself and her son – to allegorize their unity, which Valerio will very soon cruelly sever. This will send her desperately into Corrado's arms, where their sexual embrace will, temporarily, replay the beach fantasy. The failure of the paradisal cycle – like all fantasy of union, erotic relief is brief – sends her into the night and brings her back to the shop on the Via Alighieri for a scene whose symmetry with the first is strongly deliberate. Giuliana stands firm before Corrado and declares – hesitantly, then fiercely – for the rightness of her suffering, her troubled struggle, her anguished solitude. She at last dismisses Corrado, and enters into a dark dockside passage before emerging to deliver her testimony to the Turkish sailor: this is my life and all that happens to me.

Il deserto rosso is a prelude and Arrowsmith terms it Giuliana's 'individuation.' Her shop is a critical chamber on a road whose termini are invisible; though we perhaps know this to be Dante's road, we do not know where it leads. Antonioni's composition of the Via Alighieri visually 'turns a corner' and halts perspective. This is of a piece with his de Chirico motif in *Il deserto rosso*: medieval Italy appears again, but as mysterious, a stilled zone, both comforting (given the modernity his film offers as an alternative) and disturbing, unreachable but somehow there. When Giuliana first leaves her shop, in the film's fourth sequence, she immediately collapses; Antonioni blurs the image's focus, makes it grow uncertain. The passage is akin to the composition that the desperate Giuliana much later sees from the window of Corrado's hotel room, a dark, shadowed ancient street. When she at last dismisses the tempter-intruder and leaves her shop the second time, finally, Giuliana becomes the heroine of her own story; she has passed through the imagistic hell and her own paradisal fantasies into her own biography. But, as Sitney's tracking of the direct allusion at the end of the film suggests, the new earthly paradise at the end of *Purgatorio* can no longer be regarded as a stop on the way to paradise itself. The closing sequence closes a circle with the first, and Giuliana is at the portal of purgatory again – time will not stop.

At the centre of Canadian artist Bruce Elder's massive film cycle (its total running time exceeds forty hours), *The Book of All the Dead*, there is also a *Purgatorio*, *Consolations* (1988), a fourteen-hour segment of the cycle with the allusive Heideggerian subtitle *Love Is an Art of Time*. Time does not stop here either, but it radically decelerates. On one side of *Consolations* are nine heterogeneously styled films of various lengths representing the whole of Elder's production between 1975 and 1985. On the other are seven homogeneously composed pieces of uniform length (about 100 minutes each) grouped collectively as *Exultations: In Light of the Great Giving* (1990–6). It was upon exhibiting these later works that Elder announced the Dantean design for *The Book of All the Dead*.[4] Almost twenty years after its inception, *The Book of All the Dead* fell into a sequence of three 'regions': the earlier films become 'The System of Dante's Hell'; *Consolations* becomes *Purgatorio*; and *Exultations, Paradiso*.

Taken *en masse*, and allowing Elder his terminal redaction, *The Book of All the Dead* must be regarded as the most ambitious Dante film-work ever attempted. It is also the most excessively Baroque and intellectually overburdened film, weighted by its own modernity. In its complexity and stylistic variegation, the cycle must also be regarded as postmodernist; it is radically a departure from *The Dante Quartet*'s compression and Brakhage's modernist wager.[5] Instead of committing to an artist's internal imagination as Brakhage does, Elder reaches outward to compose his *Commedia* by amassing a vast assemblage of fragments, of wide-ranging appropriations and intertexts, operationally arrayed through heterogeneous 'polyphonic' formal systems.[6]

What will first impress and delight (and eventually threaten to exhaust) a dedicated viewer of *The Book of All the Dead* is the degree to which it is a work of erudition. Its vast curricula of allusions, its compendia of formal usages, its architectonics of structural remakings, all challenge conventional cinematic reception. And everywhere the cycle is punctuated with parodies both earnest and ridiculous. It is a film searching for totalism, looking for a final construct, a myth of completion that might be *equivalent* to Dante's totality. *The Book of All the Dead* is doomed to failure, accepts this fate as the cost of meeting the *Commedia*'s epic dimension, and refuses, finally, to be finished. As though it were a commandment, Elder quotes Pound's prescription that to be epic a work must include history (Shedden 99). The cycle is obsessively responsible to that obligation and its staggering problematic. Dante wrote in a believed totality *sub specie aeternitatis* enfolding history. Moderns believe history to be of active human making, and to enfold anything worth knowing. Dante knew assured hermeneutic criteria; modernity, only historicism's hermeneutics of suspicion. Indeed, modernity shatters everywhere on questions of history, of meaning, of the whole. This division is our history, and it is subtended, at best, by ideologies of historical progress; or, in Nietzsche's corrosive mediation perfectly glossed by George Grant, we figure ourselves within 'time as history' (Grant).

Elder makes this problematic Poundian ambition his guiding preoccupation, and this is plain from the early twenty-four-minute miniature of the whole cycle, *1857 (Fool's Gold)* (1981). It juxtaposes Lucretius, Pound, and Defoe's *Journal of the Plague Years*, overlaying a restricted set of optically treated images of storming seas and ocean journey. It is, in a way, his one Brakhagian film, for here meaning arises from vision in synchronous tumult, though, in other ways, *1857* is obviously a construct of textual allusion and technical visual processing hurling into time-as-history. If *The Dante Quartet* arises out of the artist's faith in imagination to overcome time internally, to rouse a space analogous to Dante's totality, Elder's *Book* is a twenty-years' cumulative, highly wrought segment serving the prospect of a postmodern hermeneutic cinema crossing over the historic chasm between the poet and us. What results is a great vault of large fragmentary *excursi*, mosaic-like structures, amassed allusions, and argumentation. The immense effort staggers gigantically toward *assembling* an epic of total redaction; it is to be a redaction of an archive of the modern itself, a huge ideogrammatic repertoire.

It is a *magnum opus*, like Pound's *Cantos*, built on and of ruins, in the sense Walter Benjamin prophesied. The salient cinematic features of the cycle – elaborate sound-and-image polyphonic montage, serial structuration, dense intertextual discursivity – all these arise from Elder's conscious awareness of the modern 'destitution' (his word) when an artist thinks himself beside Dante, and sees a great chasm of time.

Beginning with its title, *The Book of All the Dead*, Elder's cycle is founded on a consciousness (where Brakhage is heroically innocent) that he is a belated artist, and will never resurrect the Dantean vision again. Elder should, then, be paired with Antonioni, and his protagonist Giuliana, but in no way with Brakhage's vitalist-imaginative hero.[7]

So, now, erudition, energetic attentiveness, and grasping intelligence are the resources on which the postmodern artist relies, hoping to rework the modern inheritance and to stir it toward an immense – and immensely implausible – epic of recuperation. Elder assumes from the enterprise Pound embodies a presumption (however forlorn) that film can traverse an entire epoch in one work. This project is to be discovered in the ruins of time and, rooted in a negative theology, sets out the incommensurability of his construction with what it desires to make manifest. Like other large contemporary serial film-works, like Hans-Jurgen Syberberg's *Our Hitler: A Film from Germany*, Hollis Frampton's *Magellan*, and (pointedly in respect to Dante) Peter Greenaway's *A TV Dante*, *The Book of All the Dead* is erected within conditions of postmodernity. Its resources, and its laboured rigours, are conditioned by what Michel Foucault describes in connection with Flaubert's *The Temptation of St. Anthony*:

> Possibly, Flaubert was responding to an experience of the fantastic which was singularly modern and relatively unknown before his time, to the discovery of a new imaginative space in the nineteenth century. This domain is no longer the night, the sleep of reason ... but, on the contrary, wakefulness, untiring attention, zealous erudition, and constant vigilance. Henceforth, the visionary experience arises from the black and white surface of printed signs, from the closed and dusty volume that opens with a flight of forgotten words; fantasies are carefully deployed in the hushed library, with its columns of books, with its titles assigned to shelves to form a tight enclosure ... The imaginary now resides between the book and the lamp ... Dreams are no longer summoned with closed eyes, but in reading, and a true image is now a product of learning: it derives from words spoken in the past, exact recensions, the amassing of minute facts, monument reduced to infinitesimal fragments, and the reproductions of reproductions ... Only the assiduous clamour created by repetition can transmit to us what only happened once. (*Language* 90–1)

Elder's cycle begins with a fifty-five-minute autobiographical prelude, which concludes with the virtual death of the artist coincident with the discovery of his vocation. Made of split screens and a polyphonic soundtrack, *The Art of Worldly Wisdom* (1979) is no epiphanic disclosure of, nor lyrical paean to, sensibility. Instead, it offers a broken portrait of a confused student of his art come to the end of his rope. It finishes with Elder naked in a mirror wasted with disease. As his note to the film says, this is his 'dark wood' ('Note' 23): a mirror in the artist's sickroom; here is the modern protagonist – 'a body totally imprinted by history and the process of history's destruction of the body' (Foucault, *Language* 148). This overwritten and wrecked persona that Elder bears in *Worldly Wisdom* will, in the next three geometrically lengthening films, multiply into a procession of dozens of fictional pilgrims, each with a tale of misery woven amidst the innumerable philosophers and poets whose snatched texts fill Elder's long films' soundtracks and flake his images with supertitles. The artist-protagonist is one among a vast pilgrimage of the many.

The first extended film, the three-hour *Illuminated Texts* (1982), is a proper *Inferno*. The film is fitted with the familiar infernal motifs, and it is a black reverse cosmogony of modernity. Gradually accelerating montage tells the tale of our world-picture's construction, from the seeds of seventeenth-century rationalism and its severance from nature, through the objectification of the body, the hegemony of instrumental reason, and technological arrogance. It then arrives at their final destinations, collective and intimate: the Holocaust and the modern monadic subject, among whose discursive geniuses are Henry Adams, Jean-Paul Sartre, and Jacques Lacan, whose texts criss-cross the soundtrack in voice-over. As logical and familiar as a recurring nightmare and imaged as recognizably as a city street or a TV screen, the film's structure works out a succession of myth-forms, derived from Northrop Frye, to arrive at modern ideology's apocalypse. But, if Frye's literary typology, like Dante's theological typology, is a circle, the hermeneutic unfolded in *Illuminated Texts* is all trajectory, a cause-and-effect countdown to historic horrors that have dissolved all collective legitimacy of the epoch's subtending ideals and confident totalities. History, in any credible sense, has ended, and Elder intends his film as a millennial obituary. It ends in furious self-disintegration before finally arriving at the stasis of Elder himself, again mirrored, this time a ghostly image refracted off the gaping corridor of a Nazi concentration camp while an abrupt text from Nietzsche hovers on the surface of the screen: 'nostalgia, the wounds of returning.'

Elder is not done with hell. The eight-hour succeeding film, *Lamenta-*

tions: Monument to a Dead World (1985), traverses a second *Inferno*, this time of the modern imaginary's fondest counter-myths, counter, that is, to the rationalist ideologies of technology and historical progress. The relation between the two films is that between modernity as a socio-political event and high modernism as an imaginative resistance. The film explains that modernity is so intolerable that modernist fantasies persistently arise that the whole could be regained if the strongest souls undertake a mythopoeic quest back to origins, primals, beginnings, to a sacred regained. *Lamentations* plunges into this modernist-Romantic aspiration to the hilt, and its protagonist-pilgrims traverse back to start over within sacred precincts of history, ruined temples, ecstatic gestures. Not unlike Syberberg's German-Romantic *Our Hitler*, *Lamentations* mobilizes a majestic catalogue and powerfully rehearses promises of the cure for modern history. Built around the filmmaker's own ambivalently made trek across three continents' 'sacred spaces,' the film both indulges in the strong effects afforded by renewing rituals and simultaneously ironizes them, or rather deconstructs them.[8] The depressed realization of this film is that wherever Elder journeys, historicism has gotten there first; he cannot but recognize it, and so modernity proves again to have triumphed as our totality. This Elder calls 'The Dream of the Last Historian' (the subtitle of part one of *Lamentations*). Nowhere else in contemporary filmmaking is the imaginative effect of Foucault's 'constant vigilance' more rigorously realized than in Elder's corrosion of the pathos stemming from irrationalist nostalgias of modernism's counter-myths.

Illuminated Texts was, in a sense, an anguished replica and update of the classic structure of Dante's *Inferno*. *Lamentations*, however, with its full panoply of Baroque modern-filmic ordnance, is finally more penetratively Dantean in its ironies. It is the seductiveness of the damned at their most beautiful, erotic, and pathetically ennobled that sorely tests and tempts Dante's pilgrim.[9] By offering the viewer the strongest mythopoeic seductions a modern artist might offer, and to which sensitive and passionate souls have with the best intent surrendered themselves, and then by deconstructing those seductions, Elder completes the exfoliation of the infernal 'region' of his modern epic of divestiture and privation. Simply put, the gods are gone, and the sacred spaces (the sexual body, the ancient temple ruin, primitive dance, etc.), evacuated of the divine, become all the more subtle circles of demonization. This is the modern hell of counter-history at its most sincere and eager, cynical and disappointed, most luxuriant and most devouring.

In a text, of several written in a Heidegger cadence at the time he was completing *Consolations*, Elder remarks, '... our origin has fallen into our future from whence it calls us to return to our possible greatness' (Elder, 'Henderson' 4). *Consolations* is a great film of waiting. To endure its stupendous length (of some fourteen hours) is indispensable to grasping its significance. Elder tirelessly discerns how one proceeds when living in our own great chasm, our own postmodern era, between times that knew and will know enfolding cosmologies. He explains, in a summary of his intent:

> The Holocaust destroyed the Enlightenment optimism for once and all. And in destroying the Enlightenment paradigm, it brought us into the 'Between.' This I take to be the meaning of Heidegger's comment, which I have used as a note on *Fugitive Gods* (part of *Consolations*): 'It is the time of the gods that have flown and the god that is to come. It is a time of need, because it lies under a double lack and double Not. The No-More of the gods that have fled and the Not-Yet of the god that is coming.' (Shedden 105)

Antonioni styles his *Purgatorio* as the anguished achievement of a heroine who can now undertake her biography in time, the time in-between. *Consolations* responds to the same chasm of the present by slowing down its discourse to crawl, to feel time itself, to make history dissolve to another, contemplative temporality. Unlike his previous films, this work has little discernible 'structure.' It is not a film of montage collisions but of carefully woven, gossamer connections, and its metres enact momentum in reverse. Though again, like its predecessors, a work of listening and reading texts and looking at images, *Consolations* devolves into a magnificent deceleration. Massively redundant, its repetitions' minuscule variations evolve very slowly, as the film compels the viewer into meditative rhythms. The imagery is very like the previous two films. *Consolations* is a huge performative revisitation, a mammoth superimposition on the whole cycle. Of course, that has to be: *Lamentations* showed there to be nowhere else to go but modernity's here of this time and this place. Elder's treatments of the imagery and its effects differ, however. There are likewise similar characters, that procession of pilgrims, who tell their tales again on the soundtrack, but now their journeys come to hopeful irresolution. Time enters the film stripped of its familiar cinematic correlate – narrative thrust. Love becomes the art of time, and cinema serves as its medium and, at last, slips out of politics and critical philosophy, and into philosophical theology. It is still a negative theology, to be sure, and hence the predominance of Heidegger. However, its personification is the late appearance of a modern Beatrice, Simone Weil, whose texts instruct the pilgrim in the arts of 'attention,' just as Heidegger teaches him/her the necessary relaxation of striving, of allowing the flux and flow of time to be.[10]

Consolations does not arrive at paradise, but at contemplative expectation. It is a postmodern *Purgatorio*, and the most persuasive one that cinema will likely manage. It is hardly triumphant, for it refuses aesthetic heroism and takes full advantage of the disentanglement in *Lamentations* of that seductive portion of the modern imaginary. The powerful Baroque films Elder forges before *Consolations* burn a viewer with grief and indignity, but this film manifests a wiser, Dantean wish, for the poet's spirit to arise into the completion of what he cannot complete. As it ends, *Consolations* places the viewer in such a paradox, like the pilgrim finally come to the threshold of the shrine.

There is some question whether *Exultations* should be regarded as of a piece with the rest of *The Book of All the Dead*. Elder undertook this final suite of films, this sub-cycle, after abandoning the cycle as unfinishable. Although the styles among the earlier sections of the cycle varied, salient features, which I have been describing, were consistent. Now all that changes. Almost all the imagery and sound in *Exultations* are computer-processed (previously such processing was subordinate to Elder's *plein air* shooting style and his polyphonic montage), and the welter of discursive and poetic intertexts now vanishes. The look and sound – and consequently the viewer's reception of *Exultations* – undergo mutation. These films have passed through the eyes and ears of a machine. On the other hand, some other features of *Consolations* suggest a line of development. The most important is the rising importance serial form assumes. Through *Lamentations*, there is a high degree of subordination of images, texts, and sounds to recognizable structures: autobiography (*The Art of Worldly Wisdom*), apocalypse (*Illuminated Texts*), Romantic quest-narrative (*Lamentations*). However brilliantly reinventive and/or subversive their articulation, a notional progression through these familiar structures guides the viewer, and they are assimilable to models of a postmodern *Inferno*. Elder obviously regards these structures as tainted ready-mades inherited from modernity and as signs of cultural divestiture. Hence the textual violence of his remaking them and the complex proofs generating his hermeneutic intent – of murdering them. *Consolations* is different. It has no trajectory or assimilated overall structure, and it is, therefore, unresolvable. In this respect, it is the end of something, the modern forms that precede it and that know their endings. When *Exulta-tions* resumes the cycle, ending is *a priori* an impossibility, and, by beginning again with an infinite serial work, Elder innocently insists an un-endable fugue to be his terminal design.

With counterpoint lines of imagery (of which there seem to be seven sustained throughout) and a constantly transformed Bach piece for its soundtrack, each element remains unsubordinated, directed at each other and not to a subtending structure. Some lines do seem to advance in a direction: there is a journey up a mountain, shown in rapid pixelated shots (still a *Purgatorio* motif), but other lines slowly and endlessly evolve, like the dancer whose body melts into abstraction, and passages of abstract computer imagery of 'fractal' mathematics. Elder's imagery, taken as arrayed motifs (for there are no successive segments), composes visions of identities and differences, in shape and texture and other features. The identities are sometimes developed quite directly, as is the rose symbolism, key symbol in the *Paradiso*. Dante's synchronous panoply of the mystical rose reappears throughout the films as a series of improvisations constantly recomposed by computer, as Elder introduces numerous religious homologies of the shape (mandalas, cathedral stained glass, etc.). The rose and its many variants do not develop significance directly. The viewer presumably knows Dante's image, and Elder deploys it as given and then expands on it graphically, proceeding by accumulation and association across the whole tapestry of *Exultations*. Similarly, viewers are expected to recognize that fractal computer abstractions stem from a new mimetic mathematics that does not reduce natural phenomena to an abstract system – and hence to technological measurement and control – and thus serve as a metaphor of the infinite serialism of the film, and as a contemplative analogue of natural processes.

So, could this be paradise-in-a-consciousness freed of modernity? That is dubious. Elsewhere in the film, vision often slides backward into violence and ugly eroticism. Redemption is still inaccessible – the time is still between. Moreover, all that might be glimpsed is heavily, technically processed intimation. Rather than pretend Christianity can be reborn in the flesh of a film, *Exultations* is a meditation on possible cinematic forms that might find equivalence as a tissue of formal disciplines. These too are inherited, like everything in *The Book of All the Dead*, and to be remade *after* modernity. But it is in the remaking, here with computer technology, that the implausibility of entering a sustaining paradisal aesthetic looms like a barricade. Similarly to Brakhage, but at greater length and with passages of terrible awkwardness impossible to that artist, Elder's work remains in the postmodernist regime of allusion and fragment. This *Paradiso* is a contraption in homage to eternal temporal flux, a contraption of intimated infinity, and, finally, it is a simulation-coda to the meditative sublimity *Consolations* achieves. All the wagers collected, cinema remains in that purgatory across that chasm of history separating us from Dante.

Notes

1 This essay would not have even been begun without the advice and guidance of Patrick Rumble and Bruce Elder. It certainly would never have been written without the patient encouragement of Amilcare Iannucci.
2 The use of these larger formats is unusual for Brakhage, who could make only one 35 mm print, which has been fatally damaged in projection. All copies of the film now circulate in 16 mm.
3 This interpretation is most explicitly expressed by Etienne Gilson, who sees in Dante a doctrinal poet. It is challenged very idiosyncratically by Harold Bloom (*Canon* 72–97). Bloom is the leading proponent of the radical self-imagining myth of the strong poets of American literature.
4 The fullest statements appear in three unpublished texts: 'Letter to Dr. Henderson,' 'Approaching Heaven,' and 'Letter to Antonio Bisaccia.'
5 Elder knows Brakhage's film intimately; he attended its Canadian premier and has now written very insightfully on it ('A Short Note on Brakhage's Relation to Dante'). He also includes an excerpt from Brakhage's *Dog Star Man* in *Exulations*, and devotes a very beautiful and long passage to a celebratory depiction of Brakhage's marriage in 1990.
6 Elder does not regard postmodern art in the fashion made familiar by writers like Fredric Jameson, as a symptom of the collapse of historical consciousness, much less as a nihilistic mode. On the contrary, he regards postmodernism (not unlike Jean-François Lyotard has in his writings on art) as an imaginatively recuperative-redemptive mode. See Elder's remarks, in his interview with Jim Shedden, on Heidegger, Pound, and postmodernism in connection with *Consolations*. Elder's seminal book on Canadian cinema, *Image and Identity*, is devoted to disclosing how Canadian art and experimental film arose at the edge of the postmodern mode.
7 In fact, Elder has written at length on Antonioni with a special emphasis on Giuliana ('Antonioni's Tragic Vision').

8 I mean this in the strong, Derridean sense, which I have discussed in analysing *Lamentations* in Testa, 'The Tasks of *Lamentations*.'
9 'Love becomes a demon when it becomes a god' is Amilcare Iannucci's trenchant encapsulation in his illuminating discussion of these aspects of the *Inferno* 5. He furthermore explains how such love is never without its political dimension (105).
10 See Elder's remarks on Heidegger in Shedden (108–11), and his 'Thoughts Remade around Silence' and 'State/Intended,' where Elder attempts to work out discursively what *Consolations* enacts on screen.

Bibliography

Antonioni, Michelangelo. *The Architecture of Vision: Writings and Interviews on Cinema*. Ed. Carlo di Carlo and Giorgio Tinozi. American edition by Marga Cottino-Jones. New York: Marsilio Publishers, 1996.

Arrowsmith, William. *Antonioni: The Poet of Images*. Ed. and introd. Ted Perry. New York: Oxford University Press, 1995.

Bersani, Leo, and Ulysse Dutoit. *Arts of Impoverishment: Beckett, Rothko, Resnais*. Cambridge: Harvard University Press, 1993.

Bloom, Harold. *The Western Canon: The Books and School of the Ages*. New York: Riverhead Books, 1994.

Brakhage, Stan. *Metaphors on Vision*. Ed. P. Adams Sitney. *Film Culture* 30 (Fall 1963): n. pag.

– 'Note.' *Catalogue of the Canadian Filmmakers' Distribution Centre*. Toronto: Canadian Filmmakers' Distribution Centre, 1992. 11.

Carmean, E.A., Jr., and Eliza A. Rathbone with Thomas Hess. *American Art at Midcentury: The Subjects of the Artist*. Washington, DC: National Gallery of Art, 1978.

Elder, R. Bruce. 'A Short Note on Brakhage's Relation to Dante.' *Dante and the Unorthodox: The Aesthetics of Transgression*. Ed. James Miller. Forthcoming.

– 'Antonioni's Tragic Vision: Style, Form and Idea in the Films of Michelangelo Antonioni, with Especial Emphasis on His Masterpiece, *Il Deserto rosso*.' *Canadian Journal of Film Studies* 1.2 (1991): 1–33.

– 'Approaching Heaven.' Unpublished MS, 1991.

– *The Films of Stan Brakhage in the American Tradition of Ezra Pound, Gertrude Stein and Charles Olson*. Waterloo, ON: Wilfrid Laurier University Press, 1998.

– *Image and Identity: Reflections on Canadian Film and Culture*. Waterloo, ON: Wilfrid Laurier University Press, 1989.

– 'Letter to Antonio Bisaccia.' Unpublished MS, 1994.

- 'Letter to Dr. Henderson.' Unpublished MS, 1991.
- 'Note.' *Catalogue of the Canadian Filmmakers' Distribution Centre*. Toronto: Canadian Filmmakers' Distribution Centre, 1992. 23–6.
- 'State/Intended.' *Bruce Elder, The Book of All the Dead; Complete Film Retrospective*. Ed. Jonas Mekas. New York: Film Anthology Archives, 1988.
- 'Thoughts Remade around Silence.' *Descant* 50 (Fall 1985): 167–78.
Foucault, Michel. *Language, Counter-Memory, Practice: Selected Essays and Interviews*. Trans. Donald F. Bouchard and Sherry Simon. Ithaca, NY: Cornell University Press, 1977.
- *The Order of Things: An Archeology of the Human Sciences*. Trans. Alan Sheridan. New York: Pantheon Books, 1970.
Gilson, Etienne. *Dante and Philosophy*. Trans. D. Moore. New York: Harper and Row, 1949.
Grant, George. *Time As History*. Toronto: Canadian Broadcasting Corporation, 1969.
Iannucci, Amilcare A. 'Forbidden Love: Metaphor and History (*Inferno* 5).' *Dante: Contemporary Perspectives*. Ed. Amilcare A. Iannucci. Toronto: University of Toronto Press, 1997. 94–112.
Krauss, Rosalind. *The Originality of the Avant-Garde and Other Modernist Myths*. Cambridge: MIT Press, 1985.
Lyotard, Jean-François. *The Inhuman: Reflections on Time*. Stanford: Stanford University Press, 1991.
Polcari, Stephen. *Abstract Expressionism and the Modern Experience*. New York: Cambridge University Press, 1991.
Shedden, Jim. 'Interview with Bruce Elder.' *Millennium Film Journal* (1991): 98–114.
Sitney, P. Adams. '*Accattone* and *Mama Roma*.' *Pier Paolo Pasolini: Contemporary Perspectives*. Ed. Patrick Rumble and Bart Testa. Toronto: University of Toronto Press, 1992. 171–9.
- *Visionary Film: The American Avant-Garde, 1943–1978*. New York: Oxford University Press, 1979.
- *Vital Crises in Italian Cinema: Iconography, Stylistics, Politics*. Austin: University of Texas Press, 1995.
Taylor, Mark C. *Disfiguring: Art, Architecture, Religion*. Chicago: University of Chicago Press, 1992.
Testa, Bart. 'The Tasks of *Lamentations*.' *Recherches semiotiques / Semiotic Inquiry* 13.1–2 (1993): 175–87.
Voegelin, Eric. *The Ecumenic Age*. Vol. 4 of *Order and History*. 5 vols. Baton Rouge: Louisiana State University Press, 1974.
- *Science, Politics and Gnosticism*. Chicago: Henry Regnery, 1968.

Dante by Heart and Dante Declaimed: The 'Realization' of the *Comedy* on Italian Radio and Television

RINO CAPUTO

Toward the end of the month of July 1998, the municipal government of Florence organized a series of evening cultural and theatrical performances, to be presented in the city's public squares. As part of the series, Roberto Benigni, newly returned from his now world-famous cinematic successes, gave a recitation 'by heart,' to use his own expression, that is, from memory, of the fifth canto of the *Inferno*, that of Paolo and Francesca. This was not the first time the artist had performed such a feat. For some years before, on the television program *Babele* (a program of literary and cultural popularization which enjoyed a wide following, arising from its ability to sensationalize intellectual debate), Benigni had, so to speak, 'improvised' the fifth canto of the *Inferno*.

While recognizing the skill of the protagonist of these events and the importance of the mass medium involved, namely television, it might be appropriate, before reporting on the significant experiments in *viva voce* performance of the *Comedy* throughout the course of the 1980s and '90s, to make a few preliminary remarks, only apparently tangential. The first of these is that Dante is an author who commands, and always has commanded, the attention of the Italian public. The reasons for this ongoing popularity go beyond the most obvious explanation, namely the cultural and historical importance of the Florentine poet and his works. Dante, as was pointed out some time ago, is now as ever a naturally audio-visual author, admirably suited to the multimedia methods of present-day mass communication (Iannucci, 'Dante, Television and Education,' 'Dante autore televisivo'). Yet the memory of the important role played by Dante's poem in national life from the early nineteenth century on, and especially throughout the period of the Risorgimento, is for the Italian people the basis of both its emotional and media appeal.

If this were not so, it would be hard to explain the title – only apparently odd – of a recently published article in a new weekly review called *Il Diario*. The article, entitled 'Dante for President,' chronicles a 'lectura Dantis' by Vittorio Sermonti, which has reached a vast audience of listeners. It is noteworthy that this provocative title is given star billing on the cover of the issue (which contains an interview of Vittorio Sermonti by the journalist Luca Fontana) and is accompanied by the significant comment: 'In search of our language, our national identity, and our sense of community: why Dante Alighieri continues to be relevant – and fantastic!'. Moreover, the more appropriate title of the article, appearing on pages 16–24, is 'The Pleasure of Reading Dante.'

From this consolidated point of view, we may affirm that the Italians' idea of Dante is still markedly different from that of North Americans – different from the Dante of Charles Eliot Norton and Charles Singleton as well as from that of John Freccero and the last generation of Canadian and American exegetes. For Italians, right from their earliest school days, Dante is the 'Ghibelline exile,' the historically and ideologically contradictory but poetically successful Dante of the *Sepolcri* of Ugo Foscolo. This is the same Foscolo who handed on to the next generation of intellectuals and patriots, poets and soldiers (Garibaldini and regular alike), the classic formula that underpins all of Italy's civilization, and not just her literature: 'Dante for contest, Petrarch for concord.' (Dante, that is, struggles and changes the world, while Petrarch fashions verses that never impinge upon reality.) And indeed Francesco De Sanctis, the great critic and historian of the nineteenth century, with his penetrating exegesis focused on a Romantic-Risorgimental agenda, would pursue this line of thought to the point of establishing Dante as the archetypal progenitor of an Italy united as State and Nation. Hence the inordinate number of streets and squares, as any visitor to the most beautiful cities of Italy, small and large, can easily observe, that are named first of all in honour of Dante, but also for Garibaldi, Mazzini, Victor Emanuel II, and Cavour (the four most celebrated protagonists of Italy's Revival as a nation).[1] Since, therefore, the performances of Benigni are by no means the whole story of 'Dante on television,' it is possible to trace a productive process extending over at least a decade. Moreover, the more distant causes of this process are to be sought in the versatility of the medium of television, capable as it is of conveying theatre as well as poetry, movies as well as the daily news (the last-named evolving irreversibly, precisely in the past decade, in the direction of pure spectacle). In this regard, it will be sufficient to recall as examples the important television production of the *Orlando Furioso* adapted from Ariosto's poem under the direction of Luca Ronconi, the present successor of Giorgio Strehler at the 'Piccolo Teatro' of Milan, and the ever-increasing employment of great actors of stage and cinema on television, and not only in programs dedicated to cultural subjects. One need only think of Eduardo De Filippo, of Carmelo Bene, or especially of Vittorio Gassman, to whom is due, as we shall presently see, the most remarkable and sustained series of television treatments of Dante and of the *Comedy*. All this attention, moreover, has redounded to the benefit of Italian literature in general, seeing that the television treatment hitherto reserved for Dante was extended in 1998 to include all the works of Giacomo Leopardi, the centenary of whose birth occurred that year, and more especially to the *Canti*. And, once again, Vittorio Sermonti and Carmelo Bene were among the most compelling protagonists of the 1998 cultural offerings on Italian television.

However, despite the truly proverbial difficulty of presenting the *Comedy* by audio-visual means, the task has been carried out by film writers and directors, as determined as they were daring, right from the early years of this century (see the essays in Casadio). Two examples that come to mind are the *Inferno di Dante*, directed and interpreted by Giuseppe de Liguoro in 1909, and *Dante e Beatrice* by Mario Caserini in 1912 (Giammusso 67). More numerous and better known are the experiments and more substantial productions realized on both sides of the Atlantic in the succeeding decades. In Italy, one may perhaps recall the *Vita di Dante* produced in 1965, on the occasion of the seven-hundredth anniversary of the poet's birth, by the director Vittorio Cottafavi, with Giorgio Albertazzi as protagonist.

But it is odd, as has been remarked by Iannucci ('Dante, Television, and Education' 9), that the presentation of the *Comedy* on television in Italy took initial form as a predominantly academic enterprise, with undeniable intrinsic merits, but with the inevitable defect of a certain heaviness in the end result as spectacle. In fact, the preferred format of presentation is due to the late Giorgio Petrocchi, critical editor of the *Comedy*, assisted by a small and select cohort of colleagues. This format is a 'lectura Dantis' in which an exegetic 'commentary' is combined with the vocal and visual presentation of three great thespian declaimers such as G. Albertazzi, G. Sbragia, and E.M. Salerno (the last two unfortunately deceased, like Petrocchi, in subsequent years). But there is no point in pitting aesthetic sensibility against scientific rigour. To be sure, a greater degree of mutual give-and-take would have enhanced the audio-visual product, forestalling perhaps the more predictable outcome, namely, a kind of 'theatre on television' – a theatre, be it noted, quite lacking in its essential property, dramatic magnetism!

Paradoxically, what emerges from the experiment of Petrocchi and his director Marco Parodi, carried out during the mid-1980s, is precisely the natural 'orality' of the text of the *Comedy*, as though it had been written by Dante to be read aloud or declaimed. This property was clearly apparent in all the productions, both theatrical and audio-visual, which succeeded one another during those same years and in the first half of the 1990s. Think, for example, of the 'reading' of Carmelo Bene, strongly marked in rhythm and timbre, on 2 August 1981 in Bologna, organized to mark the anniversary of the tragic terrorist massacre at the railway station; of the experiment of Paolo Giuranna at the Teatro Stabile in Genoa during 1983–6; of the whole-text reading promoted by the then director of the Teatro di Roma, Pietro Carriglio, and by the poet, literary critic, and writer Giovanni Raboni in the two-year period 1991–3 (poets, writers, artists, and intellectuals read the *Comedy* on the stage every Monday – the actors' day of rest); think of the Ravenna Festival; of the reading of Leo de Berardinis at Palermo in February 1992; of that 28th day of July 1992 when, at Cividale del Friuli, with the collaboration of Edoardo Sanguineti, the group 'I Magazzini' gave an all-night reading of Dante's poem. Among this flurry of activity must be located the more substantial efforts of Vittorio Sermonti and Vittorio Gassman, of which we shall speak presently, and the unique performance of Roberto Benigni, of which we have already spoken (Giammusso 117–56).

The article in the *Diario* just mentioned is described by the editors as an 'interview with Vittorio Sermonti.' Not by chance, it deals with the most important motives that impelled such an outstanding man of letters to give public readings of Dante, culminating in the near beatifying recognition of 31 August 1997, when Sermonti declaimed and commented on canto 23 of the *Paradiso* before Pope John Paul II. It was in 1988, at Rizzoli, that Sermonti set in motion the publication in book form of his complete reading of the *Comedy*, beginning with the *Inferno*, followed two years later by the *Purgatorio*, and later by the *Paradiso*. (By 1993 there had already been at least four editions and reprintings.) In the same time period, in addition to a wide diffusion by radio, on various networks and in different time slots, Sermonti's audio cassettes were distributed commercially by the Marketing Division of the RAI. In short, one cannot help but take note of Sermonti's experiment, a true audio-visual point of intersection between tradition and innovation. Nor must we neglect the fact that this cultural operation was overseen right from the beginning by the great philologist and critic Gianfranco Contini, whose solicitous supervision would be cut short only by his death, in the midst of life's journey, so to speak, on 1 February 1990.

In his prefatory remarks, Sermonti makes it clear that his 'lectura Dantis' is intended to be broadcast on radio. But, right from the beginning of his re-evocation of the past, it is evident that Dante's text holds an enormous emotional charge for him (and it will be well to keep in mind that from now on 'Dante' or 'Dante's text' means the *Comedy*). The function of the text is that of a vehicle bringing the world into the author's youthful field of consciousness. The period of first contact is wartime, 1940–1: the young Sermonti, with Dante and through Dante, offsets the violence of men, and the *Comedy* takes on for him the value of a realm of sound-borne meaning and symbol in which it was possible to discern the voice of the world in the voice of the text:

Le parole incomprese assumevano la arbitraria e irrevocabile proprietà dei nomi propri ... il violoncello delle cicale e la romanza del conte Ugolino, le forme del fumo e il provenzale di Arnaldo Daniello, la fame e l'alcume lacerante della luce di Dio, mio padre e Dante, Dante e io. (Sermonti xv)

[The uncomprehended words took on the arbitrary and irrevocable identity of proper names ... the *violoncello* of the cicadas and the romance of Count Ugolino, the shapes of the smoke and the Provençal of Arnaut Daniel, the hunger and the lacerating intensity of the light of God, my father and Dante, Dante and me.]

We are now in a better position to understand the adult Sermonti's predilection for transmitting the voice of Dante's text. And it is well known how characteristic of the *Comedy* is the intensity of the sounds, of the phonic harmonies, even of the dissonances, all of which however contribute to the meaning. But we can detect with equal certainty, precisely in light of these preliminary acknowledgments, the degree to which Sermonti is influenced by the teaching of Contini, both by the more general doctrine which finds the artistic value of the great decadent Italian poetry of the early twentieth century (especially that of Pascoli and D'Annunzio) precisely in its phonetic symbolism (Contini, 'Il linguaggio di Pascoli' 219–45), and the more specific one that extracts, as the 'substance' of the *Comedy*, the 'realization' of that great text (Contini, 'Leggere Dante' vi). And, in fact, it is to Contini, directly or indirectly, that we owe the phonic and vocal characterization, so to speak, of the 'lectura Dantis' of Sermonti and, in the final analysis, of all the ensuing experiments. The notion of 'execution,' borrowed perhaps from the sphere of music, permits a personality like Sermonti to discount the purely academic position of the critical reader, be he or she of a literary or of a philological-linguistic bent – or, at least, to take it for granted as necessary cultural baggage – and to concentrate all the power of meaning of the text in the oral act of reading. He does this, it must be said, in keeping with contemporary theories of maximizing the diverse potentialities of the verbal text, which have managed to undercut the centuries-old notion of the sacredness of the written text, itself, after all, a verbal construct (Eco; Iser; Ong). The 'execution' of the *Comedy* is thus a product of contemporary Dante criticism, and is the current method of 'reading' (once again!) Dante, retrieving as it were Boccaccio's original method of 'exposition' of the poem.

But the real coordinates of Sermonti's reading of Dante and of the *Comedy* are derived from life (that is, from history) and from art (that is, from culture). From his autobiographical account, it is apparent that the adolescent's quasi-magical listening experience is complemented, in the cultivated adult, by the latter's assimilation of Contini's exegetic and hermeneutic principles. And if for Sermonti, as we have just seen, 'the uncomprehended words took on the arbitrary and irrevocable identity of proper names,' for Contini instead 'great poetry is in fact a poetry of names.' If the most obvious aspect of Sermonti's reading of Dante is to allow the text to resonate freely, uninhibited by immediate critical reflection, 'it is nevertheless helpful to know,' says Contini, 'that the original is subject to two bilateral tensions.' For Dante pursues 'poetry and love' while assuming the roles of 'founder and poet' (Contini, 'Leggere Dante' xii, ix, x).

For Contini, Sermonti 'has the great advantage of not belonging to any school of Dantologists.' He is a writer with the gift of irony and is, like Dante, distinguished by the 'ability to express the inexpressible.' Therefore, the great critic can assert: 'So it happens that any passage, even when detached at random from the mechanism, has its geometrically definable position' (Contini, 'Leggere Dante' vii–viii). But one should not imagine that there is here a kind of tacit deference on the part of a dilettante reader to a professional writer, critic, and philologist. Rather, the relationship, speaking allegorically, resembles that between

Dante and Virgil. Moreover, underpinning this relationshp is an emo-
tion-laden chord which is sounded when, in the first edition of the
Purgatorio in 1990, published immediately after the death of Contini,
Sermonti reports that the deceased scholar 'dictated to his son Riccardo
a very brief final note on the story of Canto xxvii,' that is, on the leave-
taking of Virgil from his disciple, the poet and pilgrim! Sermonti, on the
other hand, has his own understanding of the task of criticism. For him
it is often a question of traversing whole centuries of critical and interpretative exegesis – the 'leprosy of notes' ('Dante for President' 20) in
his own pungent expression – by means of the nonchalance of the non-
professional reader. Or, it is a matter of solving interpretative puzzles or
philological cruces with the casual ease of common sense – a common
sense founded, to be sure, on solid and varied interdisciplinary studies.
And sometimes, for the understanding of a traditionally thorny passage, the decisive factor is that particular intonation of the voice which
for Sermonti is the determining factor in his own critical reading.

A 'vocal language' is precisely what makes Sermonti the true and
worthy successor of Giovanni Boccaccio. After his experience with
radio in the 1980s, Sermonti in effect mounted another 'presentation' in
the years 1995, 1996, and 1997, thanks to the support of the Centro
Relazioni Culturali of Ravenna in collaboration with the Centro Dantesco
dei Frati Minori Conventuali, the Commune, the Province, and the
Manufacturers' Association of the city. And it is the voice that defines
an Italian language far removed from the grammar of formal written
Italian, and therefore not 'polished' by the literary and poetic tradition,
which, from Petrarch on, has been above all an intellectual one. It is
against this cultural-historical tradition, that Sermonti defines his concept of the execution of the text of the *Comedy*:

> La voce ne sa più di me, più di quanto ne so io. Mi affido a lei. È lei che
> scopre nel testo, in cesure, arsi, tesi, scarti ritmici, *l'espressione* in senso
> musicale. Ci sono delle norme che mi accorgo di applicare. 1) Non fare
> finita di essere Dante – quello che dice Io è un personaggio che lui s'è
> inventato – quell'io simula di ricordare un viaggio che ha fatto. Io mi
> costringo a un solo livello di simulazione, quello del personaggio fittizio
> che legge se stesso. 2) Non assumere l'aria pensosa del genio assoluto. 3)
> Non si devono *recitare* i discorsi diretti contenuti tra virgolette, le persone
> che parlano sono personaggi della memoria del personaggio Dante. Quando
> racconti battute depositate nella tua memoria mormori scandendo, urli a
> bassa voce, risolfeggi il testo. Insomma, non devi *fare* Ulisse, gonfiando il

tono predicatorio. Questo io intendo per lettura di contro a recitazione: *spielen* Dante, *play*, *jouer*, ma mai recitare. Mi accorgo poi che non leggo mai un canto di Dante due volte allo stesso modo. E che però, quasi sempre, dopo un lungo collaudo, tendo a mimare la primissima lettura, a regredire a quella prima stupefazione. ('Dante for President' 20)

[The voice knows more about it than I do. I entrust myself to her. It is she who discovers in the text, in *caesurae*, arses, theses and sudden shifts in rhythm, the *expression* in the musical sense. There are rules that I realize I apply. 1) Do not pretend to be Dante – the one who says 'I' is a character which he has invented for himself – the 'I' who pretends to remember a journey which he has made. I limit myself to a single level of simulation, that of the fictitious character who is reading himself. 2) Do not assume the pensive air of the absolute genius. 3) The direct speeches contained between quotation marks must not be *declaimed*: the persons who are speaking are characters from the memory of the character Dante. When you recount speeches laid up in your memory, speak softly as you pronounce them, let your screams be muted, key down the text. In a word, you must not *impersonate* Ulysses in swelling, sermonizing tones. My understanding of 'reading' Dante as opposed to 'declaiming' him is conveyed by the verbs *spielen*, *play*, *jouer* – never declaim. Finally, I notice that I never read a canto of Dante the same way twice: and yet, after lengthy trial and error, I tend to imitate my very first reading, to revert to that first state of wonderment.]

But around the middle of the 1990s, we find another Dante 'spoken' or 'read' in public, in the theatre or on television, besides those of Sermonti and Benigni: the 'Dante of Gassman,' according to the title of a valuable volume edited by Maurizio Giammusso in 1994, which, in a text sometimes limpid and sometimes dense, recounts the exceptional Dante experiment of Vittorio Gassman, appropriately defined in the subtitle – in order to dispel any misunderstanding – as 'the chronicle and history of an interpretation of the *Divine Comedy*.'

With Gassman the vocal performance or reading aloud of the *Comedy* invades the space of the theatre, audio-visual, multi-expressive, and multi-communicative, while confirming the lack of previous experiments, theoretical or practical, on the Italian scene. Nevertheless, we recall the references to the works of English-speaking writers, well known to the actor (a man of vast and varied erudition, both general and specialized, but also learned in the ways of public reading) from

Francis Ferguson and his *Idea of a Theatre* through T.S. Eliot and his 'more readable' Dante, to John Freccero and his vision of Dante's poem as a 'journey of transformation' (Giammusso 9–10, 59–68).[2] The 'reading' of Gassman, then, has its origin in his desire, perceived as an artistic and cultural challenge, to link together the theatre and the *Comedy*. To this end, besides the ideas of foreign writers, both theoretical and technical, what is important in the case of Gassman is his recovery of a certain Italian tradition, both theatrical and Dantesque, linked to the nineteenth century of Romanticism and Risorgimento, and centred in the person of the great actor (and patriot) Gustavo Modena. Modena, costumed as Dante, would recite the *Comedy* on the stage, before the Italian public, but also, after he was driven into exile, before the public of Europe and, more particularly, of England: this episode confirms, if further confirmation had been needed, the existence of an Italian-speaking and Dante-loving element established in England with the Panizzi, the Rossetti, and even earlier with Ugo Foscolo, a current which through the good offices of Longfellow and Norton, and others would take root in Cambridge, Massachusetts, and which, through its branches, would bear fruit in Charles Singleton and modern North American Dante criticism! (See Giammusso 82–105; Caputo, *Per far segno* 23–30 and 'La critica dantesca nordamericana.')

But Gassman, like Sermonti, is committed also to the more usual, age-old idea of the presence of Dante in the 'mindscape' of the educated Italian: the recitation aloud and from memory, as Gassman says, which has taken place historically and archetypally in the home and in the classroom:

Dante per lui, è un ricordo d'infanzia, il ritorno alle gare di memoria con la madre ... è il sentimento dell'adolescenza, segnata dalle lezioni al liceo Tasso del professor Vladimiro Cajoli ... leggeva soprattutto ... dando leggittimità ad una interpretazione 'ad alta voce.' (Giammusso 17)

[Dante for him is a childhood memory, a return to the contests of memory with his mother ... the poet is the experience of adolescence, marked by the lectures given at the Liceo Tasso by Professor Vladimiro Cajoli, who always used to read aloud, giving legitimacy to a *viva voce* interpretation.]

For Gassman, too, the validity of any more expert philological or hermeneutic 'interpretation' is far outweighed by his fellow-feeling for the poet-pilgrim, protagonist of the ultramundane voyage:

Quel lungo e aspro viaggio dall'Inferno al Paradiso era solo l'ultimo tratto di un percorso più lungo, cominciato chissà quando: il fiume carsico di una esperienza di vita e arte, che usciva ora definitivamente alla luce. (Giammusso 14)

[That long and arduous journey from Hell to Heaven was but the final stage of a longer voyage, begun who knows when: the underground river of an experience of life and art, which now was finally emerging into the light.]

For this reason, the 'reading,' according to Gassman, must be carried out without recourse to the usual actor's 'aids' (no cheat-sheet with the lines, no human prompter), but solely, especially when one comes to *Paradiso* 33, 'by heart,' so as to confirm once more the sacred observance of the tradition to the point of symbolizing, from time to time, a kind of renewed 'Dantemania' (Giammusso 40, 53).

In this way, the Dante-cult proves itself a precious resource of the Italian public spirit, and unites intellectual 'clerks' and common people, all of them intensely and profoundly moved by the 'execution' of the *Comedy*. Thus it will come as no surprise that the cultivated Gassman and the (apparently) uncultivated Benigni are renewing, each in his own way, the oral tradition of the Tuscan countryside and churches, as well as that of the lecterns of the learned in their academies in every part of Italy. But all this is happening more and more today in the (seemingly) virtual public square of audio-visual reality, which, thanks to Dante and his 'sacred poem' founded on 'the word made visible,' bodes well for the potential of the new virtual media.

Notes

1 For a more detailed treatment of this subject, see Caputo *Per far segno*. Giulio Ferroni's recent article 'L'Ulisse di Dante?' in *Il Corriere della Sera*, in which he rightly laments the sorry state of knowledge of Italy's national poet among young graduate students (the article was provoked by their poor showing in a university essay writing contest whose theme was the Ulysses episode in Dante's *Inferno*), does not, however, sufficiently acknowledge the wide popular diffusion of Dante among contemporary Italians.

2 For a wider overview, see Caputo, *Per far segno* and 'Easier to Read.'

Bibliography

Caputo, Rino. 'La critica dantesca nordamericana dal 1965 al 1990.' *Dalla bibliografia alla storiografia: La critica dantesca nel mondo dal 1965 al 1990.* Ed. E. Esposito. Ravenna: Longo, 1995. 217–37.

– '"Easier to Read": Poeti nordamericani critici di Dante.' *Dante: 'For Use Now.'* Ed. Annalisa Goldoni and Andrea Mariani. *Testo & Senso* [special issue] 3 (2000): 93–102.

– *Per far segno: La critica dantesca americana da Singleton a oggi.* Roma: Il Calamo, 1993.

Casadio, Gianfranco, ed. *Dante nel cinema.* Ravenna: Longo, 1996.

Contini, Gianfranco. 'Leggere Dante.' Vittorio Sermonti. *L'Inferno di Dante con la supervisione di G. Contini.* Milano: Rizzoli, 1988. v–xiii.

– 'Il linguaggio di Pascoli.' *Varianti e altra linguistica.* Torino: Einaudi, 1979. 219–45.

'Dante for President' or 'Il piacere di leggere Dante.' Interview of Vittorio Sermonti by Lucca Fontana. *Il Diario* 3.7 (18–24 Feb. 1998): 16–24.

Eco, Umberto. *Lector in fabula.* Milano: Bompiani, 1962.

– *I limiti dell'interpretazione.* Milano: Bompiani, 1990.

Ferroni, Giulio. 'L'Ulisse di Dante? I dottorandi gettano la spugna.' *Il Corriere della Sera,* 5 June 1998.

Giammusso, Maurizio, ed. *Il Dante di Gassman: Cronaca e storia di un'interpretazione della 'Divina Commedia.'* Milano: Mondadori, 1994.

Iannucci, Amilcare A. 'Dante autore televisivo.' *Le Forme e la Storia* 6 (1994): 107–24.

– 'Dante, Television and Education.' *Quaderni d'Italianistica* 10 (1989): 1–33:

Iser, W. *L'atto della lettura.* Bologna: Il Mulino, 1976.

Ong, W. *Oralita' e scrittura.* Bologna: Il Mulino, 1986.

Sermonti, Vittorio. 'L'Avvertenza.' *L'Inferno di Dante con la supervisione di G. Contini.* Milano: Rizzoli, 1988. xv–xvii.

Notes on Contributors

VITTORIA COLONNESE BENNI has undergraduate degrees from the University of Ottawa and Carleton University (Ottawa) in modern languages and literatures, with specialization in Italian and Spanish. She received her M.A. in Italian studies from the University of Toronto, and recently (1999) completed her Ph.D. at the same institution with a thesis on Dante and cinema, focusing in particular on early Italian silent treatments of Dante. She has published articles on Dante and Leopardi and is at present revising her thesis for publication.

RINO L. CAPUTO is Professor of Italian literature at DAMS (Discipline delle Arti, della Musica e dello Spettacolo) of the University of Rome ('Tor Vergata'). A Visiting Professor at Harvard, Cambridge, and McGill Universities, as well as the University of Toronto, he is mainly interested in Italian literature of the fourteenth (Dante and Petrarch), nineteenth (Manzoni and the Romantic tradition of Lombardy and Piedmont), and twentieth (Pirandello and contemporary Sicilian authors) centuries. A volume on Dante, *Il pane orzato: Saggi di lettura intorno all'opera di Dante Alighieri*, appeared recently (Rome, 2003), and another containing essays devoted to Dante and Petrarch is forthcoming.

GUIDO FINK is Professor of English literature and Director of the graduate program at the University of Florence, Italy. Previously, he was for many years Professor of American literature at the University of Bologna, from which he graduated. A frequent Visiting Professor at American universities (Princeton, UCLA, Smith, Berkeley), he was the Director of the Italian Cultural Institute in Los Angeles from 1999 to 2003. He is the author of various books and essays on American literature, on Jewish culture, and on film. Among his film studies are works devoted to Lubitsch, Wyler, and Antonioni. His latest book, *Non solo Woody Allen: La tradizione ebraica nel cinema americano*, was awarded the prize as Best Critical Book on Film published in Italy in 2002. A frequent contributor to literary and film journals, he has translated into Italian (and edited), among other works, Ford Madox Ford's *The Good Soldier*, Lionel Trilling's *Beyond Culture*, and Shakespeare's *The Comedy of Errors*; with his wife, Daniela Fink, he was responsible for the Italian (subtitled) editions of Spielberg's *Schindler's List*, Louis Malle's *Vanya on 42nd Street*, and Orson Welles's *It's All True*.

AMILCARE A. IANNUCCI is Professor of comparative literature and Director of the Humanities Centre at the University of Toronto. He has served as Chair of the Department of Italian Studies, University of Toronto, Vice-President of the Dante Society of America, and Director of the Canadian Academic Centre in Rome. He has lectured extensively in North America and Europe and has been a Visiting Professor at the following universities: Johns Hopkins, McGill, UCLA, Calabria, Rome, Siena, and Venice. A founding editor of the journal *Quaderni d'Italianistica*, he is the author or editor of numerous books, including *Forma ed evento nella Divina Commedia* (Rome, 1984), *Dante e la 'bella scola'* (Ravenna, 1993), and *Dante: Contemporary Perspectives* (Toronto, 1997), and has written dozens of articles focusing especially on issues of literary appropriation and reception. He is presently at work on a volume analysing Dante's dynamic intermingling of poetry and theology in the *Commedia*.

VICTORIA KIRKHAM is Professor of romance languages at the University of Pennsylvania. She is the author of *Fabulous Vernacular: Boccaccio's Filocolo and the Art of Medieval Fiction* (Ann Arbor, 2001), winner of the MLA Scaglione Award for a Manuscript in Italian Studies, 2000; *The Sign of Reason in Boccaccio's Fiction* (Florence, 1993); and co-author with Anthony K. Cassell of *Diana's Hunt / Caccia di Diana: Boccaccio's First Fiction* (Philadelphia, 1991). She has published articles on Dante, Boccaccio, and, more recently, the Counter-Reformation poet Laura Battiferra degli Ammannati. Her catalogue of the portraits of Boccaccio, with a monographic essay, appears in *Boccaccio visualizzato*, ed. Vittore Branca (Turin, 1999).

GABRIELLE ANNE LESPERANCE is currently completing her Ph.D. in

Italian literature at the University of California, Los Angeles, with a dissertation analysing Italian films of the 1970s and 1990s which revisit fascism. She has been co-editor of the *Atti del XVI Congresso dell'AISLLI* and of *Carte Italiane*, and has taught Italian language and cinema at UCLA from 1991 to 1998 as a teaching associate, and from 1998 to 1999 as an instructor. She has also been a lecturer at the University of Southern California and at the University of California, Santa Barbara.

DENNIS LOONEY is Chair of the Department of French and Italian at the University of Pittsburgh and Associate Professor of Italian. He has published articles on Dante, Petrarch, Ariosto, Tasso, and Ovid, among others. His book, *Compromising the Classics: Romance Epic Narrative in the Italian Renaissance* (Detroit, 1996), was nominated Finalist for the MLA's Marraro-Scaglione Prize for Italian Literary Studies. His essay 'Spencer Williams and Dante' grew out of his teaching, which explores the relationship between Italian vernacular culture and classical culture, and is part of a larger project in which he examines the surprising multitude of ways in which Dante has assumed a position of importance in African-American culture.

PATRICK RUMBLE is Associate Professor of Italian and film at the University of Wisconsin–Madison. He is the author of several articles on Italian cinema and literature, focusing predominantly on Pasolini. On the latter, he has also written *Allegories of Contamination: Pier Paolo Pasolini's Trilogy of Life* (Toronto, 1996) and has co-edited with Bart Testa *Pier Paolo Pasolini: Contemporary Perspectives* (Toronto, 1994).

ANDREW TAYLOR received his B.A. in history and Italian from Oxford University and is currently a doctoral student at the University of California, Los Angeles. His research interests include the performance of gender and the use of fictional texts as historical evidence. Both of these are incorporated into his dissertation, a commentary on Francesco da Barberino's *Reggimento e costumi di donna*, a medieval treatise for women. Mr Taylor is based in Los Angeles, where he works at the Getty Research Institute for the Arts and Humanities.

BART TESTA teaches film studies at the University of Toronto. A former book editor of the *Canadian Journal of Film Studies*, he is the co-editor with Patrick Rumble of *Pier Paolo Pasolini: Contemporary Perspectives*

(Toronto, 1994) and author of the volumes *Richard Kerr: Overlapping Entries* (Regina, 1994), *Back and Forth: Early Cinema and the Avant Garde* (Toronto, 1992), and *Spirit in the Landscape* (Toronto, 1989). He has also written numerous essays on cinema which have appeared in various anthologies and which include studies of Michael Snow, Denys Arcand, and Stan Brakhage. He is presently editing an anthology of critical texts on Antonioni.

JOHN TULK is Assistant to the Director of the University of Toronto Humanities Centre. A former Roman Catholic priest and Professor of historical theology in the Toronto School of Theology, his major interests are the humanistic disciplines and the history of Christian thought, especially the early Church and the theology of the Reformation. He is the author of studies on a range of topics including Iron Age Greece, the doctrine of Baptism in the early Christian Fathers, the Tower experience of Martin Luther, and the development of Christian humanism. He has also co-authored with Amilcare A. Iannucci *Reading and Writing the Canadian City*, a classroom text, which is responsible for his interest in Canadian cinema.

MARGUERITE R. WALLER is Professor of English, Film and Visual Culture, and Women's Studies, at the University of California, Riverside. Her publications include *Petrarch's Poetics and Literary History* (Amherst, 1980) and articles on Dante, Petrarch, Wyatt, Surrey, Shakespeare, Lucas, Rossellini, de Sica, Fellini, Cavani, Wertmüller, Nichetti, and Las Comadres, a multicultural women's art-making collective active in the U.S./Mexico border region. She is the co-editor with Frank Burke of *Federico Fellini: Contemporary Perspectives* (Toronto, 2002).

JOHN P. WELLE is Professor of romance languages and literatures, Concurrent Professor of film, television, and theatre, and Fellow, Nanovic Institute for European Studies at the University of Notre Dame. The recipient of grants and fellowships from the Fulbright Commission and the National Endowment for the Humanities, he is the author of *The Poetry of Andrea Zanzotto* (Rome, 1987), the editor of *Film and Literature: Annali d'Italianistica* (1988), and the editor and translator with Ruth Feldman of *Peasants Wake for Fellini's Casanova and Other Poems*, by Andrea Zanzotto (Urbana, 1997). He has also published articles on Dante, Fellini, Pasolini, Tessa, Sereni, Ginzburg, Fortini, and early Italian cinema. He is currently working on a book involving literary intellectuals and Italian silent film.

Index of Films

Index of Names

Numerals in bold refer to sections of works. Names of film characters are followed by film titles in italics within brackets.